CHIEFTAINCY, THE STATE, AND DEMOCRACY

T0341572

CHIEFTAINCY,
the STATE, and
DEMOCRACY

*Political Legitimacy
in Post-Apartheid South Africa*

J. Michael Williams

INDIANA UNIVERSITY PRESS
Bloomington and Indianapolis

This book is a publication of

Indiana University Press
601 North Morton Street
Bloomington, IN 47404-3797 USA

www.iupress.indiana.edu

Telephone orders	800-842-6796
Fax orders	812-855-7931
Orders by e-mail	iuporder@indiana.edu

LIBRARY OF CONGRESS CATALOGING-IN-PUBLICATION DATA

Williams, J. Michael, [date]
  Chieftaincy, the state, and democracy : political legitimacy in post-
apartheid South Africa / J. Michael Williams.
     p. cm.
  Includes bibliographical references and index.
  ISBN 978-0-253-35418-1 (cloth : alk. paper) — ISBN 978-0-253-
22155-1 (pbk. : alk. paper) 1. Chiefdoms—South Africa. 2. Local
government—South Africa. 3. Democracy—South Africa. 4. Post-
apartheid era—South Africa. 5. South Africa—Social conditions—
1994– 6. South Africa—Politics and government—1994– I. Title.
  GN656.W55 2009
  321'.10968—dc22   2009023244

1 2 3 4 5 15 14 13 12 11 10

For Rod and Marlene Williams,
who put me on the right path,

and

for Molly,
who makes the journey meaningful

CONTENTS

ACKNOWLEDGMENTS

This project has taken more than ten years to complete, and during this period I have relied upon a wonderful group of people for support and assistance. There is simply no way I would have had the stamina or fortitude to complete this book if it were not for the encouragement of this group of colleagues, friends, and family members. In the process, I am well aware that I have burdened far too many of them with the trials and tribulations of the chieftaincy in South Africa, which has always been a labor of love for me. For all of you who joined me on this long and meandering journey, I will always be deeply grateful. While my name is the only one that appears on the cover, this book reflects the time, energy, and efforts of many people— some of whom are mentioned below and many of whom will remain anonymous. The vignettes that make up the bulk of this book come from the experiences of South Africans who were gracious enough to trust me with their stories, and I have done my best to convey these accurately. Any errors of fact or interpretation, of course, are mine alone.

The opportunity to conduct the research for this project would not have been possible without generous funding from a variety of institutions. The Fulbright fellowship that I received from the United States Information Service and the Institute of International Education for my fieldwork provided me with the opportunity to collect much of the data for this book. In addition, I was able to formulate my initial interpretations of this data with a grant from the Global Studies/MacArthur Consortium Program. The University of San Diego, the institution that inspired me as an undergraduate and the one I am proud to call my academic home, has provided me with the resources to return to South Africa numerous times to conduct additional research. I particularly want to thank Patrick Drinan, Nicholas Healy, Mary Boyd, Julie Sullivan, and Mary Lyons for providing me with the financial support necessary to complete this project.

Of course, despite the care that is taken to design a coherent research project, the final result in large part depends on finding those people who are willing to take the time to answer questions and to share information. The truth is that I was very fortunate to meet a great number of South Africans who went well beyond the common courtesy that is customarily afforded to foreigners. I am grateful to the University of Natal-Durban for giving me the space and resources I needed while I was in South Africa. In particular, I want to thank the Department of Political Science, the Department of History, the Center for Social and Development Studies, and the University Library for assistance. I owe a special debt of gratitude to Sandy Johnston, Ralph de Kadt, Jeremy Grest, Heather Hughes, Suzanne Berry, Leanne Munsami, Libby Ardington, Jeff Guy, Keith Breckenridge, and Catherine Burns for their wonderful guidance and support when I made the university my home. In addition, I am grateful to the KwaZulu-Natal Provincial Administration, Uthungulu Regional Council, Inhlovu Regional Council, Ugu Regional Council, Zululand Regional Council, Durban Metropolitan Council, IDASA, the Regional Consultative Forum, Data Research Africa, and the Department of Provincial and Local Government for providing me access to information about the chieftaincy and local government. I am grateful to Slu Hlongwa, Zakhele Hlope, and Ernst Retief, who not only provided me with invaluable information but who also suggested examining issues that I had overlooked. I especially want to thank Rudi Hillerman, who has met with me on a continual basis since 1998 and who has taught me about local-level issues and how these issues fit into broader frameworks and processes in South Africa.

Of course, this book would not have been possible without the people in Mvuzane, Kholweni, and Ximba who graciously opened their homes to me and who helped me understand the richness and complexity of South African society and politics. I owe an eternal debt of gratitude to each and every one of them. In particular, I want to thank chief Bhekabelungu Biyela, chief Vincent Mtembu, chief Zibuse Mlaba, chief Victoria Dube, Simon Ngubane, and Tony Saville. In addition, the entire Thandi/Gina family graciously welcomed me into their home while I was conducting research in Mvuzane and Kholweni. There is simply no way to adequately thank Gogo Thandi, Gogo Gina, Nokothula, Ntombifuthi, Owethu, Zongile, Zama, and Lindo for the warm place to sleep and the wonderful home-cooked meals. I am also grateful to Vusi Chamane. He not only introduced me to the communities of Mvuzane and Kholweni but also has become a dear friend who continues to teach me about the challenges of rural development and the importance of local participation in development matters.

Without the assistance of Peter Zulu, however, much of this research would not have been possible. As my research assistant, Peter not only helped me to gather information, he also became my closest advisor and friend during my stay in South Africa. He enabled me to make my research ideas a reality, and he helped to shape and define the nature of this study. I was truly blessed to have met him and to have shared my fieldwork experience with him. Unfortunately, Peter did not live to see the completion of this book. While his death was tragic, his life was one that was full of optimism, laughter, and love.

There are many people who have taken the time to read various drafts of this book, and there is no doubt that because of their input, my arguments have improved—despite the fact that I would sometimes stubbornly ignore their advice and suggestions. In particular, I am grateful to Aili Tripp, Crawford Young, Barbara Oomen, Lungisile Ntsebeza, John Harbeson, Karen Flint, Kevin den Dulk, Mary Galvin, Rick Duenez, Lisa Bornstein, Mel Page, Cheryl Goodenough, Bert Kritzer, Heinz Klug, Joshua Forrest, Jeff Peires, Michael Bratton, Bruce Magnusson, Peter VonDoepp, Ann Woods, Cedric Jourde, David Shirk, Emily Edmonds, Casey Dominguez, Jim Gump, Lee Ann Otto, Noelle Norton, Randy Willougby, Vidya Nadkarni, Virginia Lewis, and Michael Pfau for providing me with constructive criticism and encouragement. I am especially grateful to Michael Schatzberg and Del Dickson, who have provided moral as well as intellectual support over the years in addition to reading multiple drafts of this book. There is no question that my arguments have benefited enormously from their many comments and suggestions.

I am also grateful to my students, who have never failed to provide me with honest and critical feedback. I am especially grateful to Paul Lenze, Kati Ansert, Chantal Francois, and Katie Briscoe, who took the time to provide me with detailed suggestions. I also want to thank Kati Ansert, Alicia Dolan, Florence So, Sarah Adams, Eric Green, Jessica von Borstel, Molly Dishman, Karen DeBolt, and Lisa DeBolt for conducting research for me over the years.

It has been a distinct pleasure to work with the editors at Indiana University Press. In particular, I want to thank Dee Mortensen for her unwavering support of this project and for her unyielding encouragement. I also thank Laura MacLeod and Carol Kennedy for their editing, the anonymous reviewers for their comments, and Em Hansen Trent for designing the map illustrations. Chapter 3 was originally published in the *Journal of Southern African Studies* 35, no. 1 (2009), as "Legislating 'Tradition' in South Africa," and chapter 4 was originally published in *The Journal of Modern African Studies* 42, no. 1 (2004), as "Leading from Behind: Democratic Consolidation and the Chieftaincy in South Africa." Permission to reproduce these chapters is gratefully acknowledged.

Of course, friends and families often bear the brunt of a project like this, and I am deeply grateful for the love and support of the McArdle family, the Martin family, David and Terri Richmond, and Rick and Kathy Sepulveda. My sister, Julie, and her husband, Eric, were a constant source of inspiration and support. I am particularly grateful to Julie for listening to my ideas about South African politics and providing me with different perspectives that I had not considered. My parents, Rod and Marlene, opened my eyes to the world at an early age and provided me with the curiosity to venture to South Africa in the first place. It is not an exaggeration to say that they have given me their full support and love to secure all my dreams, and it has been no different with the writing of this book.

I owe special thanks to Hanford for reminding me each day when it was time to leave the computer to get some fresh air in the backyard with a game of fetch or to go for a much-needed walk. To the newest members of the family, I want to thank Zack and Ben for providing me with a new perspective on life when I needed it most and for reminding me that there is no better job than being a dad.

To my soul mate, friend, and wife, Molly, I am thankful for her unconditional love, support, and encouragement in what was both an exciting and demanding period in our lives. More than anyone else, Molly experienced the full range of challenges and emotions that accompanied the completion of this study. In South Africa, not only was she a source of personal and moral support, but she proved to be a crucial research assistant whose own reflections, observations, and questions helped me to understand aspects of South African society that I would have otherwise ignored. There is no one else in the world I would want with me during this journey, and I am forever thankful that she is part of my life.

ABBREVIATIONS

ANC	African National Congress
CC	Constitutional Court
CONTRALESA	Congress of Traditional Leaders of South Africa
DA	Democratic Alliance
DPLG	Department of Provincial and Local Government
DWAF	Department of Water Affairs
GEAR	Growth, Employment and Redistribution
IC	Interim Constitution
IEC	Independent Electoral Commission
IFP	Inkatha Freedom Party
ISRDP	Integrated Sustainable Rural Development Programme
KZG	KwaZulu Government
KZN	KwaZulu-Natal
LG White Paper	Local Government White Paper
LGTA	Local Government Transition Act
NP	National Party
RDP	Reconstruction and Development Programme
SADF	South African Defense Force
SALGA	South African Local Government Association
TLGF Act	Traditional Leadership Governance and Framework Act
TLGF Bill	Traditional Leadership Governance and Framework Bill
UDF	United Democratic Front
URC	Uthungulu Regional Council
ZJSB	Zululand Joint Services Board

CHIEFTAINCY, THE STATE, AND DEMOCRACY

ONE

INTRODUCTION

The Chieftaincy, the State, and the Desire to Dominate

*Without traditional leadership, there would be no community.
It is like tea without water.*

*We, the people of South Africa, recognize the injustices of our
past; honour those who suffered for justice in our land; respect
those who have worked to build and develop our country; and
believe that South Africa belongs to all who live in it, united
in our diversity.*

The current political order in South Africa is one that
reflects both continuity and change with its apartheid
past. Its transition to democracy in the early 1990s, heralded around the
world as a "miracle," resulted in one of the most progressive constitutions in the world that sought to establish strong democratic institutions. As such, it is not surprising that the leaders of the African National
Congress (ANC), the majority party since 1994, have continually made
solemn promises to "democratize" and "transform" the lives of ordinary
citizens. Indeed, in many ways, there have been notable positive changes
since 1994, and South Africa has enjoyed nearly fifteen years of relative
stability and peace. At the same time, many of the legacies of the apartheid era remain intact and are conspicuous to citizens and visitors alike.
The economic and social legacies, such as the growing income inequality,
the rising number of shantytowns in the urban areas, and the continued
racial tensions, are the most visible, but few students of South African
politics appreciate the significance that the institution of the chieftaincy
has in the daily lives of many South African citizens. Yet as one of the
most vivid political reminders of the apartheid past, the institution of the
chieftaincy demands careful scrutiny, especially in evaluating the quality
of democracy and the nature of state-society relations in South Africa.

For the leaders of the post-apartheid South African state, there is perhaps no political institution that has caused as much contention, and as much angst, as the chieftaincy. Indeed, the more than two thousand mostly hereditary rulers that make up the chieftaincy institution have been a source of agitation for the government since the transition period in the early 1990s. For this reason, the decision to officially recognize and protect this institution in the post-apartheid constitution was itself controversial. Admittedly, given the plethora of issues that exist in post-apartheid South Africa, such an assertion might be interpreted as mere hyperbole. Yet given the ambitious goals of the ANC to fundamentally change the lives of ordinary South Africans, the potential of the chieftaincy to facilitate, or to discourage, this process should not be underestimated. Indeed, the claims of the chieftaincy that it "represents" local populations and that it should have "autonomous" authority over them are declarations that should be taken seriously, as they demonstrate the ongoing struggle between the chieftaincy and the state regarding which of these institutions has the right to exercise its authority. In short, the presence and influence of the chieftaincy in South Africa is real, and the success or failure of South Africa's democratic experiment in some ways depends on how it is incorporated into the new political order.

For many within the ruling ANC, the coexistence of the chieftaincy with more democratic institutions has been simply a short-term necessary evil, which was itself the product of a transition littered with difficult accommodations. Despite the fact that at its founding in 1912 the ANC welcomed the participation of chiefs in its organization and many chiefs were active in the ANC throughout the anti-apartheid struggle, many believed that the apartheid regime had effectively de-traditionalized and de-legitimized this pre-colonial institution. In this vein, it is the view of a number of politicians, journalists, and scholars that at some point in the future the chieftaincy must be abolished in order for South Africa to become truly democratic (Ntsebeza 2005; Mamdani 1996; Munro 1996). Depending on one's definition of democracy and one's vision of what type of social order is most appropriate for South Africa, this may be true, but whether South Africa should have recognized the chieftaincy during the democratic transition is a topic that misses more compelling issues.

The more interesting question, and the focus of this book, is how the chieftaincy seeks to establish and maintain its political legitimacy, vis-à-vis local populations as well as the state, in the post-apartheid period. Since 1994, the chieftaincy has been forced to share its authority with a new set of institutions, which are based on a set of norms, rules, and processes that are distinct from its own. For example, one obvious difference is that while post-apartheid institutions are premised on the twin principles of majority rule and free and fair elections, the chieftaincy is based on decision making through consensus and on the hereditary right to rule. Similarly, while the ANC promotes the vision of a pluralist and diverse South Africa, many people in rural areas perceive the chieftaincy as representative of the unity of the local community, and in many cases "strangers" are met with distrust.

These differences are not trivial, nor are they necessarily incompatible, but they do represent conflicting worldviews about the nature of authority and the right to rule. Thus, what is important to analyze is how the recognition and protection of the chieftaincy in the interim (1993) and final (1996) constitutions put into motion a struggle between the chieftaincy and the state over which moral-order worldview would achieve hegemony at the local level.

As this analysis reveals, there are no clear "winners" or "losers" in this struggle. Instead, one of the results of this interaction has been the mutual transformation of both the state institutions and the chieftaincy, and the blending together of the different political norms, rules, and processes associated with each. Understanding how this mutual transformation unfolds and the implications this has on the legitimacy of the chieftaincy and the legitimacy of the state are the central aims of this book.

The starting point for this analysis is based on the current political reality that the chieftaincy remains an important political force at the local level. In previous research on the authority of the chieftaincy, there is a general consensus that in much of sub-Saharan Africa, and specifically in South Africa, people still rely on the chieftaincy to address their daily needs (Logan 2009; Beall 2006; Bratton, Mattes, and Gyimah-Boadi 2005; Oomen 2005 and 2000). The reasons why people continue to access their chiefs and the question of whether people accept chiefs as legitimate rulers remain open to debate (Oomen 2005; Rouveroy van Nieuwaal 1987 and 1996). This political reality, in my opinion, requires a different type of analysis that does more than simply wish the chieftaincy away, but rather seeks to understand the process through which it continues to exercise authority.

To analyze these struggles over political legitimacy in South Africa, I examine the dynamics among the chieftaincy, state institutions, and local populations in three chieftaincies located in the KwaZulu-Natal province. My analysis situates these local experiences into the broader political environment and compares the processes of continuity and change in these three chieftaincies with what has occurred in other chieftaincies throughout South Africa. This comparative case study focuses specifically on how the chieftaincy and local populations have negotiated the introduction of specific norms, rules, processes, and institutions that are fundamental to the ANC's policies of transformation and democratization. In particular, I analyze how the introduction of free and fair elections, elected local government institutions, and development projects has affected the legitimation process at the local level. In most cases, these "modern" institutions, as well as the underlying democratic political principles, were first introduced to many rural South Africans in the post-1994 period. An examination of the struggle between the chieftaincy and the state to exercise authority reveals the syncretic nature of authority at the local level. Through a "the multiple legitimacies framework," I will explain how the chieftaincy has sought to establish and maintain its authority in the midst of these political changes.

THE CHIEFTAINCY IN SOUTH AFRICA: FACT OR FICTION?

Despite assurances that an examination of the chieftaincy in South Africa was a worthwhile research project, it was three weeks after I had arrived in South Africa, in September 1998, when I began to appreciate for the first time the complexity of the chieftaincy in the South African political and social environment. In the University of Natal-Durban bookstore, looking for recent books on the chieftaincy, I asked one of the employees if she knew where I could find such publications. After the receptionist at the front shyly confessed she was not sure, she asked another employee, in all seriousness, whether the chieftaincy would be in the fiction or nonfiction section of the bookstore.

After they shared a mutual laugh at my expense, I quietly browsed the bookstore on my own, finding a few historical accounts of the chieftaincy in the history and sociology sections, but nothing on the role of the chieftaincy in contemporary South Africa. I left wondering what I should take away from this encounter. At the time, I was embarrassed and a bit worried—embarrassed that I had shown my true colors as an outsider who knew very little about "real" South African politics and worried that this institution that I had read so much about in academic books and articles was somehow not real. Looking back, I see now that it was my first real indication that for many people in South Africa, not to mention those who live elsewhere, the chieftaincy remained a mystery and that any analysis of the chieftaincy requires an initial examination of who these chiefs are, what they do on a daily basis, and how the post-apartheid state has sought to accommodate this institution.

According to the most recent government survey, there are more than 2,400 individual kings, queens, chiefs, and headmen in South Africa, who reside in seven of the nine provinces.[1] Those occupying these positions are sometimes referred to as "traditional leaders," and the institution is often referred to as "traditional leadership." It should be noted at the outset that the use of these terms itself is a source of much political and academic dispute in South Africa. For some, the use of the term "traditional" is controversial, as it implies that this institution and its leaders have remained unchanged over time and somehow provide an unproblematic link with the pre-colonial past. Nevertheless, the terms "traditional leaders" and "traditional leadership" are in common usage in South Africa, and these terms are used in the constitution and in many statutes. In this same vein, there are many traditional leaders who find the terms "chief" and "chieftaincy" disrespectful because these are titles that were used during colonialism and apartheid.

At the local level, this issue is usually avoided as most everyone refers to the institution in his or her indigenous language.[2] While the government has officially adopted the terms "traditional leaders" and "traditional leadership," I have decided to use the term "chieftaincy" to describe the institution itself and to use the term "chief" to describe those particular leaders with this title. I have not made this choice for any normative reasons, and readers should not infer any conscious or unconscious motives other than the fact that I believe the terms "chieftaincy" and "chief" allow for a more fluid narrative. When I refer to the chief's assistants, I will use the appropriate Zulu terms: *induna* (headman), plural form *izinduna; iphoyisa* (assistant to *induna*), plural form *amaphoyisa*. In addition, there is another set of assistants to the *izinduna* who are simply referred to as "traditional councilors." There are some instances where I will refer to the chief and his assistants as a group, and for the sake of convenience, I will simply use the term "traditional leaders."

Each of the 2,400 traditional leaders mentioned above has jurisdiction over a specified territory. The eleven kings and queens rule over sizable areas of land and have authority over a group of chiefs. For example, in the province of KwaZulu-Natal, King Goodwill Zwelethini, who came to power in 1971, is the leader for the 280 Zulu chiefs who live in this territory—some of which was formerly part of the Zulu Kingdom, which was an independent political entity from 1816 to 1879. While the kings and queens are supposed to be nonpartisan and exercise mostly ceremonial responsibilities, this has not been the case in KwaZulu-Natal, where King Zwelethini has often been involved in provincial and national politics.

Each chief in South Africa has authority over a specified territory as well. Currently, there are 774 different chiefdoms in South Africa. Beginning with colonial rule in the early nineteenth century, the labels that the government has attached to these territorial units have changed. For example, during the nineteenth century, beginning with British colonial rule in the Natal and Cape colonies, chiefs were given authority over particular "reserves" or "locations." After the election of the National Party (NP) in 1948, and with the passage of the Bantu Authorities Act in 1951, these areas were renamed "tribal authorities." In addition to creating tribal authorities at the local level, this act also created "regional authorities," which consisted of a group of tribal authorities, and it also created a number of "territorial authorities" that had jurisdiction over the regional authorities and the tribal authorities (see map 1). During apartheid, many referred to these areas collectively as Bantustans or Homelands—the point being that under the apartheid regime all black South Africans belonged to a particular Bantustan, and they were required to reside there unless they received permission from the apartheid government to live and work in the so-called white areas. The areas designated as Bantustans for the 80 percent of the population that was classified as black constituted only 13 percent of the territory in South Africa, which resulted in overcrowding and overuse of the land. Those who lived in these areas were under the control of chiefs and under the jurisdiction of customary law.

Keeping track of the different labels that have been used to describe the chieftaincy areas is itself a challenging task. Most recently, with the passage of the Traditional Leadership Governance and Framework Act (TLGF Act) in 2003, what were previously referred to as "tribal authorities" were renamed "traditional councils" and the regional authorities were replaced with "local houses of traditional leaders." Because all South Africans are now recognized citizens of the Republic of South Africa, the terms "Bantustan" and "Homeland" are no longer officially used to describe the areas where there are traditional councils or local houses of traditional leaders. At the same time, the boundaries of the chieftaincies have remained unchanged from the apartheid era, despite the use of a different label. Unlike the pre-colonial period, where chieftaincy boundaries were much less defined, the current territorial units are the product

MAP 1. *South Africa Bantustans. Map designed by Em Hansen Trent and courtesy of the University Libraries, the University of Texas at Austin.*

of state law. In fact, in the offices of the Department of Provincial and Local Government (DPLG), which is the national government department responsible for the chieftaincies, there exist voluminous maps of these areas, along with files that dutifully record the exact coordinates of every territorial unit as well as the history of each "tribe."[3]

In terms of what chiefs do on a daily basis, the local people expect their chief to fulfill certain responsibilities. First and foremost, the chief is responsible to provide order and security. Ultimately, the chief is the person who is supposed to coordinate security measures at public gatherings and make sure that those who break rules are held accountable in customary or state courts. Second, chiefs are expected to solve disputes.

Whether there is a conflict over land, cattle, water, or even the placement of a development project, there is an expectation that the chief should be involved in the resolution process. Depending on the nature of the dispute, the chief may decide to hold a formal court hearing where anyone from the public may attend or to resolve the matter more informally at his homestead.

In addition to providing order and resolving disputes, chiefs are also responsible for the allocation of land in the community. In the areas where the chiefs rule, there is no individual freehold title; instead, people occupy their land with the consent of the chief. For example, if someone in the community needs more land to accommodate his family, he must ask permission from the chief. During apartheid, those who were granted land were given a Permission to Occupy Certificate from the chief that "officially" recognized this use.

Finally, a main function of the chief is to preside over ancestral rituals and ceremonies. There is a belief in many communities that the chief is the most important link to the ancestors and that the chief provides unity to his area through his connection with the supernatural world (Weir 2005; Flint 2001; Berglund 1989; Krige 1936). While the extent to which chiefs perform these ceremonial duties varies, it is common to hear people discuss how the chief's authority is based not only on what he does in the material world, but on his connection with the supernatural world as well.

The territories that the chiefs rule vary in size and in population. In the province of KwaZulu-Natal, for example, chieftaincies range in population from a few thousand people to well over thirty thousand. Each one is further divided into smaller areas, which in KwaZulu-Natal are referred to as wards. While these wards rarely appear on official maps, the boundaries between the wards are well known within the local community. Within each ward, there is an *induna*, who provides assistance to the chief. For many in the local community, the *induna* is the first person they visit when there is a conflict, and in many cases, the *induna* is able to resolve any disputes without taking the issue to the chief. While the responsibilities vary in each chieftaincy, most *izinduna* have the authority to resolve minor disputes, to make recommendations concerning development, to provide security at festivals or other gatherings, and to take the concerns of the people to the chief and to help the chief govern the area. In the past, the *izinduna* claimed their positions based on hereditary right or by appointment from the chief, but this selection process is undergoing some changes.

The Zulu king and the Zulu chiefs, especially chief Gatsha Buthelezi, have been some of the most vocal and forceful advocates of the chieftaincy, and they have sought to preserve the chieftaincy's power and autonomy in South Africa's new political order. The province of Kwa-Zulu-Natal has more chieftaincies than any other province in South Africa, with 280 recognized chiefs as well as thousands of *izinduna* and traditional councilors (who are assistants to the *izinduna*). The Zulus are also the largest ethnic/language group in South Africa, and make up almost one quarter of the total population. While most Zulus live in the province of KwaZulu-Natal, there are also sizable contingents who live and work in the province of Gauteng. Of the more than 9 million Zulus who live in KwaZulu-Natal, it is estimated that 54 percent live in rural areas (Republic of South Africa 2001a).[4] Of those, a vast majority live under the authority of the chieftaincy. It is also common, however, to find chiefs who rule in townships, which are located at the outskirts of urban areas, or to find chiefs who rule in areas that are sometimes referred to as peri-urban. For the most part, however, Zulu chiefs, like chiefs throughout South Africa, are more common in rural areas.

Since 1994, the ANC-led government has adopted numerous measures to accommodate the chieftaincy. This is not particularly surprising. According to the post-apartheid constitution, the government is required to recognize and protect all traditional leaders who claim their authority within the parameters of customary law. It is estimated that approximately 14 million people (30 percent of the total population) live under the jurisdiction of the chieftaincy, although this number does not account for those who officially live in areas where there is no chieftaincy but who may return on a regular basis to rural areas where the chieftaincy remains in power (Republic of South Africa 2002: 24).

In addition to recognizing individual chiefs and the territorial areas that they have ruled since 1994, the South African national government, as well as each of the seven provinces where the chieftaincy resides, has also established national and provincial Houses of Traditional Leadership, which consult with the elected governmental bodies on issues that affect their areas. Finally, every king, queen, and chief in South Africa earns a government salary, and they are expected to assist with development projects at the local level. The provincial government pays these salaries, with kings earning R507,038 ($45,271) per year and chiefs earning R121,702 ($10,866) per year (Republic of South Africa, Proclamation 34, No. 29166, August 29, 2006).[5] To put this in perspective, in 2001, for those individuals living in the local municipality where two of the three case studies for this book are located, only 0.002 percent of the population had an annual income of more than R76,812, and a total of 78 percent had no reported income (Republic of South Africa 2001a). In addition, there was an estimated 48.5 percent of the total South African population who fell below the national poverty line of R354 per month in 2002 (United Nations Development Programme 2003: 5–6).

Thus, for better or for worse, the chieftaincy is definitely formally entrenched in post-apartheid South Africa, and it has influence over a range of decisions that affect a large segment of the population.

WHY SOUTH AFRICA?

Because of its relative political and economic success since 1994, its strong democratic institutions, and its vibrant and active civil society, some scholars suggest that South Africa represents an "exceptional" case in sub-Saharan Africa and that the lessons of the South African experience do not travel to other countries on the continent (Mattes 2007; Villalon and VonDoepp 2005; Gibson 2004; Klug 2000). Yet despite its economic, political, and social "successes," South Africa continues to face many of the same issues that other sub-Saharan African countries face.

For example, the anti-immigrant riots in 2008 highlighted not only the xenophobia that exists in South Africa, but also the frustration of many citizens concerning the lack of employment and the growing inequality in society. There is also growing evidence that South Africans are highly dissatisfied with their democratic institutions and that despite the relative strength of the South African state, many citizens in the rural areas continue to lack basic services, such as clean water, roads, electricity, and quality schools (Crais 2002, 2006; Koelble 1998, 2005; Picard 2005; Du Toit 1995). Even more ominous was the forced resignation of President Mbeki in 2008, and the sense that South Africa has become a dominant-party state where the opposition has little opportunity to affect policy decisions (Friedman 1999; Southall 1998). As most students of African politics are aware, the issues mentioned here are common throughout Africa, which is a reminder that upon closer inspection, South Africa might not be quite as exceptional as first appearances suggest.

The example of the chieftaincy makes this point abundantly clear. An examination of chieftaincy-state and chieftaincy-societal relations in post-apartheid South Africa provides another reminder of its similarities with other African states (Mamdani 1996). Indeed, with respect to the accommodations made to the chieftaincy during the democratic transition and the decision to formally integrate the chieftaincy into the political order, the South African case has more similarities than dissimilarities with its neighbors.

For example, of the forty-eight states in sub-Saharan Africa, at least twenty of them have officially recognized the chieftaincy in constitutions or through statutes. While many African states in the 1950s and 1960s sought to abolish the chieftaincy, this trend was gradually reversed, especially in the 1990s (Rouveroy van Nieuwaal 1996). Ghana, Namibia, Nigeria, and Mozambique are just four examples of states that have incorporated the chieftaincy into their constitutional dispensation in the last twenty years (Kyed and Burr 2006; Burr and Kyed 2006; Vaughn 2003; Rathbone 2000; Vaughn 2000). Thus, it is clear that the decision to accommodate the chieftaincy in the interim (1993) and final (1996) constitutions is one that many other countries made, and the chieftaincy-societal and chieftaincy-state dynamics examined here might also shed new analytical light on similar dynamics in other sub-Saharan African countries.

In terms of the accommodations it has made with traditional leaders, South Africa provides a fascinating example of what Sklar refers to as a "mixed polity"—a democracy that combines both democratic and oligarchic features. Sklar (1999) argues that mixed polities are quite common, and he suggests that integrating indigenous political institutions, even if they are not democratic, might provide stability and promote development. Consistent with this argument, Englebert goes even further and suggests that those African states that have incorporated indigenous institutions are more likely to establish and maintain political legitimacy (2000: 129). Other scholars more generally note the "hybridity" of African regimes and the blending together of so-called liberal and illiberal politics (Villalon and VonDoepp 2005: 6). Whatever label is used, it seems clear that African states that democratized in the early 1990s often adopted sets of institutions, rules, and processes that are not easily situated into the Western notion of "liberal democracy." Recognition of this institutional integration, however, does not itself capture how struggles for authority unfold within mixed polities. This study seeks to address this issue with an analysis of how the mixed-polity system provides the context for negotiations over legitimacy at the local level.

Given the number of mixed polities that exist in sub-Saharan Africa, it is important to consider how this form of governance might affect the process of democratization. In this way, the South African case furthers our understanding of how the democratic experience is manifested in non-Western cultures. To borrow Schaffer's (1998) term, there is much to be learned about the way democracy continues to be "translated" in South Africa through an examination of the chieftaincy. Given its progressive constitution, its neo-liberal economic policy, and its rating as "free" from the Freedom House since 1994, there is a tendency to overlook the fact that South Africans, especially those in the rural areas, may define democracy differently than do those in the West. In his analysis concerning the meanings of democracy among the Baganda, Karlstrom found that "if Africans have shown themselves by no means uninterested in democracy, the democracy which they envision often does differ significantly from Western liberal conceptions" and that indigenous conceptions of democracy are oftentimes linked to pre-colonial chieftaincy institutions (1996: 1). This is equally true in South Africa, and a close examination of the chieftaincy in South Africa enables us to better understand the way democracy is internalized in the non-Western world.

MAKING SENSE OF THE RESILIENT CHIEFTAINCY: EXISTING THEORIES

Despite the recognition that the chieftaincy continues to wield authority at the local level, there is no consensus on why and how this occurs. That is, why have people remained loyal to the chieftaincy when there now exist democratic alternatives? And to the extent that people remain loyal to the chieftaincy, what is the source of its authority? Over the last fifteen years, there has been a renewed interest in these questions. The result has been a burgeoning literature that has focused on a number of factors to best explain how the chieftaincy has remained resilient during a time when Africa was becoming more democratic. In this vein, scholars have argued that its continued presence is related to the legacy of indirect rule,[6] the existence of weak post-colonial states,[7] the rise of cultural rights,[8] the allocation of land,[9] the adaptability of the chieftaincy,[10] and the rise of a neo-liberal economic order.[11] Each of these studies contributes to our understanding of the chieftaincy, and they all focus attention on how politics is practiced in those areas at the periphery of state control. Yet for the most part, each of these studies fails to examine the processes through which the chieftaincy, the state, and the local populations negotiate the interface between different types of norms, rules, and institutions. Similarly, while there have been few studies focusing on the legitimacy of the chieftaincy at the local level, there have been numerous attempts to explain its so-called resilience or revival.[12]

Of the arguments that have been advanced over the last two decades concerning the resilience of the chieftaincy, perhaps the most well known argument is Mamdani's analysis in *Citizen and Subject* (1996), where he focuses on the legacies of indirect rule. His approach focuses attention on the *forms of power* prevalent during both colonial and apartheid rule and the institutional legacies these forms of power have for post-colonial regimes. Mamdani correctly notes that chiefs were the central link between state and society during colonial and apartheid periods. With respect to South Africa, the legitimacy and stability of the apartheid system depended, in large part, upon the willingness of these leaders to implement government policies. The central state institutionalized and manipulated the ideas of custom and tradition as a means to enhance the authority of the chieftaincy (granting them complete judicial, legislative, and executive authority) and to facilitate indirect rule (Mamdani 1996). According to Mamdani, the apartheid system created a bifurcated state in which chiefs practiced "decentralized despotism," owing more loyalty to the central state than to the local populations.

In terms of the legitimacy of the chieftaincy, Mamdani suggests that the authority of this institution cannot be disconnected from the power of the central state. The colonial state utilized the "traditional" powers of the chieftaincy to help facilitate colonial rule. The chieftaincy, according to Mamdani, lacks an independent or autonomous source of legitimacy (other than a manipulated version of "customary law") and continues to exist only because the state is unwilling, or perceives itself unable, to eliminate it.

It is assumed that chiefs may exercise power, but that they do not exercise legitimate power. This is because the power of the chiefs *comes from* the state rather than from local populations. Specifically, the chieftaincy continues to control their subjects either because of the use or threat of state force and/or because these leaders rely upon the expanded definitions of "customary law" to justify and legitimate what is otherwise "uncustomary" behavior.

In short, according to this analysis, the chieftaincy should not be conceptualized as separate from the state itself, as it is nothing more than an extension of the state's authority. If Mamdani were correct, which I argue he is not, then there would be little reason to investigate the relations between the chieftaincy and local populations, as they are devoid of any authentic consent. Instead, attention would focus only on the relationship between the chieftaincy and the state.

While Mamdani's study provides a detailed examination of the relationship between the apartheid state and the chieftaincy, it does not examine these relations in the post-apartheid era (Mamdani 1996). Instead, Mamdani offers a set of hypotheses concerning the possible ways this relationship might develop given his understanding of the political dynamics of the apartheid era and the nature of the transition process. For Mamdani, the legacies of the bifurcated state and decentralized despotism suggest a certain type of political development for South Africa—one in which the lines between citizen and subject remain impenetrable. Even more importantly, Mamdani did not consider the limits of the central state's control at the local level, or the possibility that traditional leaders needed to respond to community opinions in order to maintain legitimacy (Crais 2006; Oomen 2005: 20; Herbst 2000; Hamilton 1998). In this way, his analysis largely ignores the specific struggles at the local level concerning the role of the chieftaincy vis-à-vis the state and rural populations.

More recently, Ntsebeza utilizes Mamdani's framework to examine the chieftaincy in the district of Xhalanga in the Eastern Cape. His central argument is that the chieftaincy remains an important political actor largely because of the policies of the colonial state, the apartheid state, and now the post-apartheid state. He suggests that as long as the state enables the chieftaincy to control land allocation it will remain a powerful local actor (2005: 23). Consistent with Mamdani, he concludes that the chieftaincy is not compatible with democracy in South Africa, and argues that the only reason that it remains significant in the rural areas is because it controls the allocation of land.

Ntsebeza offers a rich and detailed historical analysis of the chieftaincy, and it is an important contribution to the literature on this topic. Yet while I agree that land allocation is important, I disagree with the notion that this is the only reason that chiefs remain resilient, and I think he underestimates their continued symbolic and moral force in contemporary South Africa. In fact, his study focuses little on the ways in which the chieftaincy, the state, and citizens have interacted since 1994. To the extent that he does address the post-apartheid period, he limits his analysis to the ways in which the ANC has embedded the chieftaincy through a series of local government, development, and land policies.

Another explanation for the resiliency of the chieftaincy focuses on the existence of weak states. The thrust of this argument is that the chieftaincy remains an important institution because the central state lacks the necessary capacity to fulfill its everyday duties (Rouveroy van Nieuwaal 1996; Alexander 1995). With this approach, the chieftaincy is the fortunate benefactor of an inefficient, corrupt, and disconnected African state. State and society are the dominant concepts within this framework, and the chieftaincy is often conceptualized as the important "link" or "hinge point" between the two. In what Migdal refers to as "the triangle of accommodation," chiefs and *izinduna* are local-level "strongmen," whom the state seeks to accommodate and control at its own peril (1988: chapter 7). This is a difficult strategy to implement, as the states may be unable to "capture" chiefs completely, which then enables the chiefs to continue to exercise social control and to promote their own normative order (Migdal 1994: 26–27).

Similarly, in his study of democratic attitudes in Africa, Bratton finds that even though Africans claim they prefer democratic institutions, they still tend to interact with non-state polities, such as the chieftaincy, more than with state institutions. He attributes this to the fact that the state institutions have not shown they have the capacity to respond to the needs of the people (Bratton, Mattes, and Gyimah-Boadi 2005). With respect to South Africa, Keulder argues that the post-apartheid state is quite weak in the rural areas and that the decision to incorporate the chieftaincy was purely pragmatic, as it enabled the state to exercise at least some measure of authority through the chiefs (1998: 306). Unlike Mamdani, who sees the chieftaincy as part of the state, these studies imply that that chieftaincy is part of civil society.

While the weak-state explanation helps us to understand the ways in which the central state has accommodated the chieftaincy, and its potential political power, it focuses too much attention on interactions with the state and too little on the specific relations between the chieftaincy and local populations. This argument privileges the state as the center of political activity and does not address how these various state actions influence relations between chiefs and local populations.

The problem is that there is no attempt to explain how the chieftaincy may or may not generate legitimacy at the local level; instead, these arguments all rely on the common assumption that the chieftaincy's legitimacy results from declining, or nonexistent, state capacity. In the end, this approach cannot explain a situation where the chieftaincy continues to wield authority even though the state has capacity and is adequately providing resources and services to rural citizens.[13]

Another explanation for the resiliency of the chieftaincy focuses on specific global forces in the 1990s, such as the rise of cultural and indigenous rights and the rise of an economic and political order dominated by neo-liberal policies (Oomen 2005; Comaroff and Comaroff 2004; Koelble 2005; Koelble and LiPuma 2005). As Oomen notes, "[o]ne way in which this scramble for legitimacy in an increasingly interconnected, globalizing world was played out was through the culture card: reviving traditional systems of governance, emphasizing autochthony in politics, granting 'group rights' to indigenous peoples or 'first nations'" (2005: 3–4). At the same time that culture was becoming more important, the ability of the state to broadcast its authority into the periphery was circumscribed with the introduction of economic and political policies that actually limited the reach of the state (Koelble 2005; Booysen 2003; Motloung and Mears 2002; Cheru 2001; Koelble 1998). Koelble and LiPuma note that the nature of neo-liberal economic policies has constrained the state and limited its ability to "reach into the hinterlands" (2005: 91–92). Moreover, these "constraints imposed on governance are . . . leading to a rescaling of the critical functionalities" of the state itself (92). It is into this "political vacuum" that the chieftaincy emerges as an important social force (92). Thus, the argument is that these twin processes provided the context for the chieftaincy to stake its claim and to remain a viable actor in the post–Cold War world.

The focus on these external forces is important, and I agree that it is difficult to explain the political gains of the chieftaincy without understanding this global context. For example, there is no question that traditional leaders in South Africa utilized the rhetoric of cultural rights to their advantage during the transition period (Oomen 2005; Comaroff and Comaroff 2004; Klopper 1998; Bank and Southall 1996). It was also to their benefit that Nelson Mandela had praised the virtues of the chieftaincy both in his autobiography and after his release from prison, thereby allying himself with this global movement (1994a; Ntsebeza 2005: 259).

While these factors may provide the context for the so-called revival of the chieftaincy, how traditional leaders actually responded and adapted to this context is the focus of my analysis (Rouveroy van Nieuwaal 1996). Oomen's analysis comes closest to this approach, as she moves between the global and the local to explain how chiefs have created law at the local level since 1994. The difference between my analysis and Oomen's is that instead of focusing on the making of law at the local level, I am interested in how newly introduced norms, rules, processes, and institutions—such as elections, local government, and development projects—influences the legitimation process in the rural areas and how local populations use the chieftaincy as a lens to give meaning to these new forms of authority.[14]

Finally, some scholars suggest that the resilience of the chieftaincy is based upon its ability to successfully straddle the "modern" world and the "traditional" world. In some ways, this framework seeks to understand the authority of the chieftaincy using Weber's ideal-type dichotomy of traditional and modern legitimacy. Consistent with this argument is Rouveroy's conception of the chieftaincy as a "hinge point" between local populations and the state (1996: 46). According to this analysis, the key to maintaining authority in these situations is the ability of traditional leaders to "dispose[] of two different bases of legitimacy and authority. This permits him to operate differently towards the state and his people. A kind of hinge point, a chief tries to connect both worlds" (46). Thus, rather than suggesting that the chieftaincy's authority is rooted only in "tradition," this framework suggests a more dynamic process at work. What is most useful with this conception of the chieftaincy is that it focuses on the agency of local actors and correctly highlights that the chieftaincy, the state, and the local populations are engaged in an ongoing process through which each is attempting to exercise authority.

What this model fails to account for, however, is that the different moral orders—the "modern" and the "traditional"—actually interact and blend together in important ways. Even though most contemporary accounts of the chieftaincy eschew the use of the modern/traditional dichotomy to describe authority relations, the notion that there exist two separate worlds only serves to reinforce this idea. Rather than operating in distinct worlds, I argue that traditional leaders are involved in a process where they have been forced to incorporate particular aspects of the state's moral order to maintain their authority.

THE MULTIPLE LEGITIMACIES FRAMEWORK

While there are a number of explanatory frameworks that have been utilized to understand the legitimacy of the chieftaincy, none of these adequately captures the importance of chieftaincy-society relations at the local level, or the nature of the legitimation process. The starting point for my analysis is that in rural South Africa there are multiple sources of legitimacy that all leaders—chiefs as well as elected officials— can use to justify their rule. Each of these different sources of legitimacy offers people a particular set of set of symbols, values, political principles, institutions, rules, and processes that are central to ruler-ruled relations and interactions. Unfortunately, all too often these different sources of legitimacy are conceptualized as static, diametrically opposed categories that represent so-called traditional and modern worldviews.

Critics of this categorical approach note that such ideal-type dichotomies ignore the ways in which understandings of what is "traditional" and "modern" can change over time and the ways in which different sources of legitimacy can blend together (Economic Commission for Africa 2007; Galvan 2004; Lutz and Linder 2004; Bierschenk and Olivier de Sardan 2003; Ray 2003; Dusing 2002; Goheen 1992; Whitaker 1970). Yet while the notion of a strict traditional/modern dichotomy does little to explain the process of legitimation, it is also a mistake not to recognize the political reality that sub-Saharan Africa is replete with competing understandings of legitimacy and that achieving hegemony is one of the most daunting challenges for the post-colonial state.

In this study, the chieftaincy is conceptualized as not only an institution that performs particular functions, but one that promotes a particular set of norms, rules, institutions, and processes that are distinct from those proposed by the post-apartheid democratic state. What I refer to as the multiple legitimacies framework seeks to focus attention on the process through which chiefs struggle to promote and reproduce a preexisting set of governance norms and structures while simultaneously responding to the introduction of new norms, rules, and institutions at the local level.

Unlike previous studies, this analysis focuses on the actions of chiefs, and their assistants, as they seek to traverse a new political and social environment. It also accounts for the ways in which normative and institutional structures limit their actions (North 1990). Chiefs, local populations, and state officials are engaged in an ongoing process where specific components of the different sources of legitimacy are borrowed, reproduced, altered, and/or co-opted. Thus, these different sources of legitimacy are not hermetically sealed and resistant to change; in fact, the assumption of this analysis is just the opposite.

To maintain political legitimacy, the chieftaincy must find ways to blend its political norms and values with those of the post-apartheid state in ways that resonate with local populations. While achieving some type of congruence between the new and the old may be the objective, in many instances the result is the creation of an entirely new, and distinct, moral order, however unintended and unforeseen.

It is at the local level where one can learn the most about its legitimacy because it is at this level focus can be on what traditional leaders actually *do* and what they *mean* to those in the community. In this vein, I describe the ordinary, and extraordinary, encounters between traditional leaders, rural populations, and local government officials as a way to explain the nature of legitimacy at the local level. More generally, such an analysis provides the opportunity to evaluate the state's ability to transform societal norms, rules, and institutions that are deeply embedded and that predate the establishment of the democratic rule (Herbst 2000; Scott 1998).

To address these questions requires a challenge to common assumptions concerning the nature of the chieftaincy's political authority, as well as the conceptual connections between the state, political legitimacy, and democracy. Specifically, I do not assume that the state is the only institution with political legitimacy, nor do I assume that the introduction of democratic rules and processes automatically results in political legitimacy (Schatzberg 2001; Schaffer 1998). Instead, my framework allows for the possibility that other non-state institutions, in this case the chieftaincy, may create alternative legitimacy formulas that are distinct from what the state promotes.

This blending of different norms, rules, and institutions facilitates a legitimation process that is complex and contradictory, and challenges the conventional understanding of authority, and democracy, in South Africa. Indeed, this book interrogates the very image of a bifurcated state, where civil authority and traditional authority are kept separate and distinct and where democratic consolidation in the rural areas is presumed to be impossible (Mamdani 1996). My argument is that even though both the democratic state institutions and the chieftaincy want to exercise exclusive social control in the rural areas, the reality is that neither is able to do so completely (Koelble 2005; Comaroff and Comaroff 2004; Crais 2002). To remain relevant at the local level, both the state institutions and the chieftaincy are forced to share sovereignty, thereby blurring the boundaries between citizen and subject. Thus, rather than establishing a bifurcated state, these processes reveal the syncretism of authority relations and how the different sources of legitimacy overlap in ways that can be ambiguous, contradictory, and mutually transforming (Koelble 2005; Rouveroy van Nieuwaal 1996; Migdal 1994).

The Nature of Political Legitimacy

Political legitimacy is at the heart of this analysis. While it may be only a slight exaggeration that the issue of political legitimacy is "the master question of politics," there is no question that the nature of this meta-concept is as elusive as it is important (Crick 1959: 150). At its core, and as utilized in my argument, the concept of political legitimacy focuses attention on how political actors, such as chiefs, *justify their rule*. In other words, an examination of political legitimacy highlights the relations between the ruler and the ruled and the extent to which there exists an agreement on the basic contours of power—such as the specific norms, rules, and institutions that are utilized to compel obedience. The basic, and most critical, point here is that rulers desire to have their rules obeyed, and there is a preference to establish obedience that is voluntary rather than forced.

Drawing on these initial assumptions, I conceptualize legitimacy as an ongoing process that involves critical evaluations on the part of both ruler and ruled concerning the justifications for the exercise of power (Alagappa 1995). By focusing on the legitimation process, I am most concerned with those norms, values, myths, and symbols that rulers utilize to establish and maintain political legitimacy (Schatzberg 2001; Beetham 1991).

Given that the legitimation process focuses attention on the relations between ruler and ruled and how the exercise of power is justified, the next issue is how to best conceptualize and understand these dialogues over power. In other words, what factors determine how people evaluate political authority? While there are different ways to approach this issue, I argue that people are more inclined to follow rules if they deem the underlying moral basis of authority as appropriate and right and if the rules are made and enforced in a manner that is beneficial for the community (Alagappa 1995). Each of these considerations is a different dimension of legitimacy, which I refer to as moral legitimacy and performance legitimacy. Thus, the legitimation process consists of an evaluation concerning the exercise of power and whether or not it is justified in terms of its moral and performance dimensions.

In the case of South Africa, I argue that both the state and the chieftaincy are engaged in the legitimation process with those they are ruling. In other words, they are both simultaneously seeking to promote their own norms, rules, and processes. The notion that both the state and the chieftaincy are involved in this process should not come as a surprise. Most rulers, it would seem, at the very least want to be perceived as legitimate, and in some ways it is true that the "desire to justify one's domination is as great as the desire to dominate" (Barker 1990: 14).

As stated above, the multiple legitimacies framework focuses attention on the syncretic nature of authority in rural South Africa and highlights the dynamic interactions among the chieftaincy, the state, and local populations in the struggle for political legitimacy. Unlike other studies, where the issue of political legitimacy is raised, but rarely discussed in any depth, this analysis focuses squarely on this concept (Myers 1999: 38).

To analyze both dimensions of legitimacy, I explore the nature of political legitimacy in rural South Africa from both the bottom up and the top down. In other words, I am interested in understanding the actions that the chieftaincy takes to establish and maintain legitimacy as well as the particular meanings that people attach to the these actions at the local level. Recognizing that government policies may constrain these actions and meanings, I also analyze the ways in which politicians and bureaucrats have sought to define and limit the extent of their authority.

Moral Legitimacies in Sub-Saharan Africa

The moral dimension of political legitimacy is the underlying norms, values, myths, and symbols of the society that are used to define and evaluate "appropriate" political action. These norms, myths, and symbols constitute a worldview that helps to determine the structures of authority as well as a vision of how things ought to be and what is, according to Schatzberg (2001), politically "thinkable." In this way, the moral dimension of legitimacy includes both explanatory and normative ideas. It explicates cause-effect relationships that give meaning to complex events or change, and provides standards for distinguishing between right and wrong.

At its core, it focuses attention on the cultural determinants of authority and the beliefs that people have about authority, what Geertz refers to as the "structures of meaning," through which people make sense of their daily lives (1973: 312). According to Weber, this is crucial, as "the basis of every system of authority, and correspondingly every kind of willingness to obey, is a belief, a belief by virtue of which persons exercising authority are lent prestige" (Weber 1978: 263). Not surprisingly, numerous students of African politics, whether implicitly or explicitly, note the importance of the moral aspect of legitimacy (Schatzberg 2001; Schaffer 1998; Karlstrom 1996; Chabal 1992; Laitin 1986; Bayart 1986).

Where my definition of moral legitimacy differs from others is that I do not assume that there is only one moral order that corresponds with "a society" or even "a state." Instead, I suggest that in South Africa, there exist multiple moral orders that rulers utilize to establish and maintain political legitimacy. These competing moral orders reflect the legacy of the apartheid regime, which sought to divide people of different cultures into distinct political communities, which were presumed to be natural and timeless (Crais 2002).

The notion that there exist multiple legitimacies in sub-Saharan Africa, and that the state is often in conflict with non-state social forces, is well documented in the political science literature (Thornton 2005; Forrest 2003; Rouveroy van Nieuwaal 1999; Heywood 1998; Migdal 1994; Chazan 1988; Migdal 1988; Laitin 1986; Ekeh 1975). These studies, such as Migdal's state-in-society analysis, highlight the ways in which the state seeks to capture or co-opt non-state social forces that might threaten its hegemony (Migdal 1988 and 1994). Even more so than political scientists, however, legal anthropologists have made important theoretical strides concerning our understanding of non-state social forces. Of particular interest here is Moore's formulation of a semi-autonomous political space situated at the nexus of official state laws and informal local rules. She argues that one cannot expect the state's normative system of rules to exercise complete hegemony (1978: 3). The reality, she notes, is that we are "dealing with *partial* order and *partial* control of social life by rules," and there are multiple "reglementary processes" at work in society at once (3). These processes are defined as "all those attempts to organize and control behavior through the use of explicit rules" (3). This ongoing activity in society includes "all the ways in which conscious efforts are made to build and/or reproduce durable social and symbolic orders" as well as "[o]ther countervailing activities [which] are also ubiquitously at work which operate to reinterpret, replace, or alter these supposedly durable cultural forms whenever it is *situationally advantageous to do so*" (6 [emphasis mine]). Moreover, her recognition that these competing forces are "moving all the time, partly connected, partly autonomous" correctly anticipates the extensive fluidity of African power relations.

The most important aspect of Moore's analysis, however, is her understanding that "there can be authorities with rule-making power in many forms of organized society less complex than the state" (1978: 16). She identifies the existence of multiple semi-autonomous corporate groups in society, which make rules to bind their members.

These models highlight the fact that struggles between the state and other social forces over the ability to exercise authority are more likely to be the rule than the exception. What is less apparent is what happens when state institutions and other social forces, each with its own set of norms, rules, and processes, occupy the same social space. While each may desire to impose its own moral orders and completely transform the other, this rarely occurs (Migdal 1988 and 1994). Rather, this interface is likely to facilitate a process that involves negotiation, contestation, and "creative responses" (Galvan and Sil 2007a: 8).

Galvan's analysis of political and social change in Senegal offers a useful framework to understand these interactions. His analysis focuses on how local populations respond to the introduction of new types of property rights, land reform, and democratically elected local councils, or what he refers to more generally as "the local adaptation of imposed political . . . institutions" (2004: 2). Similar to the arguments of Migdal and Moore, he demonstrates how local populations rely upon preexisting norms and rules to make sense of new institutions. In doing so, the local populations were able to alter institutions in ways that made them more "familiar, locally meaningful, even legitimate" (2). For Galvan, the creation of these "syncretic institutions" is simply another reminder that the ideal-type categories of "tradition" and "modern" fail to adequately reflect the social and political reality in many parts of the world.

The recognition that there exist multiple legitimacies and the possibility for the syncretism of authority is particularly useful because it privileges local agency and highlights the interpretative processes that local actors employ to transform selectively newly introduced norms, rules, and processes. In this way, the multiple legitimacies approach is similar not only to Galvan's approach, but to Schaffer's (1998) analysis of the different meanings that the Senegalese attach to democracy and Schatzberg's (2001) analysis of local understandings of power throughout central Africa.

What is common in each of these studies is that they take seriously the local context and the ways in which Africans understand, define, and interpret newly introduced norms and institutions. This process is itself continual, incremental, and, at times, contradictory. Most importantly, each of these studies demonstrates how local actors are able to alter and reconfigure the efforts of the state to transform authority relations. At the same time, local actors are constrained through culture and other structures. Any analysis of the creation of syncretic institutions must take into account these limits.

Ekeh's formulation of "two publics"—the primordial public and the civic public—provides an essential starting point for understanding the origin of this phenomenon (1975: 92). According to Ekeh, unlike in the

West, where the private and the public spheres share the same moral foundation, in Africa, it is only the primordial public that "operates on the same moral imperatives of the private realm" (92). It is distinct from the civic public in that it "is identified with primordial groupings, sentiments, and activities," whereas the civic public is associated with "civil structures" such as the military, the civil service, the police, and local government structures (92). The two publics that Ekeh describes are the result of the historical legacies of the colonial bourgeoisie and the African bourgeoisie and their respective "ideologies of legitimation" (193–96).

According to Ekeh, for the African bourgeoisie, an appeal to "tradition" proved to be an effective method to achieve legitimacy as "traditional kingship and chieftaincy has always been defined in moral terms" (1975: 104). In other words, those who exercised power within the civic public could not rely upon formal institutions alone to rule. Instead, they borrowed aspects of the primordial public to justify their right to rule.

Even though Ekeh acknowledges its powerful moral basis, he does not fully develop the relationship between the chieftaincy and the primordial public. Instead, he focuses on the ways in which the African bourgeoisie utilized "tradition" to legitimize the post-colonial order.[15] This is, in my opinion, a missed opportunity to highlight the *public-ness* of the chieftaincy, as well as its distinctive *moral* appeal. Unlike Ekeh, I argue that there exist multiple sources of legitimacy in South Africa— one rooted in the civic norms of the state and one rooted in the norms associated with the chieftaincy—that are each considered moral in the so-called private realm. Indeed, one of the features of post-apartheid politics in South Africa is the struggle between these sources of legitimacy within society itself.[16]

Moral Legitimacies in Rural South Africa

In rural South Africa, there is an ongoing struggle for moral legitimacy between the norms and values of the democratic constitutional order and those of the chieftaincy. On the one hand, there are the democratic norms and values that have been introduced since the end of apartheid in 1994. As part of its transformation agenda, the post-apartheid state has rooted its claims to legitimacy in the familiar discourse of freedom, equality, and human rights. This encompasses the creation of a non-racial national identity in which "South Africa belongs to all who live in it, united in our diversity," and its success or failure depends upon the establishment of democratic institutions that promote participation, accountability, and the delivery of development resources (Republic of South Africa 1996).[17] As Mandela stated during his inauguration speech in 1994,

> [d]emocracy is based on the majority principle. This is especially true in a country such as ours where the vast majority has been systematically denied their rights. At the same time, democracy also requires that the rights of political and other minorities be safeguarded. In the political order we have established there will be regular, open and free elections, at all levels of government—central, provincial and municipal. There shall also be a social order which respects completely the culture, language and religious rights of all sections of our society and the fundamental rights of the individual.[18]

Through these comments and others, as well as through the constitution itself, the post-apartheid state has linked its moral claim of legitimacy to specific democratic norms and values.[19]

Traditional leaders, on the other hand, have rooted their moral legitimacy in a set of norms and values that they claim predate the establishment of the colonial state. For example, in the debate over the passage of the TLGF Act in 2003, ANC MP Mayosi, a member of the National Council of Provinces, made the following point: "There is a mistaken notion or belief that, from time immemorial, traditional leaders and their institutions had always been undemocratic, but this is far-fetched and far from the truth. Traditional leaders have always worked and taken decisions in councils. Hence the old adage that a chief is a chief because of his people or his respect for the word of his people" (National Council of Provinces, November 26, 2003).

The question of how such claims should be incorporated into a contemporary analysis of the chieftaincy is no doubt controversial. Building on other studies that demonstrate how pre-colonial political traditions and myths continue to help structure present-day politics, the argument here is that we cannot fully appreciate the current debates over the chieftaincy, or the nature of its authority, without an examination of these traditions and myths, whether they turn out to be "real" or "imagined."[20]

To be clear, I am not proposing that such traditions and myths are determinative or static. Rather, they simply provide a framework through which the chieftaincy, rural communities, and the state engage in the legitimation process at the local level.

The notion that a "chief is a chief through the people" is not simply political rhetoric utilized in Parliament.[21] Throughout the rural areas of South Africa, one is likely to find people using it as a way to praise or discredit their own traditional leaders. The notion that the people are bound together with the chieftaincy and that the chieftaincy gives meaning to the identity of the people is an extremely powerful idea that might be difficult for many to take seriously (Myers 1999).[22] Similar to attitudes concerning witchcraft, which South Africans utilize to shape the boundaries of their political world, the norms and myths associated with the chieftaincy provides unique challenges for those who analyze the legitimation process in the post-apartheid period (Ashforth 2005). Taking this claim seriously, however, is crucial if we want to understand the nature of post-apartheid state formation and democratization.

In each of my three case study areas—Mvuzane Tribal Authority, Ximba Tribal Authority, and Kholweni Tribal Authority—an overwhelming number of people (88 percent) wanted the chieftaincy to continue not only for what it *did* on a daily basis, but because of what it *meant* to the community in the broader sense. For example, when asked what the most important job of the chief was in the community, 35 percent mentioned resolving disputes, another 30 percent focused on development, and 12 percent suggested the maintenance of law and order. Interestingly, only 7 percent brought up land allocation or the maintenance of culture.[23]

When asked why the chieftaincy should continue, however, the responses had a decidedly different tone, which revealed its moral significance and its perceived embeddedness in society. As such, approximately 30 percent justified the chieftaincy because it leads, looks after the community, or solves community problems, and 20 percent stated that it should remain because it "has always been here." Another 30 percent, however, suggested that the chieftaincy provided discipline, dignity, and respect for the community and that there would be "disorder" without the chieftaincy.[24] Indeed, many people utilized the dichotomies of disorder/harmony and disunity/unity to describe the importance of the chieftaincy in their areas and what would happen if the chieftaincy were abolished.

The fact that rural populations continue to imagine the chieftaincy as a "symbol of unity" is at first perplexing; especially given what scholars know about the nature of indirect rule under the colonial and apartheid regimes. Such a perception challenges Mamdani's assessment that the nature of the colonial and apartheid regimes "wrenched" the practice of "traditional constraint" from rural communities. While Mamdani may be right that indirect rule altered the form of traditional rule, the evidence presented here suggests that the ideological underpinnings of the chieftaincy, which predate indirect rule, continue to provide a frame of reference for many in the rural areas. Indeed, to understand the resilience of the chieftaincy in South Africa and the struggle to transform it in the post-apartheid period requires confronting the ways in which people imagine political authority in the rural areas, even if such ideas appear more fiction than fact.[25]

While the moral legitimacy of the chieftaincy is linked to the notion that it represents "unity," it is not the case that this belief is uncontested or that it is enough for traditional leaders to invoke this myth as a means of securing legitimacy.[26] Rather, communities expect their traditional leaders to take actions that are consistent with this moral claim. Obviously, the idea of unity is inherently ambiguous, and as traditional leaders take actions in the community, these are subject to differing interpretations.[27] To suggest that traditional leaders are able to command obedience through nothing more than brute force or coercion, or that there are no constraints on their rule-making and rule-enforcing authority, does not reflect what is actually occurring in the rural areas (Oomen 2005). In addition, to argue that the chieftaincy is legitimate only because there is a weak state or only because it allocates resources, such as land, does not capture its deeper cultural significance.

By taking the moral claims of the chieftaincy seriously, we can see more clearly how its authority might threaten the sovereignty of the state. There is no doubt that "sovereignty lay at the center of modern state formation" and that it is often treated as an "ontological given" that states are the only political unit that should be able to claim sovereignty (Crais 2006: 722; Ray 1996). Nevertheless, Crais argues that through its accommodations the post-apartheid state has granted the chieftaincy "limited sovereignty" in the former Bantustan areas (2006: 722). Comaroff and Comaroff make a similar point and observe that the chieftaincy brings to the fore the "fundamental question of sovereignty: the sovereignty of African traditional governance and the kingdom of custom, in which ethnic subjects claim, and are claimed by, another species of authority" (2004: 300). Recognizing that the South African state may lack sovereignty in some areas of the country challenges some of our basic assumptions about the nature of state authority. It also raises questions as to whether the South African state shares sovereignty with the chieftaincy or whether sovereignty is actually divided between the state and the chieftaincy (Herbst 2000; Ray 1996: 181). Questions concerning sovereignty, however, require that we analyze what the chieftaincy actually does at the local level and what it means to local populations.

Performance Legitimacy in South Africa

The performance dimension of political legitimacy involves an analysis of the actual implementation of rules, institutions, and policies and refers to the manner in which power is used and how those in society evaluate this process. It focuses attention on the degree to which rulers and ruled agree that the political system is working in the best interests of the community at large. In some cases, rulers lacking institutional capacity will nonetheless promise certain projects and create expectations that, in the short-term at least, they hope will generate trust in institutions as well as trust in the moral order. The political changes in 1994 have resulted in greater expectations for both the delivery of development and the promise of more accountable and participatory politics. Obviously, in the long-term, legitimacy must be based on something more than performance or expectations of performance, but in the short term, it is possible that rulers can generate trust if they are able to deliver the political and economic goods that are promised (Alagappa 1995).

In South Africa, the issue of performance is directly related to the delivery of development resources and services (Hemson and O'Donovan 2006). Given the importance of development to those living in the rural areas, both traditional leaders and local government officials have sought to take credit for successful development projects and to shift blame where there is failure. Further, depending on the local dynamics, there has been both cooperation and conflict over development issues. In short, the relationship between traditional leaders and local government officials concerning development is complicated and complex. In many cases, local government officials must seek "permission" to enter the chief's area, mainly because he is considered the owner of the land. Even if this protocol is done out of respect rather than because of a legal or constitutional requirement, it signals to the community that the chieftaincy still matters. At the same time, due to a lack of resources, traditional leaders usually have no choice but to allow development in "their areas," especially if those living in the area expect the traditional leader to secure development for them. In the end, the expectation that both the chieftaincy and local government officials should bring development projects to the rural areas has meant that performance, or lack thereof, has become a critical part of the overall legitimation process.

With this in mind, it is not surprising that one of the main areas of dispute between the chieftaincy and the state is the implementation of development projects in rural areas and the role of local government institutions in the delivery of these projects. Both the chieftaincy and the state wish to provide the development and receive credit for its effective implementation. The ability of traditional leaders to maintain jurisdiction over development projects is part of the struggle for political legitimacy, and it demonstrates, in particular, their desire to control the rule-making and rule-enforcing process at the local level. In many cases, the struggle to make rules concerning development has meant that the local understandings of "tradition" have been altered.

The process of redefining tradition in order to get more control over the implementation of development projects is a result of pressure from rural communities that traditional leaders provide for their needs. In this way, one finds that the legitimation process is not a one-way process and that to maintain political legitimacy, traditional leaders must respond to the rising expectations in their communities.

Finally, the performance dimension of legitimacy focuses our attention on the importance of rules. In times of political change, it is common to find conflicts over the meaning and application of rules to arise as new rules, often accompanied by a new set of norms and beliefs, are introduced to replace preexisting ones. This is especially the case in South Africa, where the post-apartheid government has introduced a set of new rules and institutions at the local level. Because rules help to shape the public realm and are the foundation on which new political institutions are established, they have an added significance. Commenting on why this is the case, Hyden suggests the following:

> The answer is that they [rules] matter to most people, but not all the time. Rules are typically stable, and as long as they serve their purpose, people, including politicians, do not care much about them. But if circumstances in society change, and rules get interpreted as constraining or outdated, they become targets of political mobilization. Since much of the legitimacy of those in power rests with how well they make use of existing rules, they have a vested interest in paying attention to them. If they overlook them, however, civil society responds through the activation of organized groups demanding change. (1992: 7–8)

Given the importance of rule making and rule enforcing for the performance dimension of legitimacy, I focus on how traditional leaders behave as both political actors and judges. This includes how traditional leaders seek to fashion new rules, or adopt old ones, concerning development, local government, and elections, which are consistent with the existing moral order.

To summarize, the multiple legitimacies framework focuses on how the chieftaincy maintains authority in the rural South Africa. It is based on the assumptions that there exist various sources of legitimacy and that political actors must make decisions consistent with both the underlying moral and performance dimensions to remain legitimate. This includes how decisions are made at the local level, as well as the way in which norms, rules, institutions, and processes constrain behavior. While the ANC has sought to control this process with the incorporation and accommodation of the chieftaincy through the establishment of a mixed polity, I argue that the chieftaincy has been able to circumvent and alter some of the changes that were envisioned.

This framework highlights how the chieftaincy has selectively transformed and adapted to the post-apartheid political while simultaneously promoting, and reproducing, those pre-existing values that continue to resonate with local populations. It also clarifies why the chieftaincy cannot simply rely upon some static notion of "traditional" legitimacy and expect to remain relevant by focusing attention on how it must engage with new forms of authority. Finally, much like Schatzberg's (2001) moral matrix of legitimacy and Galvan's (2004) syncretic institutionalism, this framework is not predictive. Rather, it is a heuristic device to situate the chieftaincy's moral claims and actions so that the processes of rural politics become more legible.

METHODOLOGY AND INTRODUCTION OF CASE STUDIES

A large portion of the data for this inquiry is based on research conducted in South Africa from 1998 to 1999, when I conducted fieldwork in three tribal authority areas in KwaZulu-Natal: Mvuzane Tribal Authority, Ximba Tribal Authority, and Kholweni Tribal Authority. Subsequently, I have returned to South Africa numerous times between 2003 and 2009 to conduct follow-up research in KwaZulu-Natal as well as other provinces.

One of the advantages of focusing on these case studies is that they offer rich, descriptive accounts of the dynamics between the chieftaincy, the post-apartheid state, and local populations that highlight broader theoretical concerns. At the same time, I recognize some of the limits of this case-study approach, and I have supplemented it with other in-depth studies of the chieftaincy in different regions of South Africa as well as national economic and survey data (Beall 2006; Beall, Mkhize, and Vawda 2005; Oomen 2005; Ntsebeza 2005; Thornton 2005; Goodenough 2002; Dusing 2002; Bennett 1998; D'Engelbronner-Kolff, Hinz, and Sindano 1998).

Each of these case studies demonstrates the diversity that exists between different tribal authority areas (Oomen 2005; Thornton 2005). At the same time, they also suggest that there exist important similarities concerning the legitimation process in South Africa. Despite the fact that I supplement my three case studies with other studies on the chieftaincy, one of the possible limitations of this study is that I am unable to make the type of empirical generalizations that more quantitative studies offer (Englebert 2000). On the other hand, through the "thick description" of the three case studies, I have constructed a narrative that privileges the voices of South Africans at the local level. The stories of these people, I believe, are both captivating and instructive. In the end, the design of this inquiry is such that I provide important theoretical generalizations that help us to understand the legitimation process in South Africa more clearly.

Through a comparative examination of the implementation of democratic elections, local government institutions, and specific development projects, I tell the stories of real South Africans dealing with the everyday struggles that exist in the post-apartheid dispensation. The decision to focus on elections, local government, and development as the main sites to examine the legitimation process of the chieftaincy is based on the realities of local politics that I discovered in 1998 and that persist today.

While traditional leaders spend time on so-called traditional functions, such as land allocation, dispute resolution, and structuring of ceremonial or religious events, they are also increasingly engaged with "modern" issues and institutions. At the local level, people in the rural areas consider the chieftaincy's ability to deal with "modern" issues and institutions to be as important as their ability to handle so-called traditional responsibilities. The chieftaincy's ability to address issues concerning the introduction of elections, local government institutions, and development projects is central to the legitimation process at the local level. As it turns out, a closer analysis of the effect these more "modern" functions have on the legitimation process also reveals the contours and substance of what we often refer to as the "traditional" aspects of the chieftaincy.

To learn more about this process, I spent approximately three months living in each of the three case-study areas. While living in the community, I conducted interviews, attended meetings, and visited the tribal courts to gather archival information. In total, I interviewed approximately two hundred people between 1998 and 1999 in these three areas. Of this group, 45 percent were male and 52 percent were female. Approximately 25 percent were below the age of forty, 35 percent were between the ages of forty and fifty-nine, and 40 percent were above the age of sixty. In terms of occupations, the most frequent responses were pensioner (26 percent), unemployed (20 percent), and employed (11 percent). Most of the informants had limited formal education, with only 10 percent who had passed the matric exam (equivalent to a high school exit exam) or earned a post-secondary degree.

Upon entering a community, the first person whom I asked to speak with was the chief. This was the protocol, and in order to do research in an area I was expected to receive "permission" from the chief. I did not experience any problems getting this permission, and in fact, as word spread of my research in the area, other chiefs approached me and requested for me to visit their areas as well.

The interviews consisted of open-ended questions, and it usually took two hours to complete one interview. While I speak conversational Zulu, I relied upon a translator to assist me with every interview that was conducted in Zulu. As every tribal authority area is subdivided into different wards, I made an effort to visit as many wards as possible. I soon realized that attitudes about the chief seemed to vary with respect to whether one lived near the chief's homestead, and thus, I made it a point to visit the wards that were furthest away from the chief's homestead as well as those closest to his homestead.

In each of the three tribal authority areas, there were only dirt roads, and most people lived well beyond these roads. On most days, my research assistant and I would drive my car down a dirt road into the desired ward. We would drive the car as far as we could, and then we would park and start walking. We would usually walk for an hour or so into the community and make note of the different homesteads in the area. We would then randomly pick homesteads and request an interview with any adults who were at home. We were rarely denied our request to conduct an interview, and many people were very excited to talk about their lives and the community.

In addition to these interviews, I also conducted interviews with the chiefs, and with as many of their *izinduna* and traditional councilors as I could find. While interviews with these leaders were extremely helpful, it was also interesting to note how different their perceptions were compared to those who were not in positions of authority.

In addition to conducting interviews in the three tribal authority areas, I also conducted interviews with officials at the national, provincial, and local levels of government. Early in my research, I tried to meet with nonprofit organizations that did work in the rural areas to get their impression of the chieftaincy as well. During subsequent visits to South Africa, I have interviewed approximately two dozen other informants who lived in KwaZulu-Natal as well as other provinces.

While the interviews were the most important source of information, I also engaged in participant observation and attended numerous meetings at the tribal courts as well as local government meetings. It was through these observations that I was able to evaluate what chiefs did, as opposed to what they said they did, and this proved to be very helpful. Finally, I conducted archival research at the tribal courts and the magistrate courts, and at libraries in Durban, Pietermaritzburg, and Pretoria. Going through the volumes of records on the many South African "tribes" provided me with a way to put the current issues into a broader historical context.

The Case Studies

All three case studies are located in the province of KwaZulu-Natal (KZN) and all were part of the KwaZulu Bantustan government (KZG) until 1994. Under the KZG, there was a hierarchy of institutions, which included a territorial authority, 20 regional authorities, and 280 tribal authorities (map 2).

Each of the case studies varied in important ways that allowed me to control for certain political, economic, and social factors. For example, while the IFP was the majority party in both Mvuzane and Kholweni, the ANC was the majority in Ximba. In terms of development, Ximba had much greater access to resources than Mvuzane and Kholweni, and there were many more development projects in the former than in the latter. Ximba also was under the jurisdiction of the Durban Metropolitan Council,[28] and thus was able to benefit from the benefits of a much stronger state. Finally, the chief in Mvuzane had ruled for over thirty years through hereditary right, while the chief in Ximba was officially a regent—serving as chief only until the "rightful" chief was the appropriate age. Finally, because Kholweni was located on missionary land, the church committee "elected" the chief in 1978, and thus he did not claim a hereditary right to rule (see maps 3 and 4).

As mentioned above, there are currently 280 chieftaincy areas in KwaZulu-Natal and over 800 throughout the entire country (KwaZulu-Natal Government 2000). Two of the case studies, Mvuzane and Kholweni, are adjacent areas that are located near the town of Eshowe in northern KZN. In 1998–99, they were both under the jurisdiction of the Inkanyezi Regional Authority and the Uthungulu Regional Council (local government).

MAP 2. *KwaZulu Regional Authorities. Map designed by Em Hansen Trent and courtesy of the KwaZulu-Natal Department of Local Government and Traditional Affairs.*

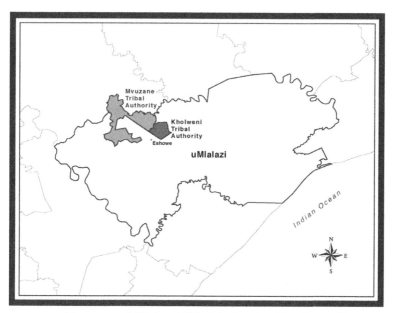

MAP 3. *Mvuzane and Kholweni Tribal Authorities. Map designed by Em Hansen Trent and courtesy of the KwaZulu-Natal Department of Local Government and Traditional Affairs.*

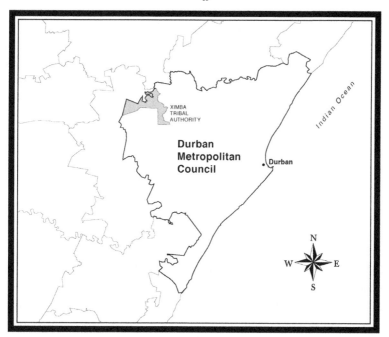

MAP 4. *Ximba Tribal Authority. Map designed by Em Hansen Trent and courtesy of the KwaZulu-Natal Department of Local Government and Traditional Affairs.*

Both areas consist of local populations that in each of the first five elections (1994 national election; 1996 local elections; 1999 national elections; 2000 local elections; 2004 national elections) had voted overwhelmingly for the Inkatha Freedom Party (IFP).[29] The two chiefs from Mvuzane and Kholweni were both members of the IFP, and by most accounts, so are a majority of chiefs in this northern area of KwaZulu-Natal.

The chief in Mvuzane was Bhekabelungu Biyela. He was born in 1929 and received no formal education. He acknowledged that the only training and education he received while growing up was from his father and his father's *isigungu* (the chief's council). After working for a brief period in Durban as a police officer, Biyela was appointed chief in 1966 at the age of thirty-seven. He was not a member of the KwaZulu Legislative Assembly, as only three to four chiefs from each regional authority were chosen to be a part of this body. He did not own a car, and he lived in a modest rondavel on a hill above the Mvuzane River. His home did not have telephone service or electricity, but in the early 1990s he did acquire access to clean water through a project co-sponsored by the Zululand Joint Services Board. The fact that chief Biyela had access to clean water, while the vast majority of the people in Mvuzane did not, caused some controversy in the area. As a gesture to the community, chief Biyela allowed his neighbors to use the water free of charge.

Mvuzane itself was the most isolated and desolate of the three case studies. There was one main road that went through the area, but it was a dirt road and became impassable during the rainy season. While there was no accurate census data on Mvuzane per se, it was estimated that approximately fifteen thousand people live in this area. Of these, the vast majority were unemployed or relied upon monthly pension stipends (R550/$92) for their basic necessities.[30] Except for a handful of sugarcane farmers, most people did not have access to clean water, electricity, or telephone service. For the most part, Mvuzane represented a "typical" tribal authority area in KwaZulu-Natal. Using 1991 census data for 173 of the tribal authorities in KwaZulu-Natal, Klitgaard and Fitschen found that the average per capita income in these areas was R541 (1997: 365). They also found that the median literacy rate was 48 percent and the median percentage of those with secondary school education was 9.2 percent. While they also find significant variations between tribal authorities, they concluded that "[a]ll of the poorest traditional authorities are located in what would be considered 'deep' rural areas" (369). The socioeconomic evidence, which was available on Mvuzane, along with my own observations, suggested that Mvuzane should be categorized as such.

While Kholweni bordered the western side of Mvuzane, it was located much closer to the town of Eshowe and was linked to this town by a tarred road. Approximately nine thousand people lived in Kholweni, and according to the most recent census information, it has a larger proportion of people under the age of thirty, has a higher degree of literacy, and has a higher per capita income than does Mvuzane. These data correspond with my own observations in the area as well. Unlike Mvuzane, there were many people who had access to clean water, electricity, and telephone service in Kholweni, although these services were still considered a luxury by most of the population. Perhaps because it was closer to Eshowe, compared to Mvuzane, I found more people in Kholweni who worked in town or in Durban. Also, because of its higher elevation and closer access to the local sugar mill, I found many more sugarcane farmers in Kholweni as well.

The chief in Kholweni was Vincent Mtembu. He was born in 1928 and was appointed as chief in 1974. Unlike Mvuzane or Ximba, Kholweni does not have a hereditary chieftaincy. What is now known as Kholweni was part of the Ntuli chieftainship until King Mpande granted the Norwegian missionary Hans Schreuder an area of land to build a mission in 1852.[31] The legend is that Schreuder had been in the Zululand area since 1844 but that he could not get permission from the Zulu king for a mission at Ntumeni (the Ntumeni mission is in Kholweni). Around 1850, Schreuder provided King Mpande with "prayer and his medicinal knowledge" and successfully alleviated the King's case of rheumatism. As payment for this treatment, King Mpande granted Schreuder the land in 1852, and the first official church was established in 1863. The missionary leaders established a non-hereditary chieftaincy in Kholweni and established a church committee to choose the chief. Except for the manner in which the chief was chosen, there was little difference between Mvuzane and Kholweni as to what the chiefs and their assistants did on a daily basis, the values the institution promoted, or the manner in which the community interacted with the chieftaincy.[32]

The third case study, Ximba, was located in southern KZN and was approximately forty miles from Durban and thirty miles from Pietermaritzburg. In the late 1990s, approximately forty thousand people lived in Ximba. The area has voted predominantly for the African National Congress (ANC), and the chief, Zibuse Mlaba, was a member of the ANC. He was born in 1956 and has been serving as "acting" chief since his brother was killed in 1988. He was appointed as acting chief until his nephew was of the proper age to be appointed himself.

Chief Mlaba received his matric diploma (i.e., high school diploma) and attended university. He was also a member of the KZN provincial legislature—an office for which he ran for in 1994, 1999, and 2004 as an ANC candidate.

What was most notable about Ximba, as compared to Mvuzane and Kholweni, was the extent to which people had access to clean water, electricity, telephones, paved roads, and newly constructed schools and creches. Given Ximba's proximity to both Durban and Pietermaritzburg, according to Klitgaard and Fitschen, this was to be expected (1997: 372). In addition, to some extent, this was a direct result of local state capacity. Ximba was under the jurisdiction of the Durban Metropolitan Council, which had access to greater resources and had a more established infrastructure. Not only did the Durban Metropolitan Council implement more development projects in Ximba than Uthungulu did in Mvuzane and Kholweni, the other result was that it had a much greater physical and ideological presence in the community. Most notably, there was a local government office within the tribal authority itself where the elected councilor had his office and was able to hold meetings with his constituents. Thus, while there were important socio-economic and institutional differences between each of the three areas, in each the chieftaincy was considered a central pillar to the local populations. Understanding why this was the case, and what is the nature of chieftaincy-state and chieftaincy-society relations, is the focus of the remaining chapters.

"THE BINDING TOGETHER
OF THE PEOPLE"

The Historical Development of the Chieftaincy and the Principle of Unity

*"[T]raditional" institutions such as chiefship need[] to be
cleans[ed] . . . of all the undemocratic attributes that were
imparted to it both by colonialism and apartheid.*
                                                    —SKWEYIYA 1993: 1

*[Before colonialism] political leadership was personal. . . .
A chief (and even the king) was supposed to deal with his
people himself and should not altogether delegate this duty.
Chiefs and* indunas *knew most of their subjects, with their
relationships and ancestry. . . . The Zulu sum this up by
saying "the people respect their chief, but the chief ought to
respect his people."*   —GLUCKMAN 1940A: 44

In the current debates in South Africa concerning the chieftaincy, the past is prologue, to the extent that the positions that many politicians, journalists, and academics take on whether
the chieftaincy should exist in post-apartheid South Africa are based on
their interpretation of chieftaincy-societal and chieftaincy-state relations
in the past. This is why the debates over the chieftaincy often allude to
how the chieftaincy governed before colonialism and how these governing norms and practices were altered during apartheid.

Numerous scholars argue that pre-colonial norms and values might
continue to influence present-day politics (Schatzberg 2001; Herbst 2000;
Heywood 1998; Schaffer 1998; Geschiere 1997; Vansina 1990; Laitin 1986).
At the same time, while scholars often have an "intuition that African
politics must have deep continuities," there is also the reality that colonial
regimes sought to alter pre-colonial norms and institutions (Herbst 2000:
29). In this way, both the continuities with and the changes from the past
relate to the claims that chiefs currently use to maintain legitimacy.

First, I begin to develop what I refer to as "idea of the chieftaincy" as
a central cultural and institutional aspect of local political life. Contrary

to what some studies contend, communities oftentimes respect the "idea of the chieftaincy" more than particular individual officeholders.[1] The norms, values, ideas, and symbols embedded in the chieftaincy provide the nexus point where more general understandings of power, fairness, representation, and justice are continually defined and debated. In the end, the "idea of the chieftaincy" operates as a prism through which many people define and interpret present-day political transformation in South Africa.

Second, I explore the ways in which particular "traditions" associated with the chieftaincy have been malleable and fluid over time, even when confronted with colonial and apartheid regimes that sought to freeze notions of custom (Hobsbawm 1983; Ranger 1983). Similar to Vansina, I think it is more useful to conceptualize "traditions" as processes, which must continually change to remain salient, than to assume "traditions" are fixed practices or ideas (1990: 258). To understand these processes, I argue that we must examine how chieftaincies and their communities reconciled the gap between preexisting political traditions (i.e., indigenous rules, processes, and ideologies) and official state rules concerning "tradition" (i.e., "customary law").

The colonial and apartheid governments manipulated certain aspects of tradition—especially relating to indigenous political ideology—to facilitate their authority. In many cases, however, studies addressing the political salience of tradition fail to examine why some political norms, ideas, values, and symbols resonate with people while others do not (Hamilton 1998; Young 1993a; Fields 1985). In other words, to what extent is the state actually borrowing particular norms and symbols rather than inventing them? With respect to chieftaincy-societal relations, the questions are even more specific: what are the acceptable boundaries of political action and debate, who makes or remakes these boundaries, what are the available remedies if one crosses these boundaries, and how did indirect rule and apartheid affect these boundaries? To answer these questions requires an understanding of the pre-colonial political traditions and how these have continued to develop over time as these traditions "act as a touchstone for proposed innovations, whether from within or from without" (Vansina 1990: 259).

THE IDEOLOGICAL AND POLITICAL IMPERATIVES OF "UNITY"

The concept of unity, or in Zulu, *simunye* (we are one), is the dominant cultural and political theme structuring chieftaincy-societal relations in

KwaZulu-Natal.[2] Broadly speaking, political decisions must appear to achieve or maintain unity if they are to be "acceptable" or "thinkable" to the community at large. Over time, this idea not only justified the centralization of power, but it also helped to give meaning to ruler-ruled relationships and the allocation of social space. As new political and economic structures developed in the nineteenth century, the identity of the people became inextricably linked with that of their king and chiefs. This linkage was important for relations not only in the natural world, but in the supernatural as well, which, unlike in the West, are not treated as separate and distinct spheres, but rather, interconnected. Political power in the natural world is oftentimes dependent upon the supernatural as most Zulus believe the ancestors "choose" those who are to rule (Berglund 1989; Krige 1936: chapters 13–14). Over time, important symbols and rituals have been established to highlight the unity between the ancestors, the king, the chiefs, and the people, and thus, to help legitimate chieftaincy-societal relationships.

Indeed, from both the primary and secondary sources on Zulu politics and culture, one is struck by the recurring theme of "unity" as a way to describe and explain relationships between ruler and ruled and the attempts by successive Zulu leaders—including kings, chiefs, and commoners—to promote and give meaning to this idea. From the time of Shaka through the current leadership of chief Buthelezi, unity has proven to be a central component of Zulu political consciousness. For example, the main themes of Zulu praise poems about chiefs and kings focus on the measures these rulers must take to ensure the unity of the group (T. R. Cope 1968). In addition, one scholar notes that the founding of Inkatha KaZulu in 1924 represented a "new wave of Zulu unity which was currently sweeping through the Zulu-speaking people" (Nicholas Cope 1990: 43). Fifty years later, Buthelezi justified the creation of "Bantustans" based on the "historic" unity of the Zulu people and the need for independence (Temkin 1976: 119–20).

While the idea of unity was, and continues to be, central to the establishment of legitimate political relationships, Zulu history is replete with examples of chaos, disorder, and division. There is no question that the significant geographic, political, cultural, economic, and societal divisions among the Zulus themselves have impeded the actual achievement of unity. In addition, to facilitate their rule, colonial powers sought to utilize the idea of unity where expedient, and to de-emphasize it where it was deemed dangerous. Despite the difficulties of achieving actual unity, and despite the manner in which this idea was manipulated by the colonial state, I argue that it still resonates in rural South Africa and structures the legitimation process.

Not surprisingly, the idea of unity provides only a rough guideline to the actual legitimation process at the local level. For many people, the goal of unity in the community is so obvious that it seems like common sense that traditional leaders should promote it, and yet, it is too ambiguous to help resolve everyday political issues or disputes. Rather communities rely on a set of more concrete principles that help to give meaning to the idea of unity. In particular, I argue there are four important principles that both rulers and ruled attach to the idea of unity in present-day KwaZulu-Natal.[3] While in practice they are often interrelated, for the purposes of analysis, they are treated as distinct concepts. The principles that are central to understanding how the idea of unity manifests itself in chieftaincy-societal relationships are:

(1) the maintenance of order;
(2) community consultation and participation in decision making;
(3) impartial and unbiased decision making by rulers; and
(4) promotion of community welfare before individual gain.

These principles inform the legitimation process and provide a set of standards from which political decisions and behavior are evaluated. Yet these principles do not predetermine political decision making. While individual traditional leaders must exercise their rule-making and rule-enforcing authority with these principles in mind, each one will undoubtedly interpret "order," "consultation," "impartiality," and "community welfare" differently under particular circumstances. Nonetheless, traditional leaders must justify their actions based on these principles and cannot simply choose to ignore them or consistently make and enforce rules that are at odds with these principles. Thus, traditional leaders often invoke these principles, and their interpretations of them, to assert their authority. At the same time, those under the jurisdiction of the chieftaincy also utilize these principles to limit the authority and check the abuse of power. In the end, the nature of chieftaincy-societal relations will vary as there is no particular "right" or "wrong" way to interpret these principles—rather, such determinations depend on context, local experiences, and particular political alliances (Thornton 2005).[4]

In addition, the notion of unity and the political principles listed above do not represent timeless qualities of the political past. There is no doubt that the experience of indirect rule and apartheid as well as the significant social and economic changes that have occurred over the last two centuries have altered the content of many of these principles. It is important to analyze the tensions, contradictions, and points of contestation inherent in these principles as they have adapted over time (Laitin 1986). While these concepts have been redefined over time, and remain fluid, they continue to structure how people understand authority relationships and the wider world around them.[5] What is equally important is that because the chieftaincy is one of the most dominant structural presences in many rural areas and because the chieftaincy dominates both "private" and "public" spheres of activity, the idea of unity and its underlying principles are often transposed for understanding other social and political phenomena.[6]

UNITY IN THE MAKING: POLITICAL LEGITIMACY PRIOR TO COLONIALISM

According to traditional ideals, a chief could never force his people to do what they did not want to do; he was a leader rather than a ruler, relying for his position on influence rather than force.

—BOURDILLON 1976, CITED IN AYITTEY 1991: 93

The Rise of the Zulu Kingdom

An abundance of historical literature has been written on the formation of the Zulu kingdom in the early nineteenth century and its development as an autonomous polity until the British effectively dissolved it in 1879 (Laband 1995; Gump 1990; Guy 1979; Omer-Cooper 1966; Morris 1965). Unfortunately, these studies rarely discuss the question of political legitimacy and the formation of pre-colonial ideologies. In many cases, scholars assume political legitimacy existed as a result of fear, coercion, or military success. Yet what we know about chieftaincy-societal relationships from this period suggests that the establishment and maintenance of legitimacy was much more complex than this. In addition to the threat or use of force, the legitimation process also depended on the use of particular rules, processes, symbols, and rituals.

Before the establishment of chieftaincies, the basic social unit of the Nguni people, which include the Zulu, was the homestead (*umuzi*). Homestead units were kin-based social structures consisting of both immediate and extended family. Political authority rested with the eldest male of the homestead, and he was responsible for ensuring the security and prosperity of those living with him. Over the course of the seventeenth and eighteenth centuries, individual homesteads combined to create larger clan groups, and these clan groups formed into chieftaincies led by one clan that was politically dominant (Guy 1979: 27). For example, the name Zulu refers to a particular clan, which inhabited an area on the White Mfolozi River near the present-day city of Ulundi. The Zulus most likely descended from a man who lived in this area over three hundred years ago and developed as most other chieftaincies in the area (Guy 1979: xvii).

Within the chieftaincies, political leadership was hereditary and was transferred through the male line (Guy 1979: 23). As more independent chieftaincies began to appear in the mid to late eighteenth century, these groups ceased to be merely kin-based social structures. People frequently moved to different chieftaincies in search of chiefs who could offer more cattle, more land, or better security (Marks 1970: 28; Omer-Cooper 1966: 15–16). The process of pledging allegiance to a chief involved asking for permission to live in the area and providing some type of tribute (*khonza*). Boundaries between chieftaincies were not precise, and most commentators suggest that chiefs exercised authority over people rather than over a distinct area of land (Lambert 1995; Marks 1970). Thus, the people living under the authority of a particular chief were most likely from a diverse set of kin groups and were able to leave the jurisdiction of the chief if this leader proved unsatisfactory for any reason.

As the leader of the group, the chief held considerable power over his followers. Not only did he exercise a combination of what might be referred to as executive, legislative, and judicial authority, but, more importantly, he also was an important link to the ancestors, and his natural powers were not easily separated from these supernatural connections. More specifically, he determined the distribution of land and the nature of agricultural production. He resolved disputes in the community and punished those who violated community rules and standards. He required those living under his jurisdiction to provide him with tribute, and in turn, he protected them from possible harm. Finally, he led the community in rituals that connected them with the ancestors and protected them from supernatural evils (Schapera 1956; Krige 1936).

Even with these powers, however, the chief was unable to rule over all his followers without assistance, and thus, he depended upon a decentralized system of authority to administer the day-to-day affairs of his area (Omer-Cooper 1966: 17). In most cases, assistants, such as *izinduna,* exercised authority over subsections of the chief's area. Eileen Krige, an anthropologist who studied Zulu politics and society, describes the duties and powers of the *induna* in the following way: "[H]e is the father of the kraal but he is also the ruler who keeps order and deals with any disputes or quarrels that arise. . . . But though he is the head, he is expected to consult the adult members of the kraal (the *ibhandla*) on all kraal matters, and is therefore never an absolute ruler" (1936: 51). Thus, the functions of the chief were reproduced at the *izinduna* level within the political context that the chief (or later, the king) was the final decision maker. The position of the *izinduna*, as well as the chief, was hereditary, although it was not uncommon for ineffective leaders to be replaced with other relatives, or in some cases, an entirely new lineage (Krige 1936: chapter 10; see also Comaroff 1978 for similar examples involving the Tswana).

One of the important consequences of the mixture of different clan groupings as well as the decentralization of power was that most chieftaincies were "fluid communities with ill-defined jurisdiction" (Lambert 1995: 24). Individual chiefs struggled to exercise their authority over all of their people while also recognizing the power and influence of the *izinduna* who administered local affairs. Despite the continual fission and fusion of communities, this structure of rule remained relatively stable until a combination of socioeconomic, political, demographic, and geographic changes began to reshape the boundaries of political authority at the turn of the nineteenth century.

In this period, there emerged three large kingdoms in the area, which battled for political and economic supremacy: the Ndwandwe kingdom, led by Zwide, the Mthethwa kingdom, led by Dingiswayo, and the Ngwane kingdom, led by Sobhuza (Omer-Cooper 1987: 54). After Zwide defeated the Ngwane in a battle for land on the Pongolo River, near present-day Swaziland, he fought and defeated Dingiswayo and the Mthethwa kingdom in 1817. At this time, the leader of the small Zulu chiefdom was Shaka ka Senzangakona. Shaka was the junior son of Senzangakona, who was a ruler of the Zulu chiefdom, which was at the time part of the larger Mthethwa kingdom. As a child, he was driven from his father's homestead because his mother had an "uncontrollable temper" and because she was not married when she became pregnant with Shaka (Omer-Cooper 1987: 55). Shaka was thus considered to be "illegitimate" and was not raised in his father's area. Instead, he grew up in Dingiswayo's court and fought bravely with his forces in many battles. When Senzangakona died, Shaka claimed the chieftaincy of the Zulus, and with the assistance of Dingiswayo, he killed his senior brother and was made chief. Soon thereafter, Zwide killed Dingiswayo and defeated the Mthethwa kingdom. Shaka then mobilized his forces and successfully defeated Zwide, thus becoming the most powerful leader in the area. He immediately began to expand his rule by conquering surrounding chiefdoms.

This period prior to and extending through the rise of Shaka is referred to as the *mfecane*. While the specific causes of the *mfecane* are subject to debate (Hamilton 1995; Duminy and Guest 1989), there is no question that the *mfecane* resulted in the migrations of tens of thousands of people in the area. In many cases, these migrations helped to reconfigure preexisting political relationships in significant ways. In particular, there was increased fear and disorder in the region as people sought to escape Shaka's rule. Out of this disorder and chaos, Shaka founded the Zulu kingdom, and he established himself as the king of the many, previously autonomous, chieftaincies. As will be discussed below, understandings and interpretations of the *mfecane,* and the nature of Shaka's authority, provided the colonial state with a powerful framework to understand and categorize both the Zulu kingdom and the chieftaincies residing in the area south of the Thukela River known as Natal (Hamilton 1998).

One of the most dramatic results of Shaka's rise to power was the transfer of power from the individual chieftaincies to Shaka's royal court and appointed advisors. No longer could chiefs rule their territories without recognizing the ultimate authority of the king. In this new dispensation, there was no question that the king was the center of the Zulu kingdom—symbolically, economically, and politically—and that he commanded the highest level of respect and deference. While in the past the chief may have promoted the unity and general welfare of his particular group, Shaka sought to unify the differing chieftaincies into a single political entity. At least in theory, his powers were all-encompassing and covered daily activities in both the "public" and "private" spheres. These powers ranged from determining agricultural production to arranging marriages, maintaining law and order, ruling on disputes, declaring war, linking the community with the ancestors, and curing the community from sickness (Krige 1936). He was simultaneously a military, administrative, political, economic, and spiritual leader. In short, according to both Krige and Gluckman, he was considered the "representative of the unity of the tribe" (Krige 1936: 233; Gluckman 1940a: 154). Indeed, the establishment and maintenance of unity between ruler and ruled was the central political imperative of the newly formed Zulu polity and continued to be the guiding principle of successive Zulu rulers.

To this end, one of the most important political structures of the newly formed Zulu polity was the *amabutho* age-regiment military system (Omer-Cooper 1966: 27). This system not only helped to expand the military, but also provided the ideological and political foundations for the establishment of a new polity (Guy 1979; Webb and Wright 1976). The *amabutho* was essentially a military organization that all males had to join. When instructed to do so, the chief assembled the group and gave it a name. This group would then fight together until it was time to marry. This military service replaced circumcision and ritual selection as a means of initiation to manhood. Women as well as men were formed into age-sets. While the corresponding male groups served in the military, the women provided agricultural produce for them. After the military service ended, Shaka allowed the marriage between the men and women from similar age-sets (Gump 1990: 136). In addition, it was an ideological mechanism used to promote a sense of unity among the men and women from different areas of the territory who were brought together (Omer-Cooper 1966: 27). Upon conquering new areas, Shaka usually left the existing chief in place but took the young men with him to join the *amabutho* system. During Shaka's reign, more than one hundred chiefdoms were brought under his rule and controlled in this manner (Omer-Cooper 1966: 57).

In addition to the *amabutho*, Zulu rulers, including the king and the individual chiefs, also based their authority on their connection with the ancestors and their ability to control supernatural forces in addition to natural ones. The king's power with respect to the supernatural world, and specifically medicine and healing, was particularly important. Krige notes that the king was the "great medicine man of the tribe" and that two terms were interchangeably used to refer to the king: *inkosi enkhulu* (great king) and *umthakathi omkhulu* (great sorcerer). While the word *umthakathi* was considered a harmful insult if applied to a commoner, it was considered acceptable to refer to the king in this way because he exercised exclusive control over good and evil (Krige 1936: 242–43). The control of *muthi* (medicine) was important to heal or destroy not only the physical body, but the "body politic" as well (Flint 2001: chapter 3). As Flint notes, "[a]cquisition of proper *muthi* and powerful doctors, who administered it, were considered essential to a chief or king's rise and maintenance of power" (chapter 3). Similarly, only in the king's court were rainmakers allowed to practice their skills, as it was believed that only the king had control over the heavens (Krige 1936: 247).

Secondary sources suggest that within pre-colonial Zulu political ideology there was little distinction between "earthly" authority or "supernatural" authority (Weir 2005; Flint 2001; Berglund 1989; Krige 1936). Both aspects were part of the legitimation process, and chiefs often relied upon each to maintain support. Zulu oral tradition teaches us that chiefs had authority to rule because they were "raised up" by the ancestors through the king (Gluckman 1940a: 36). The chief was "the living link between the community and its ancestors [and] he was the chief celebrant in many important rituals and even such specialist activities as the detection of sorcerers or the magical summoning of rain, which often fell outside his competence, were undertaken under his authority and control" (Omer-Cooper 1966: 17). Of the rituals that the chief led, the two most important were the rainmaking ritual before planting and the first fruits ceremony (*umkhosi*) after the first harvest. This power was so great that "[n]o one could plant or eat the harvest before the chief sanctioned it" (Gump 1990: 53).

Perhaps one of the most well known symbolic examples of unity in KwaZulu-Natal is the *inkatha yezwe* (grass coil of the nation). The origin of the *inkatha* can be traced back to the time of Senzangakona (Shaka's father), and it continues to be an important symbol of the Zulu "nation" (Webb and Wright 1976: 40). The *inkatha* was a coil that consisted of grass and vomit from each of the men who served in the Zulu regiments. The ritual vomiting exercise took place whenever the Zulu army was about to leave for a battle (41). The *inkatha* was passed down to successive rulers until it was destroyed during the Anglo-Zulu War in 1879. Baleni ka Silwana, one of Stuart's informants, suggested that, "the *inkatha*'s purpose is to keep our nation standing firm. The binding round and round symbolizes the binding together of the people so that they should not be scattered" (41). It is also a grass ring placed on the head for support when carrying heavy objects, and "[t]hus the word '*inkatha*' carries a double entendre; it is both a sacred emblem of Zulu unity and a support when under stress" (Harries 1987; Forsyth 1992). In the twentieth century, King Solomon (1913–1933)[7] and chief Mangosuthu Buthelezi (1975–present), as well as other Zulu rulers, invoked the imagery of the *inkatha* when they formed their respective political organizations (Nicholas Cope 1993; Mzala 1988; Mare and Hamilton 1987).

One scholar describes the creation and importance of the *inkatha* in the following way:

Zulu izinyanga [doctors] directed the ceremony by administering an emetic to assembled regiments. Each man then vomited into a straw-filled pit. The doctors bound the affected straw into a thick coiled mat, adding to it bits of material drawn from the regimental huts. . . . The *inkatha* was kept in a special hut under permanent guard. It existed as a visible expression of Zulu corporate unity. (Gump 1990: 142)

This symbolic expression of unity appears to have reached the local level as well, and in the Stuart archives, we find many references to the *inkatha*. For example, Sivivi, one of Stuart's informants, stated that "[p]eople were said to be bound up into it" (quoted in Gump 1990: 142). Another informant, Baleni, added that "[t]he binding round and round symbolizes the binding together of the people" (Webb and Wright 1976: 40).

In spite of these attempts to unify the different chieftaincies into a larger polity, there remained significant resistance. Because the chieftaincies remained somewhat autonomous and continued to exercise authority over their followers, the king's power was limited. Even the military *amabutho* system, which was effective at producing a sense of common identity during times of battle, was subject to the inherent strains of the decentralized nature of authority. For example, after completing their service to the kingdom, these men and women were married and returned to their original communities. Omer-Cooper notes that "[t]his meant that a sense of identity that these previously separate polities was not entirely lost but remained an important element in later politics of the Zulu kingdom" (Omer-Cooper 1987: 57). Marks comments further that the process of creating a Zulu identity—from the very beginning—was marked by a constant tension between fission and fusion and that leaders were always fearful of the kingdom splintering into its original clan groupings (Marks 1970: 33). In fact, on numerous occasions, powerful chiefs led their followers away from the king's control and oftentimes sought refuge in Natal.

Thus, despite the centralization of power, the use of the *amabutho* system, and other symbolic devices to promote unity, there were significant cultural and structural pressures threatening disunity of the kingdom. In this vein, Gluckman described the Zulu political system as a "federation" of different groups (1940a: 41). Zulu kings realized that they did not have the means to rule personally over such a large territory. This political reality led Shaka to employ his own policy of indirect rule to help facilitate central authority (Ayittey 1991: 439; Omer-Cooper 1966:

34). Rather than attempting to recreate completely the political structure anew, Shaka utilized the decentralized political system that he inherited and relied heavily on chiefs and *izinduna* to help maintain political, social, and economic control (Guy 1979; Marks 1970; Gluckman 1940a; Krige 1936). For example, upon conquering the people under the chief Kutshwayo, Shaka did not have the chief killed but instead, "like many others, was attacked merely to make him pay tribute, i.e. reduce him to become a subject and then instate him as an *induna*" (Webb and Wright 1976: 187). In other cases, he would replace a hereditary chief with a different lineage or an advisor from his royal court.

Thus, Shaka used both hereditary chiefs, whose lineage in some cases stretched far back into the eighteenth century, as well as appointed chiefs to maintain social control. The appointment of chiefs was based on different factors such as relation to the royal (Zulu) family, loyalty, or military skill (Marks 1970: 30–31). As the leader of a new "federation," Shaka was most concerned with chiefs whose loyalty was questionable, and he would not hesitate to replace an existing chiefly lineage with one that was more amenable to his rule (Guy 1979: 32). In most cases, the power of individual chiefs over their populations decreased as Shaka controlled the military establishment (Omer-Cooper 1966: 34). As Gump notes, "through a series of checks and counterchecks, Shaka reinforced the ties of dependency that confirmed his power and fostered the integration of his state" (1990: 133).

Order, Consultation, Impartiality, and Community Welfare in the Pre-colonial Period

In this new political dispensation, chiefs were both autonomous from and dependent on central authority. In terms of wielding authority in this political context, it is not surprising that chiefs used both command and consensus to rule, and thus it is difficult to categorize them as either "genuine" democrats or despots.

Given the disorder and chaos in which the Zulu kingdom emerged in the nineteenth century, it is not surprising that the political legitimacy of Zulu traditional leaders was largely based on their ability to provide safety, security, and order in an ever-changing and sometimes bewildering world. Indeed, in her work on the nature of Shaka's rule and political legitimacy, Hamilton focuses on the importance of order and discipline in Zulu society during both the pre-colonial and colonial periods (Hamilton 1998). She concludes that Shaka's legitimacy was based on his achievements and successes, rather than birthright, and on his ability to provide order and discipline in the midst of extraordinary social change. Isaacs stresses this even more succinctly when he states: "[t]he king (or his government) apprehends no danger from his civil subjects; the only check to his power is his warriors, who are formidable" (Isaacs 1966: 296). Even though Hamilton's study criticizes the manner in which the colonial authorities exaggerated the violent nature of Shaka's rule, she also notes how pre-colonial Zulu political ideology was structured around this notion of order. Indeed, there are many examples that support this argument.

In the first instance, the maintenance of order was considered a community responsibility. There was a sense of collective responsibility in many chieftaincies that meant that "the whole kraal [was] responsible for the misdeeds and debts of any one of its inmates. . . . The result [was] that every man in the tribe [was] a policeman" (Krige 1936: 223). This notion of collective responsibility is also revealed in that no distinction was made between criminal and civil offenses in pre-colonial KwaZulu-Natal (Krige 1936: 223). In addition, what often might be considered personal disputes could quickly become public (Ayittey 1991: 9). The colonial and apartheid policies challenged this understanding as they conferred on chiefs limited "civil" and "criminal" jurisdiction over certain issues.

According to Krige, the three crimes that threatened the order and harmony of the community the most were witchcraft, incest, and treason (1936: 224). Witchcraft was treated as a serious offense although communities did not hold the normal meetings or trials for witchcraft cases, but instead, relied upon special "doctors"—known as *izinyanga*—to "smell out" an accused witch (Flint 2001). Unlike many other types of cases, which were not reviewable by the king, a witchcraft case could be appealed directly to the king for his immediate review (Krige 1936: 225). With respect to treason against the chief, it was also treated as a serious offense that demanded swift attention. According to Krige, "treason against the chief is the same as treason against the whole people, for the chief is the symbol of the unity of the tribe and as such is sacred" (1936: 224).

Finally, there are numerous examples where Zulu traditional leaders were either deposed or killed because they were causing more disorder than order. For example, the legend surrounding Shaka's death suggests that his close advisors and brother decided to assassinate him after Shaka continued to wage unsuccessful military battles that were disrupting the community. Shaka's praise poems suggest that many people viewed him as a brutal ruler who stressed the importance of order and discipline at the expense of other important principles (T. R. Cope 1968). Indeed, some historians have noted that Dingane relaxed the military requirements on the people to distinguish himself from Shaka's rule (Thompson 1995; Omer-Cooper 1987).

While order was an important aspect of Zulu political life, Zulu traditional leaders were not expected to rule without consulting with the people. This occurred both at the royal court and at the local level with individual chiefs. Despite the increased centralization of power, the king rarely made decisions without consulting his most important advisors (*izikhulu*). The *izikhulu* consisted of important chiefs, members of the royal family, or those who had shown great skill on the battlefield (Guy 1979: 29–30). This body met in a general meeting (*ibhandla*) where all issues of "national" importance were discussed. The king could not pass any new laws, or even make a declaration of war, without the consent of this body (Krige 1936: 219). Thus, even though the king held many powers, he could not exercise these powers without the approval of his numerous assistants, who were, theoretically at least, representing the kingdom as a whole. For those "ordinary" people who were not part of the *izikhulu*, there existed what one scholar has referred to as "selective consultation" (Gluckman 1940a: 42). For example, there is evidence that everyone could speak at the *ibhandla* but that the people were not allowed to criticize the king. At the same time, the king was aware that his power was limited if he did not respond to their concerns (44).

There is evidence that these channels for participation and consultation were also present at the local level within individual chieftaincies. Omer-Cooper argues that the chief's position was "far from absolute for he was expected to rule with the advice of the leading men and in accordance with . . . the general consensus. . . . Though the chief always had the last word and could theoretically override the sentiments of any of these councils and assemblies, public opinion was supported by the sanctions of assassination, civil war or secession" (1966: 17). Consultation between the chief, the *izinduna*, and the community at large was important for several reasons. First, it enabled the chief to learn about the concerns of the community and to get advice on which decisions were most appropriate. Because the chief delegated authority to the individual *izinduna*, and because some chieftaincies were too large for the chief to actually visit all of the areas on a regular basis, ongoing consultation was a necessary means to acquire important information about his followers.

Second, ongoing consultation meant that the *izinduna* and the community at large could prevent the chief from abusing power (Ayittey 1991: 95). While the chief may have had the power to make decisions without consultation, he could very rarely act against the wishes of the majority of the *izinduna* or the community. With respect to the Tswana, Schapera notes that if a majority of the *izinduna* were against a particular decision, the chief "must abide by their verdict, unless he is looking for trouble" (1956: 78). Indeed, this appears to apply to the Zulus as well (Krige 1936). One scholar adds that "the Chief is in strict theory able to override the wishes of the people, but in practice he rarely ventures to do so. Their co-operation is essential for the successful government of the tribe; and should any Chief act contrary to the public opinion as here expressed the result would be disaster" (Olivier 1969, quoted in Ayittey 1991: 102–103).

Finally, the ultimate goal of consultation was not merely to know what the majority of people wanted, but to reach a unanimous decision—this was especially the case with a meeting between the chief and his *izinduna*. Again, the idea of unity seems to be central for the relationships both between the traditional leaders themselves and between traditional leaders and commoners. The more unified the community was the easier it would be to enforce a decision and the easier it would be to protect the community from harm (Ayittey 1991: 100). Some scholars go as far as to claim that consultation between ruler and ruled was "mandatory," but I have been unable to find evidence in KwaZulu-Natal to this effect (Ayittey 1991: 125). In any case, even Theophilus Shepstone, the architect of indirect rule in Natal, recognized the importance of consultation and consent when he noted that the chief does possess "all power, but practically, that power cannot be exercised by him safely, except with the consent of the people" (quoted in Ayittey 1991: 125).

When matters of dispute or disagreement arose, the chief was expected to resolve disputes in a manner that did not show favoritism or bias to any one individual or group. One goal of dispute resolution was to restore harmonious social relationships and to prevent personal conflicts from becoming public ones (Ayittey 1991: 9). One scholar compares the chief to an umpire, who must remain impartial in his decision making (Ayittey 1991: 125). The nature of judicial decision making was non-adversarial and communal. All witnesses for and against the accused were allowed to speak, and the chief usually waited until others had spoken to voice his opinion. In most cases, his decision in a case would reflect the consensus of those at the meeting, and if consensus was not reached, the decision was postponed. We find these trends not only with the Zulu but with other groups in southeastern Africa as well (Peters 1994; Rose 1992; Chanock 1985).

Lastly, chieftaincy-societal relations were premised on the assumption that the welfare of the community must come before the needs or desires of any one individual. This assumption applied equally to both traditional leaders and commoners, and the perception that traditional leaders were accumulating wealth or power for selfish motives led to suspicion and contempt. As mentioned above, the nature of the political community has adapted from one that was based purely on kinship ties to one that was based more on choice. The ability of people to move between chieftaincies and become a member of a new community through the act of pledging allegiance to the chief meant that communities were in a state of constant flux. This only increased with the rise of the Zulu kingdom. Despite the fluid nature of what constituted the community, the traditional leaders' responsibility to promote the welfare of the community was considered to be crucial. This manifested itself in several ways.

For example, the importance of promoting the community welfare over individual gain has been well documented with respect to rules and procedures of dispute resolution within chieftaincies. While there is no question that powerful members of the community can use these proceedings to their own advantage, they must nonetheless use the language and symbols of community to justify their claims or decisions. When scholars have looked more broadly at political decision making within chieftaincies, they have found that there is a common understanding that no one, not even the chief, should benefit at the expense of the community as a whole.

This was especially the case with respect to the accumulation of wealth. In the area of KwaZulu and Natal, wealth was measured in terms of cattle and land. With respect to cattle, it was expected that the chief would have the largest herd in the community so that they could be loaned to others in the community in times of misfortune or economic hardship. Cattle were used to pay bride-wealth—*lobola*—and chiefs also used them to facilitate a social exchange called *sisa,* where cattle would be loaned to individuals who for whatever reason did not have any of their own (Gluckman 1940a: 45). In addition, the chief was not allowed to amass personal property while in office. Rather, the wealth he accumulated, whether in terms of cattle, land, or tribute, were to be shared equally with the community (Ayittey 1991: 130). The chief was expected to share his wealth with the community, and he was expected to live modestly like his followers (Ayittey 1991: 121; Gluckman 1940a: 154). In these ways and many others, the welfare of the community was considered paramount to any individual—including the chief.

Decentralization and Contextual Authority Relations

The maintenance of order, consultation, impartiality, and community welfare were both helped and hindered by the fact that the traditional leaders were so closely connected to the entire community. One of the consequences of the decentralization of power was that those rulers who were closest to the people exercised significant authority, sometimes at the expense of superior power. Just as the king was the center of the larger Zulu community, the chief was the center of his own area, and the *induna* the leader of his. In fact, at each level, the functions and responsibilities of each stratum of leaders were similar (Krige 1936: 218 note 2). In similar fashion, Krige notes that "[t]he chief is to the tribe what the umnumzane [*induna*] is to a kraal [village]; he is the 'father' of his people, and his ancestors regulate the welfare of the whole tribe" (1936: 218). Gluckman argues that the chief symbolizes the community identity and that he was "the center of the tribe's unity" (Gluckman 1940b: 149). The chiefs, as well as the *izinduna,* were powerful and influential leaders within their own area of control, and thus, were somewhat autonomous from the king. At the same time, however, all these relationships were based on dependency. The chief was dependent upon the king, the *izinduna* dependent on the chief, and the king dependent on both (Marks 1970: 32; Gluckman 1940a: 43). Krige refers to the chiefs as the "eyes and ears of the king" (1936: 220).

The fluidity of authority relations meant that local populations were meant to have loyalty to different political leaders at the same time (Gluckman 1940a: 43). Depending on whether a person was in the presence of the *induna,* the chief, or the king, the deference and obedience displayed would vary. In this sense, authority relations were contextual. While this was beneficial from a point of view of administration—that is, establishing authority over a host of different clans and chieftaincies—it was also dangerous to the extent that it was much easier for dissatisfied factions to break away or threaten to destroy the "unity" of the entire structure (Gluckman 1940b: 152; Marks 1970: 33).

This contextual understanding of authority was also evident between traditional leaders themselves. For example, when a chief was residing at the king's residence, or was in the presence of the king, he was referred to as *induna*. If he was in his own area without the king, he was called *inkosi* (chief). Similarly, when the chiefs' assistants were in their own area, they were referred to as *abanumzane,* but when they were with the chief, they were called *izinduna* (Guy 1979: 29–30). These labels, then, do not refer to a static status group that has a consistent identity; instead, they refer to a set of duties and functions determined by context and situation.

The Limits of Authority

The idea of unity and the principles of order, consultation, impartiality, and community welfare also suggest some inherent boundaries of political authority. While the imperative of unity—at the level of both the "state" and the chieftaincy—necessitated, and even justified, the centralization of power to a small group of rulers, this process coexisted with a shared understanding of chieftaincy-societal relations that set the boundaries of authority. While the king, the chiefs, and the *izinduna* had extraordinary power vis-à-vis their community, there were also important limits to their authority. Those living under these rulers expected them to promote unity, harmony, and the general interest of the community. They were also expected to administer the law fairly and consult the community before making important decisions. The most significant recourse any member of the community had against these rulers not fulfilling their duties was to simply to leave the area and pledge allegiance to another chief (Ayittey 1991: 125; Omer-Cooper 1966: 17–20; Gluckman 1940b: 148). Because the chiefs relied upon taxes, tributes, and labor from their followers to maintain authority, the threat of members of the community leaving the area was taken seriously.

Other ways in which the members of the community checked abusive chiefs was to sue a chief in the king's court or to simply force a chief to resign his position (Gluckman 1940a: 43). The situation described by Comaroff (1970), concerning succession disputes among the Tswana, apply with equal force with respect to the Zulu. While there were set rules concerning who could serve as chief (the most important being that the older son of the "great wife" was the legitimate heir), these rules could be interpreted and used to replace chiefs as well (Comaroff 1970).[8] Shaka himself did not have a hereditary right to the position of chief, but rather, attained this position only with the help of Dingiswayo. As

Hamilton notes, Shaka did not believe that chiefs were born, he believed they could be made, and thus, unmade (see also Webb and Wright 1976: vol. 1, 115–16). Chiefs were well aware of the fact that if they could not garner community support, their position would no doubt be threatened. Thus, there was an incentive for chiefs not only to provide order but to make decisions fairly with the input of the community.

In addition, as mentioned above, the decentralized system of power meant that people could take their problems or cases to a variety of rulers, including the chief, the *izinduna*, and in extreme cases, the king. Thus, there was an important institutional check built into the system itself. The decentralized structure of the chieftaincy meant that people could create divisions and factions in the community in certain circumstances. For example, those unhappy with the chief might decide to rely upon the *induna* to resolve disputes rather than going to the chief. The existence of kinship ties, which did not necessarily overlap with the chief's jurisdiction, was another manner in which divisions could be formed (see Ayittey 1991). Lastly, given the fact that people could pledge allegiance to another chief, there was an incentive to satisfy the people's needs. In this way, "chief was balanced against chief, for the unsatisfactory chief lost followers to a more popular neighbor" (Gluckman 1940b: 148).

The Idea of the Chieftaincy

One of the more instructive insights concerning the complex and deep connections between ruler and ruled in KwaZulu-Natal is the distinction most people made, and continue to make, between individual chiefs and the institution of the chieftaincy itself. As Omer-Cooper notes, the "[c]hieftaincy was regarded as inhering more in the royal lineage than in any particular individual. Though there was a definite law of succession it was not regarded as absolutely sacrosanct and where an heir was judged incapable or otherwise undesirable he might be passed over in favour of some other member of the royal family" (Omer-Cooper 1966: 19). While it was not uncommon to replace bad or inefficient chiefs, it was less common for the institution of the chieftaincy itself to be challenged. Gluckman's observation of this phenomenon led him to argue that the Zulus "could be rebels but not revolutionaries" (Gluckman 1940b: 152). While people were expected to respect and show loyalty to an individual chief, the deeper attachment was to what the chieftaincy itself represented—which transcended the individuals who occupied the positions of leadership at any one moment. In short, the idea of the chieftaincy took precedence over individual officeholders within the institution itself.

The evidence suggests that the "structures of meaning" in pre-colonial Zulu society were complex and contradictory but that political debate and structure centered on the notion of unity. Pre-colonial relations between ruler and ruled were based upon a decentralized, yet hierarchical, system of control. The authority of chiefs was founded upon a diverse set of factors, ideas, and structures. While the chiefs exercised legislative, executive, and judicial power vis-à-vis their own communities, they were also expected to be the king's obedient assistants and to balance community needs against the needs of the larger kingdom. Similarly, *izinduna* were expected to assist the chief in the administration of the area but were also granted discretion to make decisions, resolve disputes, and represent those living in their distinct area.

While studies that focus on the importance of order and discipline in pre-colonial Zulu society are important, the historical record also suggests that order was only one of several political traditions that can be traced to this period. More specifically, there is significant evidence that the way rulers attempted to secure order and discipline was constrained by a set of equally important principles. Thus, even though the establishment of order was critical for maintaining political legitimacy, only when this goal was achieved within the proper procedural and symbolic framework would there be unity. My argument is that Zulu rulers, even at this early period, could not rely upon only force and coercion to maintain political legitimacy. Instead, they relied upon other methods and practices to help foster and maintain political legitimacy. The introduction of indirect rule and apartheid policies, however, altered these dynamics and changed the nature of the legitimation process.

REMAKING UNITY: INDIRECT RULE, APARTHEID, AND THE APPROPRIATION OF POLITICAL TRADITIONS

I believe that the power of Chiefs will become extinct from the force of circumstances.

—THEOPHILUS SHEPSTONE, QUOTED IN WELSH 1971: 115

The Bantu form of government is the traditional Bantu democracy, and the Tribal Chief, together with his Tribal Council, provides the protective shelter under which the highest and the lowest can feel at home and find self-expression and fulfillment. For this reason this form of government is the only suitable line of approach for the full development of a community of their own.

—REPUBLIC OF SOUTH AFRICA 1960–62: 1 (DEPARTMENT OF BANTU ADMINISTRATION AND DEVELOPMENT. ANNUAL REPORT, HEREINAFTER BAD ANNUAL REPORT 1960–62)

[T]he wrath of the people will not be directed at the oppressor but at those who will be burdened with the dirty work of manipulating the detestable Rehabilitation Scheme, the collection of taxes and other measures which are designed to keep down the people?

—NELSON MANDELA, QUOTED IN MZALA 1988: 65–66

The Establishment of Indirect Rule (1845–1948)

While in 1845 the chieftaincies residing north of the Tugela River, and thereby, within the boundaries of the Zulu kingdom, remained beyond the control of the newly established British colony of Natal, those within the colony's boundaries were the first to experience Shepstone's policy of indirect rule.[9] Even before it was annexed in 1845, Natal was the scene of intense conflicts between the newly arrived Trekboers, the British, and numerous chieftaincies who were either indigenous to the area or who migrated to the area to escape the control of the Zulu authorities (Lambert 1995; Welsh 1971; Brookes and Webb 1965).[10] Both Dingane, the Zulu king who succeeded Shaka in 1828,[11] and the chieftaincies within Natal, held discussions with both the Trekboers and the British—each attempting to use the wealth and power of the newcomers to provide security or economic benefits (Brookes and Webb 1965).

As the British settlers began to occupy the area around present-day Durban, there was considerable fear of the autonomous Zulu kingdom to the north and much confusion over what to do with the chieftaincies in Natal. It is well known that the "native question" in Natal ultimately came under the exclusive jurisdiction of Theophilus Shepstone, who was sent to Natal in 1846 as a diplomatic agent to the native tribes.[12] Where many white settlers saw risk, Shepstone saw possible opportunities. The key was to devise a policy where in the short term chiefs could provide order and where the responsibilities placed on the state—in terms of both financial and personnel—would be minimal. With respect to knowledge about Zulu politics, society, and culture, Shepstone believed he understood the Zulus better than most. In fact, Shepstone was raised in the eastern frontier region of the Cape Colony, was the son of a Wesleyan missionary, and learned Nguni languages at a young age (Thompson 1995: 97). Initially, his paternal instincts to "civilize" the Africans led him initially to promote a policy where Africans would enter a program of Western education, which would hopefully lead to economic development. In the end, this type of policy proved impossible to implement due to serious financial constraints on the colony (Thompson 1995: 98; Brookes and Webb 1965: 58–59).

Without a strong police force, civil servants, or financial assistance, Shepstone relied upon the preexisting chieftaincy system to govern over the "natives." This was difficult, however, as the chieftaincies in Natal were in a state of disarray and confusion following Shaka's wars and policies, and the resulting migration of people (Brookes and Webb 1965: 59). At the center of Shepstone's proposal was the demarcation of specific "locations," or "reserves," which were to be set aside for the chieftaincies and their followers. White settlers immediately criticized this plan, fearing that the locations would occupy too much land and that they would interfere with their ability to acquire cheap labor and that the locations were much too large (Brookes and Webb 1965: 60). In addition, many white settlers and administrators cautioned that Shepstone's proposal, where chieftaincies were given limited autonomy, would lead to a situation where they would most likely "set up their own authority in direct opposition to that of the Government" (Welsh 1971: 15). Shepstone believed this would not happen in Natal, based on his impression that the Zulu had "notions of most implicit obedience to their rulers" that was not found among "natives" in the Cape (Welsh 1971: 19). Nevertheless, the 1846 Locations Commission, which established the demarcated areas, stated in its report that the authority of the chieftaincies would eventually diminish and other authority structures would replace them (Brookes and Webb 1965: 58–59).

In the end, Shepstone's idea of utilizing chiefs to help implement colonial rule proved to be successful in that it helped to maintain order and facilitate economic expansion for the white settlers. It would take nearly fifty years, however, until the colonial regime implemented indirect rule in the Zulu kingdom north of the Tugela, and this did not occur without the use of force. In 1879, the British defeated the Zulus at the Battle of Ulundi, thereby destroying their capital city and the *inkatha* that had been handed down to successive kings after Shaka's death. King Cetshwayo was sent into exile, the monarchy dissolved, and the British created thirteen independent chiefdoms that were ruled by both hereditary and appointed chiefs (Laband 1995; Guy 1979). This new political dispensation proved to be unworkable, and a civil war ensued. In 1887, the British took over the administration of what was referred to as Zululand, and after the colonial government incorporated Zululand into Natal in 1897, the rules and processes of indirect rule were applied in full force to this area. Thus, unlike the chieftaincies in Natal, which experienced indirect rule from the mid-1840s, those living in Zululand had a much longer period of political autonomy.[13]

With the political union of the country in 1910, South Africa ceased to be a colony in the normal sense as Britain transferred most legislative and executive power to more autonomous political structures. From this period to 1948, the newly established segregationist state established the legal foundation of the subsequent apartheid state. In 1927, with the passage of the Native Affairs Act, the South African government implemented the "Shepstonian" system of indirect rule throughout the Union. This act, along with the 1913 Land Act, continued the reserve policy of the Natalian administration and left many of the boundaries unchanged. Following the victory of the Nationalist Party in 1948, the government passed the 1951 Bantu Affairs Act. This piece of legislation, more than any other, laid the foundation for the emerging apartheid policy and reestablished the chieftaincy as the vital link between the people and the government. Under this legislation, the government established a hierarchy of authorities consisting of tribal authorities, regional authorities, and territorial authorities. At the apex of this hierarchy, however, were the white officials from the Department of Bantu Affairs (BAD) who supervised their activities. While the department was omnipresent, it was not omnipotent, and many daily struggles in the local Bantu areas remained separate from its directives (Evans 1997).

The government justified this system as providing more self-governance and political autonomy. As members of Parliament argued at the time, the act was important in order to "have a basis on which the Native will henceforth be able to give expression to his own inner self to develop his family life and his national life" (quoted in Butler, Rotberg, and Adams 1977: 28). Chiefs controlled all levels of this structure. They appointed the members of the tribal authorities and controlled the regional authorities, which consisted of two or more tribal authorities. Territorial authorities represented all tribal and regional authorities, and with the passage of the 1959 Promotion of Bantu Self-Government Act, could eventually reach the status of an independent and sovereign state. Unlike three other Bantustans, the Kwazulu Bantustan never sought the status of complete independence. Instead, in 1970, the government established the KwaZulu Territorial Authority, and in 1972, it achieved self-governing status and established the KwaZulu Legislative Assembly (KZLA).

Order and Unity: The Ideological Foundations
of Indirect Rule and Apartheid

There is no question that the experiences of indirect rule, the segregationist state, and apartheid altered the nature of the legitimation process at the local level. Chieftaincy-societal relations, as well as chieftaincy-state relations, had to be adjusted to meet the new demands caused from the reallocation of space and power. What is less clear, however, especially given the survival of the chieftaincy after the end of apartheid, is how these experiences affected the nature of pre-colonial understandings of authority and ruler-ruled relations. More specifically, what happened to the idea of unity during this period and the principles of order, consultation, impartiality, and community welfare? Did these concepts remain important during indirect rule and apartheid? Did the colonial state utilize any of these concepts to help facilitate their control? To emphasize the importance of continuity, even in the middle of ruptures caused by colonialism, one scholar notes that the colonial and apartheid states attempted to establish a "chord of familiarity amongst the oppressed . . . to [better] facilitate social control" (Hendricks 1990: 15).

While many studies examine how the policies from colonial rule through apartheid affected the chieftaincy, much of this literature utilizes a top-down approach in which official rules, laws, and decrees are offered as evidence of chieftaincy-societal relations at the local level (Mamdani 1996; Welsh 1971). Many of these studies assume that any pre-colonial political ideologies were effectively abolished or reinvented anew during these periods and that chieftaincy-societal relations, if such relations even existed, were based on a new set of norms or values. There is evidence, however, that the actual implementation of indirect rule and apartheid was much less coherent than sometimes assumed and that there often existed a significant gap between official law and actual political behavior (Crais 2006; Crais 2003a; Crais 2003b; MacKinnon 2003; Evans 1997; Clough 1990).

This does not mean, however, that there is no place for official rules, laws, or decrees in an analysis of the chieftaincy. There is no question that official rules were extremely important concerning chieftaincy-state relations, and that both state officials and chiefs utilized the law in many ways to effectuate political decisions (Gluckman 1940b). We must not assume, however, that these official rules affected chieftaincy-societal relations in the same degree (Moore 1986). Indeed, numerous studies show how the chieftaincy, to maintain legitimacy, was forced into the difficult position of representing two different groups—the state and their local populations (Rouveroy van Nieuwaal 1996; Marks 1970, 1986). This precarious nature of chieftaincy-state and chieftaincy-societal relations is where there may exist important gaps between the official rules and actual interactions that could help us understand how colonialism and apartheid transformed pre-colonial political ideologies (Marks 1986).

An analysis of official state rules, laws, and decrees is instructive as they illustrate how the colonial, segregationist, and apartheid states utilized particular principles embedded in pre-colonial political ideologies to help facilitate rule. Such an examination reveals that these states utilized the idea of unity and the principle of order to justify their policies. Focusing on indirect rule and apartheid in their ideological form, rather than just their institutional form, demonstrates that while unity and order were exaggerated in the new political dispensation, consultation, impartiality, and community welfare were largely ignored. In the process, these ideas were altered and given new meanings, but they remained important to local communities.

For example, in *Terrific Majesty*, Hamilton (1998) examines how the colonial state appropriated ideas and images of Shaka to construct indirect rule and how this adaptation process worked. More specifically, she is concerned with how Zulu ideas about power and authority were utilized to structure colonial rule (99). In her analysis, Hamilton focuses on the importance of discipline and social order in the Zulu political consciousness and how Shepstone based his proposals on these values. Even though the principle of order is only one of several that are crucial to the overall legitimation process, Hamilton's study provides an important starting point to understand how the colonial state incorporated pre-existing Zulu political principles to maintain social control.

Comparing what she saw in the Zulu kingdom versus Natal, Hamilton notes that Shepstone interpreted the former as characterized by order and the latter by chaos. This dichotomy was central to Shepstone's own understanding of the political situation as well as a way for him to "sell" his policy to a skeptical white population. While this dichotomy was no doubt politically prudent for Shepstone, it is interesting that he used the familiar ideas of order/chaos as opposed to other dichotomies colonial authorities often utilized, such as West/other or civilization/barbarism (Hamilton 1998: 91). The colonial state recognized the importance of order to the ongoing legitimation process in the region, and thus it was continually stressed.

In this vein, there are numerous examples that demonstrate how the colonial and apartheid states utilized general understanding of Zulu ideas of order to justify their policies. In particular, the chieftaincy-state relationship was meant to mimic the king-chieftaincy relationship as colonial officials envisioned in Zululand. Understanding the central importance of the king as the symbol of unity for the Zulus, colonial officials attempted to appropriate this to their own advantage (Nicholas Cope 1993; Marks 1970; Gluckman 1940a). As early as 1849, for instance, Shepstone declared himself to be the "Supreme Chief" and "Father" of the Zulus in Natal and assumed the powers of the Zulu king (Welsh 1971: 119–20; Hamilton 1998). With respect to the authority of the chiefs, Shepstone stated that "everything affecting life and property and the peace of the country which the chiefs have hitherto done on their own responsibility, must now be done on the authority of the Government appointed over them" (Welsh 1971: 20–21). The 1891 Natal Code of Native Law expanded the power of the supreme chief and gave him the power to appoint and depose chiefs and divide or amalgamate "tribes" as he saw fit. The position of supreme chief and his powers were applied to all of South Africa in the 1927 Native Administration Act and again in the 1951 Bantu Authorities Act.

These powers were conferred on the state even though it was well known that Zulu kings and chiefs did not, and could not, rule without due regard for public opinion (Marks 1970: 40). In fact, in his testimony to the 1883 Cape Native Laws and Customs Commission, Cetshwayo, the former Zulu king, was asked if he could act independently when appointing chiefs. His response was revealing: "No, the King has not the power of electing an officer as chief without the approval of other chiefs. They are the most important men. But the smaller chiefs he can elect at his own discretion" (quoted in Marks 1970: 40). According to the 1891 Code, however, the supreme chief could appoint all chiefs. In addition, rather than recognize the autonomous position of many chiefs in the pre-colonial Zulu kingdom, the code provided the chiefs were the "minor deputies" of the supreme chief and were given a small salary for their duties (Marks 1970: 43).

Utilizing an unrestricted conception of order, the colonial and apartheid states routinely demonstrated the full force of their authority. For example, in 1846, in one of his first acts in Natal, Shepstone deposed chief Fodo for fighting with his neighbors despite warnings from the state not to do so. After exercising this authority, Shepstone commented that "they saw in it what might have taken years to show them so clearly by other means, that the Government intended to be supreme in its own territory, and that all independent action on the part of Chiefs and Tribes would be prohibited and punished" (quoted in Welsh 1971: 20). Again in 1857, Shepstone broke up two chieftaincies and had their property confiscated for disobeying orders. One scholar notes that there was no precedent in African law for this "eating up" of chieftaincies and that Shepstone was "acting as autocratically as Shaka" (Lambert 1995: 31). One of James Stuart's informants stated that the "[g]overnment is expanding every few years. The Government resembles Tshaka, for he never got tired. Its army is money" (Webb and Wright 1982: 29). Such coercion continued throughout the colonial era and reached even more brutal proportions in the apartheid era, when many chieftaincies were dissolved, amalgamated, or "resettled" to different areas (Yawitch 1981).

It is also interesting to note how the colonial and apartheid states appropriated particular symbols, images, and rituals associated with the Zulu tradition of order to facilitate its rule. In the colonial era, the use, and misuse, of these symbols and images culminated in 1873 when Shepstone attended the coronation of King Cetshwayo and "officially" installed him as ruler of the Zulu kingdom "as Shaka" (Hamilton 1998: 73). In addition, during both indirect rule and apartheid, people were instructed to address government officials with the customary Zulu salute of *Bayete*. In the past, this salute was usually reserved for only the king and was meant as a show of respect to the person who symbolized the unity of the people. The use of this salute symbolized the superior status of the government and its role as a unifying force (Gluckman 1940b).

At the same time, the colonial and apartheid states limited or banned other symbols and rituals they deemed dangerous. For example, chiefs were allowed to form an *amabutho* only with the permission of the colonial government (Natal 1891: S.156; Lambert 1995: 29). Because the *amabutho* was intimately associated with the Zulu military, as well as with chiefly power, colonial officials often looked upon it with suspicion. The dismantling of the *amabutho* was also one of the central aspects of the British ultimatum to King Cetshwayo and the Zulu kingdom just preceding the Anglo-Zulu War in 1879 (Omer-Cooper 1987: 114). The king responded that he could never agree to this request as the *amabutho* was materially and symbolically tied to the Zulu kingdom (Omer-Cooper 1987: 114). The apartheid state continued this trend and banned other activities such as the brewing of beer, the possession of Zulu "cultural" weapons, and specific battle cries (Union of South Africa 1957: S.16[a–c]). In this way, the colonial and apartheid states continually sought to appropriate those symbols and rituals that perpetuated their rule and discourage, or simply ban, those that were perceived as a threat.

At the local level, the colonial state focused exclusively on the ability of chieftaincies to maintain order and increased their powers in this regard. Until the passage of the 1927 Native Affairs Act, however, the powers of the chieftaincy over matters not directly relating to law and order were diminished. The following list of the official powers of the chiefs during this period demonstrates the state's primary concern with order: in 1888, chiefs were not allowed to take a household under their control without sanction of the secretary of native affairs; in 1893, chiefs lost jurisdiction over their followers residing on private lands; in 1894, a law was passed that allowed *izinduna* to try civil cases without reference to the chief, and new *izinduna* could be appointed only with the approval of the magistrate; in 1896, a new law extended to appointed chiefs the same *lobola* privileges as hereditary chiefs, and magistrates were given power to decide numerous cases in the reserves including land matters (Lambert 1995: 124). Given the nature of these changes, Lambert suggests that chiefs had become nothing more than policemen, whose sole responsibility was to ensure order (124). In the late nineteenth century, one critic of these new rules stated that "[i]f we do away with these little matters, which are really the only things in which the chief has any authority, then I say we are striking at the root of our own policy" (124). In fact, one chief actually sought to resign his chiefship in the late 1880s because he was not able to provide basic services or meet the growing demands of the state (124). There is no question that in the early 1900s, the official authority of the chiefs was diminishing under the pressure of colonialism (179).

This trend was reversed, however, with the 1927 Native Administration Act and the 1951 Bantu Authorities Act. Each of these acts sought to enhance the authority of the chiefs vis-à-vis their communities. Specifically, the segregationist and apartheid states each believed that chiefs needed more authority over such issues as land allocation, dispute resolution, and development to ensure the continued maintenance of law and order. Thus, what we find with these acts, and the subsequent regulations, are rules that enable chiefs to hear more types of cases, inflict stricter punishments, and enforce a broader range of criminal laws. For example, in the 1960–62 Bantu Affairs Annual Report, the minister noted that the chiefs "are the Government's representatives in the areas concerned and as such have to ensure, in general, that effect is given to all laws, instructions and requirements concerning the administration and control of the Bantu in their areas" (BAD Annual Report 1960–62: 2–3). This policy echoed the 1852–53 Native Affairs Commission report when it said that "[t]he point upon which the whole of the Kafir law hinges are [sic] mutual responsibility and unquestioning obedience to the order of the chief—his word is law, his power is absolute" (Natal 1852–53: 21; Marks 1970: 38).

This trend continued during apartheid and even with the establishment of "self-government" in KwaZulu. For example, in 1976, the KwaZulu government proposed that the fine for "insolence" increase from R4 to R100. The central state responded to this request by raising it to R200.[14] For those who could not afford such a fine, corporal punishment was used instead (Mamdani 1996: 125–26). In general, the apartheid state afforded chiefs much more authority, over a wider degree of issues, than was the case previously. In the 1974 KwaZulu Chiefs' and Headmen's Act, many of the duties previously outlined by proclamation by the central government were repeated. Most importantly, chiefs were responsible for "maintain[ing] law and order and report to the Government, without delay, any matter of import or concern, including any condition of unrest or dissatisfaction" (KwaZulu Legislative Assembly 1974: S.6(d)). Chiefs were also confirmed to have he power of arrest (S.6(e)(i)), search and seizure (S.6(e)(ii)), and reporting to a "competent authority . . . any pretended witchcraft or divination" (S.6(f)(iii)). Thus, in the end, the KwaZulu Bantustan mimicked the apartheid regime's tendency to selectively appropriate those aspects of the Zulu past that were most congenial with its desire to maintain control.

Redefining Consultation, Impartiality, and Community Welfare under Indirect Rule and Apartheid

Given the almost exclusive focus on order, Mare and Hamilton note that "[t]he powers that were given to chiefs by the colonial authority were of a different nature to the powers they had had in independent pre-colonial societies; the effect was to undermine the legitimacy of their position because such absolute power would not have been countenanced" (Mare and Hamilton 1987: 18). While the state surely influenced chieftaincy-societal relations by focusing almost exclusively on the chiefs' duty to maintain order, there is also evidence that suggests chiefs, and the state, needed to respond to other norms and values to ensure compliance. On this point, Lambert reminds us that during the period of indirect rule in Natal "even powerful chiefs lacked the coercive powers necessary to rule without some degree of popular consent, while a chief who did try to impose his will risked having people transfer their allegiance elsewhere" (Lambert 1995: 28). In fact, Lambert gives numerous examples where people changed their allegiance because a chief was excessively cruel or was not adequately protecting the community (28). In addition, there are numerous examples in Zululand and Natal where local communities resisted orders from the state and their chiefs that were not perceived to benefit community welfare (Lambert 1995; Beinart 1982; Beinart and Bundy 1987; Yawitch 1981; Lodge 1977). Thus, Mare and Hamilton's statement, as well as Shepstone's premonition that indirect rule had "entirely changed the political relationship between Chiefs and people," requires further examination (Welsh 1971: 125).

Let me be clear, however, that the argument here is not that indirect rule or apartheid had no affect on chieftaincy-societal relations. There is no question that colonialism did influence how chiefs and their followers interacted and the nature of the legitimation process. The boundaries of the chieftaincies' power expanded, and the state weakened those mechanisms to restrain this power. The issue that is raised here is whether those pre-colonial governing principles, other than the maintenance of order, remained important to local communities in spite of the colonial experience. Much of the literature on this topic, with its focus on official rules rather than local chieftaincy-societal relations, assumes that these principles simply faded away with colonialism (Mamdani 1996). Based on my field research, however, this proposition seems unlikely. The point here is to locate the ways in which these principles remained salient and the processes through which they were redefined or were adapted to new circumstances. For example, Thornton's (2005) research in Mpumalanga and Limpopo finds that despite the experiences of apartheid, for chiefs to remain legitimate they must continually earn the respect of their populations. Not surprisingly, unlike the maintenance of order, the official rules have comparatively very little to say on the principles of consultation, impartiality, and community welfare. Rather, the interactions between the state, chiefs, and local populations provide the means to assess the extent and nature of the gap between official rules and the dynamics of local politics. While the arguments below would greatly benefit from more historical research highlighting the voices of both chiefs and their followers at the local level, one scholar who has conducted such research notes that

> the colonial state became, in effect, a parasite drawing its lifeblood—legitimacy—from the chiefs. If the state had abolished the chieftaincy and refused to recognize chiefs, it would have had to develop its legitimacy all by itself, a daunting task indeed, and one that few chose to undertake. . . . The state had to keep chiefly legitimacy more than a mere fiction if it was to continue to benefit from their existence. It therefore preserved some real sense in which chiefs were responsible to their subjects. Chiefs, in turn, were thus given the space in which to exercise some autonomy from the colonial state. (Mahoney 1998: 25)

Even though the maintenance of order was the primary concern, the importance of consultation and participation was not lost on early colonial administrators. For example, Shepstone was known for traveling great distances to hold meetings with chiefs, and he often consulted with them on various matters. There is evidence that this consultation was considered an important aspect of chieftaincy-state relations. At the 1881–82 Natal Native Commission, numerous chiefs complained that Shepstone's successor, his son John, did not consult with them and did not appear to represent their interests (Lambert 1995: 58). In fact, once Theophilus Shepstone left his position in 1876, the government failed to hold meetings with chiefs. Instead, the government established a board to issue new rules and procedures without any consultation with the chiefs (Lambert 1995: 59). Not only did this breakdown in communication result in political uprisings involving chiefs, such as the Bambatha uprising in 1906, but it also eroded any trust chiefs and their followers might have placed in the government.[15]

More importantly, however, even with the presence of the colonial state, consultation, impartiality, and community welfare remained important principles at the local level. One example comes from what is now known as the Mvuzane Tribal Authority under the Biyela chieftaincy.[16] What happened in Mvuzane is not unique; similar examples can be found in the archival material. From 1925 to 1935, the community was involved in a succession dispute between two of chief Hashi Biyela's sons (Hashi died in 1925). The archival information about this dispute, which contains memoranda, minutes from meetings, letters from the different participants, and communications between colonial administrators, represents a wonderful opportunity to hear the voices of both the local state officials and the Africans involved. It demonstrates the complex interactions between the state and the chieftaincy and the extent to which chiefs and *izinduna,* as well as magistrates, relied upon a combination of formal rules, threats, consultation, and community consent to implement their decisions. The dispute involved two sons, Zimvu, the eldest son, and Zalaba, a junior son, who each claimed his father had chosen him to be the next chief. In the end, after a formal enquiry with witnesses, lawyers, and colonial administrators, the government supported Zalaba's claim even though the majority of the community claimed they supported Zimvu.

In a memo dated December 17, 1925, the chief native commissioner of Natal, stressing the importance of autonomy and community decision making on the issue of succession, wrote that "[i]t is of course desirable that the people concerned should come to an amicable arrangement amongst themselves if possible" (Correspondence, December 15, 1932).[17] By 1930, however, the Eshowe magistrate warned that this matter would not be resolved peacefully and that it would be a "grave error" if someone was appointed without a full investigation (Correspondence, April 15, 1930). Many witnesses came forward with their interpretation of the facts, and a majority of the *izinduna* told the magistrate that they favored Zimvu. In many of the meetings with colonial officials, the *izinduna* on each side of the debate invoked the will of the people to justify their position. For example, *induna* Mdumeli, who was acting as chief during the dispute and supported Zimvu, told the magistrate that "my duty is still to the late Chief Hashi, and that I must look after the interests of all his children. It is not correct that I favour Zimvu, but the matter has been brought up to me, and I must therefore voice the feelings of the people. I have done this in the interests of the tribe because they are the ones who will be ruled by whoever is appointed, and I feel I must convey their feelings" (Memorandum, April 22, 1931). He added, "[T]he tribe should be allowed to vote for whom they want. If they choose Zalaba well and good and vice versa. This would settle the matter permanently, and would also prevent the aspirants from losing their property by engaging lawyers etc." (ibid.).

In most meetings on this issue, both chiefs and *izinduna* stressed the voice of the people and claimed the people should ultimately decide the issue. Of course, how to interpret these voices was a point of ongoing contestation. One *induna,* for example, suggested that if Hashi did name Zimvu the heir, and not Zalaba, the people did not properly understand this, and thus, could not have agreed with it (Memorandum, April 22, 1931). To settle this matter, the magistrate arranged a formal enquiry into the succession dispute. At the public meeting held as part of the enquiry, over 1,700 people were in attendance, including Zimvu and Zalaba, all the *izinduna* from Mvuzane, and eight chiefs from neighboring areas. The report noted that the "interest shown by the Natives was extraordinary" (Proceedings in an Enquiry, August 8, 1932).

During this enquiry, after it was apparent the government supported Zalaba's claim, Zalaba spoke of the importance of gaining the confidence of the people but was concerned he could not do this if Mdumeli and Zimvu remained in the area. He wanted the government to remove them so he could establish better relations with the people. The magistrate agreed with Zalaba and ordered Zimvu to leave the area. One chief added that "[i]t is a very hard punishment, but if obedience is not shown to the Chief they must go." The magistrate then warned, "[Y]ou men today see what has happened to one man. He must go to another District, and if you do not listen, especially *indunas*[sic], it will happen to you also. . . . Those who refuse to support the Chief in the future will be sent away. The decision from the Supreme Chief must be obeyed" (ibid.).

While the chiefs and *izinduna* spoke of the people's wishes and interests, the government stressed obedience and threatened punishment. After formally choosing Zalaba, one chief noted that "[a]lthough I do not know what the Biyela people have to say, we are prepared to accept the decision which cannot be disputed and we hope that the people will also accept it" (Appointment, September 23, 1932). In one last attempt to sway the officials, Zimvu, through his attorneys, suggested that the tribe be subdivided so that he could be appointed chief over the members who supported him. Zimvu said that he was entitled to represent the 75 percent of the tribe who favored his claim. The government did not agree to this, and at a subsequent meeting, Zimvu agreed to the government decision. He said he would do so "as I am a child of the Government and will listen to the Government. . . . [But] the settlement of this matter was not in accordance with Native custom" (Memorandum, October 1932).

Even after Zimvu left the area, the matter was still not completely resolved. In 1933, chief Zalaba asked the government to dismiss a majority of his *izinduna* as they had not acknowledged his chieftainship, and they disliked him. The magistrate noted that if this was indeed the case, it was unacceptable as the *izinduna* were supposed to "assist and advise him in all matters; and pull together as one" (Meeting, November 2,

1933). When the magistrate confronted the *izinduna* about this matter in front of Zalaba, they all claimed they did respect his authority. Zalaba argued that "[o]nce they are at home they will be talking something different" (ibid.). This was supported by another person at the meeting, who argued that "I say all these *induna*s [*sic*] are only speaking favourably today because our Magistrate is present. I know as soon as they reach home they will start changing colours" (ibid.). Despite these concerns, the magistrate decided not to dismiss the *izinduna* because "it is not an easy matter to deprive them of this dignity" (ibid.). Two years later, however, after numerous fights between Zalaba's and Zimvu's supporters, the *izinduna* were dismissed and replaced with people who supported Zalaba.

This scenario demonstrates the complexities of both chieftaincy-state and chieftaincy-societal relations.[18] This succession dispute highlights the various governing principles that were simultaneously at work. While the state provided numerous forums in which all participants could voice their opinion, these situations were also meant to demonstrate the importance of order and obedience. The chiefs, *izinduna,* and commoners, on the other hand, suggested that the most appropriate way to ensure order was to make decisions based on consultation, participation, and the community sentiment. In the end, the result of the government's decisions, at least in the short term, was to produce disorder, disunity, and bloodshed. What is most important, however, is that this scenario makes it clear that there were ways in which the principle of consultation could coexist with order, even when the state obviously stressed the latter. These divisions in Mvuzane, which are rooted in this succession dispute, continue to manifest themselves to the present day. There are still discussions concerning the "secession" of one part of Mvuzane Tribal Authority, and the present chief must convince these people that it is to their advantage not to do this.

Other evidence suggests that the principle of participation and consultation continued to be important even at the height of apartheid. After the passage of the 1951 Bantu Authorities Act, very few chiefs in KwaZulu or Natal elected to form tribal authorities. The act stated that the formation of such entities would be voluntary and would not be done until the government had "consulted" with the chiefs. In 1955, Dr. Verwoerd, the secretary of native affairs and the architect of the Bantu Authorities Act, held a meeting near the town of Nongoma about the act. There were approximately three hundred chiefs there as well as King Cyprian. Dr. Verwoerd was obviously frustrated that very few chiefs had established tribal authorities, and after giving his speech, he suggested that he would need an immediate answer as to whether the chiefs in attendance would agree to the formation of tribal authorities. Much to his dismay, one chief rose and stated that none of them could agree to any policies until they consulted their communities—to which the other chiefs agreed (Mzala 1988: 57). King Cyprian, however, who was in favor of the act, told the chiefs they needed to decide immediately and reportedly stated that "[a]s I am your child and can therefore not speak on your behalf, I ask you to consider this request and to decide for yourselves" (57).

A decision was delayed until 1957, when King Cyprian called a special meeting to announce that the chiefs would accept the act. Out of the approximately 288 Zulu chiefs, only 72 attended (Mzala 1988: 61). It is probably no mere coincidence that this meeting followed the promulgation of Proclamation 110 in the same year, which required every chief or headman to constitute his followers into a tribal authority within thirty days. If this was not done, the minister would do it himself. According to the government, the previous meeting with Dr. Verwoerd in 1955 was considered to be the "consultation" needed to meet the required statutory demands.

With respect to the issue of impartiality, the ability of chiefs to resolve disputes was also affected under colonialism and apartheid. As the Mvuzane example demonstrated, given the influence of the colonial state, it was more difficult for chiefs and *izinduna* to function merely as an "umpire." Their jurisdiction changed substantially, and their followers were able to appeal unfavorable decisions to the magistrate.[19] Not surprisingly, the colonial and apartheid states were concerned with the chiefs' judicial powers only to the extent that they helped to facilitate order. Unlike the legislative and executive guidance concerning the maintenance of order, there is relatively very little official pronouncement on the issue of impartiality.

In 1927, the Native Affairs Act established that chiefs could hear all civil cases arising out of "native law" or "custom" that were brought to the chief by two natives who were both residents in his area. These powers were meant to allow chiefs to control people in their areas, to more effectively levy taxes, and to emphasize the chief's role as the arbiter of disputes. Yet again, that these judicial functions were intimately intermingled with administrative ones meant that neutrality was difficult to maintain. One clue that the colonial state did not necessarily consider neutrality as important as maintaining order was that the 1927 act did not require chiefs to keep a written record of the proceedings or the evidence they heard concerning a case (Mzala 1988: 42). This meant that challenging the impartiality of chiefs was even more difficult. In addition, what we find after 1951 is a general strengthening of the chiefs' power to decide various criminal and civil matters, with little guidance as to the proper procedure for these decisions.

While there are numerous studies demonstrating the importance of chiefs appearing to remain impartial throughout southern and eastern Africa (Rose 1992; Moore 1986; Chanock 1985; Gluckman 1965; Schapera 1956), there are surprisingly few examinations of this issue specifically in Zululand and Natal (but see Krige 1936). Thus, we know relatively little about the processes of dispute resolution in Zululand and Natal during colonialism and apartheid.[20] What is interesting, however, is how the colonial state redefined the principle of impartiality to apply more to the practice of politics than to the administration of law. For example, Proclamation 110 of 1957 forbade chiefs to join any political organization deemed by the minister of native affairs to be "subversive of or prejudicial to constituted government or law and order" (S.18). Further, a chief could be dismissed from office if he disobeyed this law.

This wall of separation between the chieftaincy and politics was a recurrent theme during apartheid and continues to structure much of the debate on the chieftaincy in present-day South Africa. In 1965, for example, before the establishment of the KwaZulu Territorial Authority (KZTA), one report stated that some Zulu thought it was "undignified for chiefs to sit in a Legislative Assembly, exposing themselves to heckling. A bicameral assembly might be preferable, with chiefs sitting in a Upper House" (South African Institute of Race Relations 1965: 134). With the establishment of the KZTA and the KwaZulu Legislative Assembly, however, chiefs were continually exposed to heckling and politics, but argued they could remain impartial as long as they did not join a political party. Clearly, the issue here is one's definition of "politics" and whether this definition is consistent with impartiality or another important principle. For example, in 1995, one member of the KwaZulu-Natal Legislative Assembly stated:

> The question is whether Amakhosi should be involved in politics or not, whether Amakhosi should be members of political parties or not. The ideal situation would be that Amakhosi should continue to be involved in politics. In politics insofar as to fight for the rights and development of all their people without being members of a political party. That is the idealistic situation. (KwaZulu-Natal Legislative

Assembly, KwaZulu-Natal Legislative Debates [hereafter KZNLA Debates] 1995: 1620)[21]

Implicit in these arguments is the idea that engaging in politics, and thus sacrificing the principle of impartiality, would be detrimental to the goal of unity. The best example of this is the debates that took place in the 1970s between Paramount Chief Zwelethini and the KwaZulu government over his participation in politics. While the KwaZulu constitution stated that "[t]he Legislative Assembly shall consider the Paramount Chief of the Zulus personifying the unity of the Zulu nation aloof from Party politics and sectionalism" (KwaZulu Constitution 1972, S. 2.1), many accused Zwelethini of helping to form and joining a political party. In addition, Zwelethini had attended certain functions that the KwaZulu government considered to be political in nature, and thus, unacceptable behavior. In his own defense, Zwelethini stated that, "I was requested by the people, as their father, to address them, therefore I said something, but I know that I said nothing political in that speech" (KwaZulu Legislative Assembly Debates [hereafter KZLA Debates] 1979: 838). Further, he argued that he "helped this House in breaking down or squashing these [opposition political] parties, because we are fighting for unity" (836). In the end, one member suggested that the unity of the Zulu nation was dependent on the unity between Zwelethini and chief Buthelezi:

> May I suggest here that as your late father did, you make a resolution to yourself, that henceforth you will do precisely what you father did, that is, to follow the advice of the Chief Minister [Buthelezi], who is in fact a blood relation of yours and a father to you. Walk hand in hand with him and do whatever he advises you to do, as your father did. Let the world and let the people see the two of you walk together hand in hand, and then you will hear the applause that comes as a result of this. (KZLA Debates 1979: 858)

Thus, the importance of unity and impartiality is invoked, but at this moment of history, it is used to justify the authority of the KZLA over the paramount chief and the fact that chief Buthelezi, rather than Zwelethini, symbolizes the unity of the Zulu people. What is interesting, however, is that these ideas and images, while the substance has clearly been transformed, still resonate with chiefs and their followers.

Finally, there is the issue of community welfare. At the turn of the nineteenth century, chieftaincy-societal relations were in a constant state of flux, with people often choosing to move between different chiefs. While the principle of promoting the community welfare over that of any one individual was crucial, what actually constituted a community was less clear. In some ways, the belief that chiefs were raised up by the ancestors to rule, the *amabutho* system, and festivals such as the *umkhosi,* were all part of an ongoing process to establish a sense of community and unity. The pressures of indirect rule, however, put such immense pressure on intra-community relations that one *induna* told the 1906–1907 Commission, just following the Bambatha rebellion, that Africans no longer "know one another and to whom they belong" (Lambert 1995: 181). The sense is that the attempts to redefine community, and the role of the chief, had failed.

Using the ideas of unity and community as justifications, the colonial state attempted to redefine the nature of chieftaincies and their followers, and thereby make them easier to control. For example, in the 1891 Natal Code of Native Law, a tribe is defined for the first time as "a number or collection or body of natives forming a political organization or community, and composed of not less than twenty kraals under the government, control, or leadership of a chief, and which organization or community has been recognized by the Supreme Chief" (Natal 1891: S.1, chapter 1). In this definition, we see the establishment of a rigid structure of hierarchical authority—from the supreme chief to the chief to the community—which in the past was much more fluid. In addition, "community," "political organization," and "tribe" are seen as interchangeable concepts as long they have been "recognized or established by the Supreme Chief" and each consists of "not less than twenty kraals" which are under the "control or leadership of a chief."

To facilitate the formation of such tribes, the colonial government also reconfigured territorial space. Again, utilizing the ideas of unity and community, each chief was given a specific area of land within a location, or reserve, where their followers could reside. These definitions and rules established a "territorial definition of chiefship" which had not existed before (Lambert 1995: 30; Welsh 1971: 119). Eventually, people would be confined to these areas and would be unable to move between chieftaincies without permission from the government. This new restriction on movement enabled the colonial state to introduce the hut tax and *isibhalo* (a form of forced labor) shortly thereafter, in 1848. Even though chieftaincies were no longer kin-based structures, the colonial state utilized the notion of "tribe" to create a sense of long-standing social and political cohesion, which was in many cases absent (Lambert 1995: 24).

With the passage of the 1951 Bantu Authorities Act, the notion of "tribe" was again at the forefront, although the idea of community was conceptualized in much different terms. For example, the act states that the responsibilities of the tribal authority are to "generally administer the affairs of the tribes and communities in respect of which it has been established; render assistance and guidance to its chief or headman in connection with the performance of his functions" (Union of South Africa 1951: (S.4(1)(a–d)). With respect to understandings of community and the principle of community responsibility, it is notable that the act defines the chief as one member of the tribal authority, who should expect "assistance and guidance" from those living in his area. Rather than focusing on the duties and functions of the individual office holders, this act focuses attention on the duties and functions of the community as a whole. The idea of community responsibility was at the center of this law. Still, these communities needed the chieftaincy because they were still at the "tribal stage of development, and only chiefs were to be their natural rulers because Africans did not have the ability to elect representatives to democratic institutions or organs of government, and they also did not have the necessary sense of responsibility" (Mzala 1988: 50).

This act was controversial in KwaZulu and Natal, and it took many years before tribal authorities and regional authorities were established. For example, after the passage of the Bantu Authorities Act in 1951, the first regional authority, Inkanyezi, was not established until 1959, and as of 1965 only 102 tribal authorities and 12 regional authorities were formed with approximately one third of the chiefs refusing to follow the king's instructions. Nevertheless, in his 1959 New Year's address, the king noted how the act would promote community and order in society: "The South African government's policy of Separate Development offered the Zulu people a chance to regain their former self-respect and national pride. We have been living in a state of uncertainty for many generations. In terms of the present policy in this country the road before us is clear. Development on separate but parallel lines makes for orderly society" (quoted in Mzala 1988: 73). Thus, in the end, the pursuit of order and unity, ironically, entailed the policy of "separate development."

With the end of formal apartheid in 1994, and the introduction of a new set of ideological and institutional principles based on democratic ideals, chieftaincy-societal relations are again in the process of readjusting. Just as with the founding of the Zulu kingdom, the introduction of indirect rule, and the establishment of apartheid, we should expect this process to be uneven and contradictory as both rulers and ruled attempt to make sense of the new political dispensation. The colonial experience in KwaZulu-Natal highlights the tensions between those dominant pre-colonial cultural and political traditions and the changing physical realities resulting from the presence of the colonial, segregationist, and apartheid states.

The historical evidence suggests that chieftaincy-societal relations are embedded in a mixed political culture accommodating both authoritarian and participatory principles. As is the case in most societies, these principles are inherently ambiguous and are open to constant interpretation and reinterpretation. In addition, the pre-colonial institutional design of the chieftaincies promoted both centralization and decentralization, and thus, the maintenance of contextual authority relations. Indirect rule and apartheid utilized certain aspects of these cultural and institutional qualities to establish social control. Not surprisingly, the colonial and apartheid states privileged those principles that helped to facilitate social control, and ignored or downplayed those that were considered less important. What was once a mixture of ideas that were complex and open to interpretation became "closed, static, structured, and simple" under colonialism and apartheid (Hamilton 1998: 128).

Specifically, while in the pre-colonial period the idea of unity was ambiguous enough to incorporate a host of political goals and practices, the colonial state focused on the significance of order as the only acceptable manifestation of this ideal. Still, the evidence suggests that colonialism did not necessarily "invent" an entirely new set of authority relations, but rather, relied upon preexisting principles and ideas to facilitate its rule (Hamilton 1998; Fields 1985).

While the chieftaincy is first and foremost a political institution, it also has a much deeper meaning, and local populations perceive it as something much more than a set of rules or processes or a set of individual leaders. Rather, its importance and centrality in the community transcends the sum of its parts—it represents the importance of unity in political and social life. Mahoney captures this notion when he suggests that the "chiefship was the primary vehicle for these people's political imaginings" and that while there is often contestation over which individual is best suited to be the leader, "[r]elatively uncontested . . . were the ideas that people should have chiefs, and that chiefs should rule through particular rites and ceremonies and political structures" (1998: 27–28).

While the experience of colonialism and apartheid altered the content of these principles, the importance of unity, order, consultation, impartiality, and community welfare, as frames of reference for local populations, continued to structure chieftaincy-societal relations. Chieftaincy-societal relations were changed because of these experiences, but the type of change was not always intended or anticipated (Evans 1997; Lambert 1995; Clough 1990; Greenberg 1987). Pressured from both the state and their followers, chiefs and *izinduna* learned to selectively invoke particular principles and ideas in different circumstances. Indeed, as I demonstrate in subsequent chapters, these historical lessons are important to the analysis of present-day chieftaincy-state and chieftaincy-societal relations. Similar to the experiences under indirect rule and apartheid, communities are reinterpreting the idea of unity and the principles of consultation, impartiality, and community welfare, given the new political dispensation, while simultaneously continuing to respect the idea of the chieftaincy.

THE MAKING OF A MIXED POLITY

The Accommodation and Transformation of the Chieftaincy

In a purely republican democracy . . . , no constitutional space exists for the official recognition of any traditional leaders.

There is no reason why African customs and traditions should be seen to be in conflict with the demands of modern governance. What is required is an innovative institutional arrangement, which combines the natural capacities of both traditional and elected local government to advance the development of rural areas and communities.

It is the Department's considered view that the institution has a place in our democracy, and has a potential to transform and contribute enormously towards the restoration of the moral fibre of our society and in the reconstruction and development of the country, especially the rural areas.

This chapter examines the national debates concerning the chieftaincy in the 1990s and how the chieftaincy has been officially integrated into the post-apartheid constitutional order, from the writing of the 1993 interim constitution to the adoption of the TLGF Act in 2003 and the Communal Land Act in 2004. I argue that through a series of policies the post-apartheid South African government has sought to simultaneously accommodate and transform the chieftaincy as it has attempted to introduce democratic norms, processes, and institutions into the former Bantustan areas. In short, its aim has been to create a mixed polity where the chieftaincy and democratic institutions exist together. An analysis of these formal arrangements, as well as the debates surrounding them, highlights the competing, and sometimes conflicting, visions that exist at the national level concerning the appropriate role of the chieftaincy in the post-apartheid era. It also reveals the inherent tension between accommodation and transformation and the unanticipated results of such a process.

For the African National Congress, the end of apartheid encompassed more than the repeal of segregationist legislation or the establishment of one person, one vote. Instead, it signaled the beginning of a "transformative movement" that it hoped would alter preexisting political, social, and economic relations.[1] As Thabo Mbeki stressed at the end of the Fiftieth National Conference of the ANC in 1997,

> we must transform the machinery of state as speedily as possible to ensure that this becomes an instrument that serves the interests of the people . . . we must continue to pursue the objectives of high and sustained economic growth and development to achieve a visible improvement in the standard of living of our people, with special emphasis on the poor . . . [and] we must continue the struggle to devote greater and greater amounts of public resources to the goal of meeting the social needs of the people. (Mbeki 1997)

Likewise, in the 1999 State of the Nation Address, he stressed the "the enormity of the challenge we face to succeed in creating the caring society we have spoken of." It was something that could "not be carried out by the government alone"; instead,

> it is a national task that calls for the mobilisation of the whole nation into united people's action, into a partnership with government for progressive change and a better life for all, for a common effort to build a winning nation. The Government therefore commits itself to work in a close partnership with all our people . . . to ensure that we draw on the energy and genius of the nation to give birth to something that will surely be new, good and beautiful." (Mbeki 1999)

Of course, the chieftaincy has not escaped the reach of this transformation process. Not surprisingly, the ANC has argued that the transformation process is not intended to destroy the chieftaincy, but rather, to reestablish its dignity and respect, which were wrenched from it during colonialism and apartheid.[2] More specifically, the ANC has asserted that the transformation of the chieftaincy will only restore its legitimacy, which was lost during apartheid. Thus, in the Draft White Paper on

Traditional Leadership and Governance, the DPLG stated that the central objective of the policy framework was to "define the place and role of the chieftaincy within the new system of democratic governance, transform the institution in line with constitutional imperatives, and restore the integrity and legitimacy of the institution of the chieftaincy in lines with customary law and practices" (Republic of South Africa 2002: 7).

Despite promises that the government did not intend to use the policy process as a way to abolish them, traditional leaders remained skeptical—to say the least—of any reforms that might affect their power at the local level. One of the results was that they vigorously opposed any policies that were intended to alter the status quo, oftentimes threatening to disrupt elections if their demands were not met (Beall 2006; Oomen 2005). Obviously, such a threat strikes at the very core of South Africa's democratic order, and the ANC took such threats seriously. In fact, local government elections were delayed both in 1995 and in 2000 because of the demands of traditional leaders.

In the end, while traditional leaders have been unable to stop the implementation of reforms completely, they have definitely demonstrated the ability to slow down the process. Over the years, the pressure they have exerted has become more organized and more unified. In the early 1990s, the Inkatha Freedom Party (IFP), led by chief Gatsha Buthelezi, spearheaded the effort to ensure that the chieftaincy's powers would be secure in the post-apartheid regime. Given the IFP's electoral strength in KwaZulu-Natal during this period, controlling the provincial government from 1994–2004, the ANC offered some important concessions to the chieftaincy. From 2000, however, the chiefs in KwaZulu-Natal have shown a propensity to work with chiefs from other provinces, who may be members of the ANC or Congress of Traditional Leaders of South Africa (CONTRALESA), and this has only increased their influence at the national level. While many chiefs still profess loyalty to either the IFP or the ANC, in many instances, chiefs are working together through a new organization, the Coalition of Traditional Leaders, which was established in 2000.

One of the major advantages for traditional leaders has been that until 2003 they continued to exercise authority through the former Bantustan structures, such as the tribal authorities and regional authorities. The irony is that the very structures that many traditional leaders fought against in the 1950s because they were not indigenous or authentic have now become sacred and the institutional basis of their "traditional" authority. Even more importantly, for many people at the local level these structures remain meaningful, and the existence of these structures has made the transformation process even more difficult.

As the previous chapter demonstrated, the process of syncretism and the struggle for legitimacy at the local level were central features of the colonial and apartheid periods. While my analysis focuses on the post-apartheid period, the processes I describe are actually part of an ongoing struggle and have linkages to the past. As such, it is imperative to analyze the current legitimation process as one where the chieftaincy has the ability to alter and reconfigure newly introduced norms and institutions—just as they did in the past. In the national debates concerning the chieftaincy in the 1990s, however, policymakers seemed oblivious to this possibility. Instead, they assumed the traditional leaders lacked all semblance of "real" legitimacy at the local level and remained important only because no other options existed for rural populations or because they fulfilled particular "traditional" functions. Traditional leaders, however, had utilized the apartheid system to become important political and public authorities at the local level, and they were not willing to give up this status without a fight.

THE NATIONAL DEBATE ON THE CHIEFTAINCY AND THE POLICY OF INCREMENTALISM

As noted above, it was not until 2003, with the passage of the TLGF Act, that the precise role and functions of the chieftaincy were set forth in national legislation. In this act, as well as in the others that preceded it, the ANC-led government sought to adopt and implement an institutional arrangement that would simultaneously accommodate and transform the chieftaincy. For their part, traditional leaders welcomed the recognition and protection provided in the 1993 interim constitution and 1996 final constitution but resisted attempts of the ANC to threaten their autonomy at the local level and the authority they wielded over their rural populations.

Given that it took the ANC almost ten years to formalize the relationship between the chieftaincy and newly established democratic institutions, its policy has been one of incrementalism, as opposed to swift action. The fact that it took the ANC so many years to formalize the relationship between the chieftaincy and democratic institutions was a net benefit for the chieftaincy. As I discuss in subsequent chapters, while the government was slow to formalize these relationships, at the local level there were important informal relationships being formed. This policy of incrementalism that the ANC adopted enabled the chieftaincy to alter those new norms and institutions that threatened its authority.

The Recognition and Constitutionalization of Culture

In the midst of the political changes that swept through South Africa in the late 1980s and early 1990s, traditional leaders sought to redefine themselves for the new political order—resurrecting the idea that they were, and always had been, bound up with the people. Thus, rather than puppets of the apartheid system, they argued that they were liberators. Contrary to the claims that they were "decentralized despots," they argued that they were one of the last remaining vestiges of authentic African democracy. And rather than accepting assigned ceremonial and customary functions, they insisted that they must be allowed to provide for the needs of their communities and help administer and implement development projects.

Traditional leaders relied upon two organizations to lobby the government on their behalf. The first was CONTRLESA, which a group of traditional leaders from the KwaNdebele Bantustan established in 1987 as a way to oppose the efforts of their homeland government to gain independent status from the South African state (Bank and Southall 1996: 415). The official aim of this organization, consistent with that of the ANC, was to achieve a "unitary, non-racial and democratic South Africa." Obviously, by making such a claim, this organization sought to situate the chieftaincy within the broader anti-apartheid movement. By 1990, the group had expanded to represent traditional leaders from across South Africa except for a majority of traditional leaders within the KwaZulu Homeland, which supported the IFP.

Similar to CONTRALESA, the traditional leaders in KwaZulu had argued since the 1970s that they were fighting against the apartheid state and that they were liberators rather than collaborators (Bank and Southall 1996). In 1975, chief Buthelezi established the Inkatha National Cultural Liberation Movement, which was based on an association that King Solomon had created in 1924 to represent the Zulu people. One of the main objectives of the Inkatha National Cultural Liberation Movement was to protect "culture" and protect the authority of the chieftaincy. In addition, until 1979, Inkatha worked closely with the ANC in exile to resist the apartheid government. After a falling out, however, Inkatha and the ANC became fierce rivals within the province, and the violence in KwaZulu and Natal resulted in more than twenty thousand people losing their lives. In 1990, the IFP was formed as a political party, but the violence in the province continued through 1994.

The friction between the IFP-aligned traditional leaders and the non-IFP-aligned traditional leaders has declined in recent years. In fact, in 2000, a new organization, the Coalition of Traditional Leaders, was formed to represent all traditional leaders in South Africa. While traditional leaders still belong to CONTRALESA or the IFP, as we will see later in this chapter, they are much more likely to work together now than they were in the past.

In retrospect, given Nelson Mandela's respect for the chieftaincy institutions, it is not surprising that upon his being released from prison, one of the first groups that he met was CONTRALESA (Bank and Southall 1996).[3] In his autobiography, Mandela describes the proceedings at the Thembu Great Place at Mquekezeni as "democracy in its purest form": "There may have been a hierarchy of importance among the speakers, but everyone was heard; chief and subject; warrior and medicine man, shopkeeper and farmer, landowner and labourer. People spoke without interruption, and the meetings lasted for many hours. The foundation of self-government was that all men were free to voice their opinions and were equal in their value as citizens" (1994a: 610).

Thus, with Mandela's release, both CONTRALESA and the IFP lobbied extensively for formal recognition and protection in the new constitutional order. Attempts to guarantee such status, however, were largely unsuccessful at the beginning stages of the negotiations. When the first round of negotiations began between the National Party and opposition groups in 1991, traditional leaders were not invited. This move was more of a surprise to CONTRALESA than to the IFP, as the former believed they had the support of the ANC (Friedman 1993). During the second round of negotiations in 1993, however, traditional leaders were invited to participate. While CONTRALESA attended these negotiations, the IFP refused to take part because of an argument over the proposed method of representation. Utilizing the existing apartheid demarcations of authority, the IFP argued that there should be three separate delegations from KwaZulu: one for King Zwelethini, one for the KwaZulu Homeland government, and one for the IFP. Unsatisfied with the prospect of only one delegation, the IFP chose not to take part at all in the formal negotiations. The result was that the IFP's influence on the drafting of the interim constitution was quite limited.

Despite the absence of the IFP, traditional leaders, working through CONTRALESA, not only secured protection and recognition in the interim constitution, but also guaranteed that they would be protected in the final constitution with the inclusion of a constitutional principle concerning their authority. Constitutional principle XII(i) reads as follows:

> The institution, status, and role of traditional leadership, according to indigenous law, *shall be recognized* and protected in the constitution. Indigenous law, like common law, shall be recognized and applied by the courts, subject to the fundamental rights in the constitution. (Republic of South Africa 1993 [emphasis mine])[4]

This principle, although it does not explicitly state how traditional leaders are to be "protected" in the constitution, was a major victory for traditional leaders as it guaranteed that they would be an officially recognized institution in the post-apartheid state and confirmed the establishment of a mixed polity in South Africa. While the IFP was not officially involved with the negotiations leading to these protections, they were nonetheless exerting significant pressure on the parties—especially at the end of the process. For example, up until two weeks before the first all-inclusive elections in April 1994, the IFP was threatening to boycott the elections, and more importantly, to secede from the new South African state and establish an autonomous Zulu state. It was not until the ANC and the National Party (NP) agreed to a constitutional principle that guaranteed that the Zulu monarchy would be recognized and protected in the newly formed KwaZulu-Natal province that the IFP agreed to participate in the elections. In addition, the KwaZulu Legislative Assembly passed the KwaZulu Ingonyama Trust Act, which guaranteed that all of the land within the KwaZulu Bantustan would be held in trust by King Zwelethini and that this land would not be alienated in any way without the permission of the king (KwaZulu Legislative Assembly 1994).

After the election, however, there was pressure from women's organizations, progressive ANC members, and other civil society organizations to limit the authority of the chieftaincy in the final constitution. These reactions against the chieftaincy did have some success. For example, between the adoption of the interim constitution in 1993 and the adoption of the final constitution in 1996, the members of the newly elected parliament changed the extent to which traditional leaders were entrenched in the new political order. Without exception, the changes that were made decreased the powers and authority of the chieftaincy.

Nonetheless, the final constitution recognized the chieftaincy and customary law. Customary law is protected in chapter 2 (the Bill of Rights), and the chieftaincy is protected in chapter 12. The pertinent sections of chapter 12 state the following:

> (211) (1) The institution, status and role of traditional leadership, according to customary law, are recognized, subject to the Constitution. (2) A traditional authority that observes a system of customary law may function subject to any applicable legislation and customs, which includes amendments to, or repeal of, that legislation or those customs. (3) The courts must apply customary law when that law is applicable, subject to the Constitution and any legislation that specifically deals with customary law.
>
> (212) (1) National legislation *may provide* for a role for traditional leadership as an institution at local level on matters affecting local communities (Republic of South Africa 1996: chapter 12, section 211) [emphasis mine].

In addition, this chapter provides that the National Assembly "may" adopt legislation to establish houses of traditional leaders that would have the ability to comment on legislation affecting customary law. In 1997, the national Parliament, under the leadership of the ANC—it occupied 252 of the 400 seats in Parliament—created a national House of Traditional Leaders. In addition, soon thereafter, those six provinces that had traditional leaders in their jurisdictions adopted legislation to establish provincial houses of traditional leaders. Similarly, in each of these provinces except KwaZulu-Natal, the ANC was the majority party.

A closer look at the changes made from the interim constitution (IC) drafted in 1993 to the final constitution in 1996 demonstrate how the ANC sought to reign in the chieftaincy, if only minimally, after the election in 1994. One of the most important changes concerned the extent to which traditional leaders were allowed to be involved with the new local government institutions that were going to be established immediately following the election. The IC had provided that traditional leaders "shall *ex officio* be entitled to be a member of that local government [provided for in the Constitution], and shall be eligible to be elected to any office of such local government" (Republic of South Africa 1994: section 182). The 1996 constitution, however, provided that the president has the discretion to decide the status of traditional leaders at the local level (Republic of South Africa 1996: section 212(1)). In addition, the

IC provided that provincial legislation must establish Provincial Houses of Traditional Leaders to deal with matters relating to the chieftaincy or customary law. The 1996 constitution, on the other hand, provides that provincial legislation "may" create such houses through legislation. Finally, while the IC established a Council of Traditional Leaders (now called the National House of Traditional Leaders) that had the authority to review national legislation that affected the chieftaincy, the 1996 constitution provides that the national government "may" establish such a body.

Not surprisingly, most traditional leaders, whether they were aligned with CONTRALESA or with the IFP, were not pleased with the final wording of the constitution, and many believed they were betrayed. Many traditional leaders argued that it harkened back to the way in which the chieftaincy was institutionalized under apartheid (Beall, Mkhize, and Vawda 2005; T. W. Bennett 1995). That is, traditional leaders analogized that making the functions of the chieftaincy and the rules of customary law subject to the constitution was effectively equivalent to repugnancy clauses, which were utilized by colonial and apartheid courts to void any customary law that was against the norms of society. Instead, traditional leaders wanted "customary law" to trump other constitutional provisions, such as the equality clause. In the end, the ANC refused to negotiate on this issue, and the constitution makes clear that customary law must conform to the other provisions of the constitution.

During the certification litigation to determine the validity of the final constitution, CONTRALESA made a number of arguments along these lines to the Constitutional Court (CC).[5] Its main contention was that the constitution did not establish an "entrenched function" for traditional leaders, and thus, it was invalid because it did not meet the standard set by Constitutional Principle XIII. The CC disagreed with this argument and ruled that chapter 12 was consistent with this principle, and therefore valid. In reaching its decision the CC relied on two separate arguments—each of which highlights the issue of sovereignty in post-apartheid South Africa as well as the tension between accommodation and transformation. First, the CC stated that the objections raised by CONTRALESA were misplaced because it has been settled that "*no-one exercises power or authority outside the constitution*"—not even traditional leaders (*Ex Parte Chairperson, Certification Judgment* 1996 [hereafter *CJ* 1996]: 58; emphasis mine). Secondly, the CC suggested that traditional leaders should be grateful for what protection they did receive because— "[i]n a *purely republican democracy* . . . , no constitutional space exists for the official recognition of any traditional leaders" (*CJ* 1996: 5; emphasis mine). Thus, the CC made it clear that traditional leaders would have to learn to fit within a democratic order, not the other way around. The broader conclusion that can be reached is that while traditional leaders have a long historical linkage with local governance, and even though the 1996 constitution protects the institution to some degree, there is an underlying belief (at least among those in the CC) that the role of the chieftaincy will be limited by the 1996 constitution.[6]

With this said, however, the CC did not deny that traditional leaders are oftentimes perceived as the legitimate form of government at the local level. It noted that during the apartheid era these leaders played a crucial and critical role, both de jure and de facto, in the operation of local government. Along these lines, the CC stated that "traditional forms of government . . . have deep historical roots in the country and . . . continue to have direct relevance for millions of people, particularly many living in rural areas, *where the perceived reality of government is the traditional authority rather than the modern state*" (*CJ* 1996: 57; emphasis mine). Such a "perception" is no doubt a threat to the legitimacy and sovereignty of the post-apartheid state. At the same time, if utilized correctly, this "perception" might also enable the government to gain access to rural areas and implement development projects and local government institutions with the cooperation of the chieftaincy.

THE ESTABLISHMENT OF LOCAL GOVERNMENT AND THE NECESSITY OF ACCOMMODATION

While the constitution guarantees a place for traditional leaders in the new order, it fails to delineate the precise nature of its authority and its relationship with other state institutions. From 1993, however, it was clear that the chieftaincy would no longer be the only institution in the rural areas and that it would have to coexist with other state institutions, specifically local government. From the early 1990s, traditional leaders strenuously fought against the idea of "wall to wall" local government in their areas. The establishment of local government not only would force traditional leaders to share power with another institution but would also entail drawing new boundaries that would cut across their tribal and regional authorities. In the end, if they could not keep local government out of the rural areas, they were determined to forge accommodations, both formal and informal, in order to maintain their authority at the local level.

For the most part, the ANC has welcomed the idea of accommodation and has sought to facilitate it through legislation. One of the reasons this has transpired is that the South African state, similar to other African states, has found it difficult to broadcast its authority to the rural areas and has sought to utilize the chieftaincy for this purpose (Picard 2005; Herbst 2000; Du Toit 1995). Specifically, as early as 1994, the government sought to establish institutional arrangements so that the chieftaincy would provide assistance to local government institutions with the delivery of development projects. These arrangements were largely ad hoc, and they varied throughout the country. The other advantage to making such arrangements was that it enabled political parties to make, or maintain, important links in the rural areas that were crucial for elections (Munro 1996). Yet rather than pass legislation directly addressing the authority of the chieftaincy and its relationship with other institutions, the government initially focused on local government and development legislation that dealt with the chieftaincy indirectly. Thus, to understand the accommodation of the chieftaincy we must examine in more detail the debates concerning the making of local government.

The Making of Local Government: The Transition Period

The creation of permanent local government institutions was a gradual and incremental process divided into three different phases.[7] At each critical juncture during this period, which includes the elections in 1995/96, the publication of the Local Government White Paper in 1998 (Republic of South Africa 1998b, hereafter LG White Paper), and the establishment of permanent local government institutions in 2000, traditional leaders staked out an aggressive negotiating stance, and they consistently warned the ANC that its policy was unacceptable and that if it were implemented, it would lead to the demise of the chieftaincy.[8] More specifically, often citing apartheid-era legislation and regulations, traditional leaders argued that there was no need for local government in the rural areas as they were already fulfilling this role through the tribal and regional authorities. When the argument for complete and unfettered autonomy failed, traditional leaders then advocated for a role on these bodies. In particular, they argued that they must be given official representation in the local government institutions.

At first, the government was hesitant to provide traditional leaders with an official status on the local councils. As we have seen, while the interim constitution guaranteed them "ex officio status" in local government institutions (IC, clause 182), the final constitution provided that the president would have the discretion to decide the status of traditional leaders at the local level (Republic of South Africa 1996: section 212(1)). In 1995, after traditional leaders in KwaZulu-Natal had successfully delayed local government elections in the province, the government amended the Local Government Transition Act (LGTA) and granted traditional leaders throughout the country the ability to serve on the new local government institutions (section 9a, Act 89/1995; Ntsebeza 2005: 277–78; Oomen 2005: 51).

These amendments, however, limited their representation to no more than 10 percent of the total of each council. Under this rule, it was often the case that not all traditional leaders would be able to sit on the councils. One of the results was that many councils were purposively designed to have a large number of representatives and thereby allow for as many traditional leaders as possible. For example, the KwaZulu Provincial Government wanted all 280 traditional leaders to have official status, and therefore, created local government institutions, which were called regional councils, that were large enough to accommodate the 10 percent rule. In some cases, this meant that the councils consisted of 250 to 300 members. As we will see, the ways in which these councils were designed definitely affected how South Africans came to understand the nature of "democratic representation."

Even this accommodation, however, met with some degree of hostility on the part of traditional leaders. As set forth in the amendments to the LGTA, the 10 percent rule applied not only to traditional leaders but to other groups as well, such as women, farm laborers, and levy payers. Many traditional leaders were insulted that they were treated as just another "stakeholder group" and believed this demeaned the status of the chieftaincy.[9] In other words, traditional leaders perceived themselves as something more than another group in civil society and demanded that they receive the respect that should be afforded to their status as the leaders of the community. Through both IFP structures and the ANC-dominated CONTRALESA, traditional leaders voiced their anger at the new local government institutions. One of the main fears was that local government institutions would eventually gain control over land allocation in the rural areas. For example, KwaZulu-Natal Chief Hlengwa stated, "I will have no land; no people and no control. I will become a councilor to the mayor, and then too I will be one of many councilors. When I die, who on the council will come along to say my son should take over, and if so, to do what?"[10] Seeing this as a zero-sum process, chiefs used more combative rhetoric, calling on every household to be "mobilized" for the "continuation of the battle" started at the Convention for a Democratic South Africa (CODESA).[11] In this vein, Chief Holomisa, who has been an ANC MP since 1994, said that, "It's becoming clear that the government listens only if you are aggressive. We want to co-operate but we are the guarantors of the rights of our people."[12]

What the LGTA did not do, however, was to set forth how local government institutions and the chieftaincy would actually cooperate at the local level. The result was considerable confusion as this legislation had created over eight hundred newly elected local government institutions that were simply superimposed over preexisting tribal authority and regional authority boundaries. Without any assurances as to how the new situation would actually work, traditional leaders feared that the new institutions would limit their autonomy and authority at the local level, even with formal representation. While traditional leaders decided to participate with the newly formed local government councils, they also continued to rely upon the tribal authority and regional authority structures. In some cases, traditional leaders refused to discuss certain issues at the local government meetings and required elected representatives and NGOs to meet with them at these other venues.

Another important feature of this transitional phase was the degree of institutional diversity at the local level. In some cases, councils consisted of a majority of traditional leaders, thereby diminishing the authority of the elected leaders (Oomen 2005: 61). In other cases, traditional leaders remained in the minority but were able to secure positions on the all-important executive councils. To add to the confusion, some national and provincial leaders interpreted "ex-officio status" to mean that traditional leaders would be observers rather than voting members, and councils adopted a variety of policies on this issue (Oomen 2005: 62). There were also cases where traditional leaders were allowed to vote but chose not to because they did not want to appear political. In the end, the result of the establishment of these temporary local government institutions was considerable confusion at the local level. For example, I visited local councils where traditional leaders were active in the decision-making process, but I also visited ones where they were not involved. Even with these formal accommodations, traditional leaders believed that the government had violated the provisions in the constitution that guaranteed their protection and that the government's reforms were disrespectful to them as the leaders of the community.[13]

As the government developed its permanent local government institutions, which would be established in 2000, it sought to clarify the formal relationship between the local state and the chieftaincy. As this debate unfolded, traditional leaders argued that they wanted to be recognized as a separate tier of local government and thereby reestablish their autonomy.[14] In the scheme of cooperative governance established in the constitution, local government is defined as the "third tier" of government, which the government claims is closest to the people. Traditional leaders have stressed that they were actually closest to the people and that the chieftaincy should be recognized as a formal tier of government. With the aim of maintaining as much autonomy as possible, they have wanted to utilize the tribal and regional authorities to receive direct funding from the state, to direct development projects, and to replace the local councils. Traditional leaders have argued that as the de facto local government institution during apartheid and as the true representatives of the people, they were now entitled to have this position formalized under the new dispensation.[15] Recognizing the fact that elected local government institutions would be formed in their areas, traditional leaders have sought to guarantee that they would have as much autonomy as possible within this new design and that they would exercise "real" power as opposed to ceremonial functions.

With formal legislation concerning the specific powers of traditional leaders not yet completed, the 1998 LG White Paper was the government's clearest statement on what the boundaries *should* be at the local level when the permanent institutions were established in 2000, and thus was an incredibly important document to all stakeholders. It is also important to keep in mind that this LG White Paper was released for public comment two years after the establishment of the transitional structures and two years before the establishment of permanent institutions—after many informal accommodations had already formed at the local level. It addressed the functions of both the chieftaincy and local government as well as the sources through which each secured its authority. Even though a certain degree of cooperation and consultation between local government and the chieftaincy was expected, the drafters of this document believed (or hoped) that because each group were responsible for doing different duties in the community, and because each relied upon different sources of authority to rule, that there would be little overlap or conflict between the two (Beall, Mkhize, and Vawda 2005: 763).

This notion that the local state and the chieftaincy had different sources of political legitimacy was most clearly expressed in the concluding remarks of the LG White Paper:

> There is no reason why African customs and traditions should be seen to be in conflict with the demands of modern governance. What is required is an innovative institutional arrangement, which combines the *natural capacities* of both traditional and elected local government to advance the development of rural areas and communities. The cooperative model proposed here provides a constructive role for traditional leadership at local level in the governance and development of rural communities. (1998: 78; emphasis mine)

But what were these "natural capacities" and who had the power to define them? At the outset, there was a disjuncture as to what was happening on the ground and the nature of the moral order in which the chieftaincy rooted its authority. In addition, the state's desire to delineate between the two moral orders demonstrates that it had not anticipated the process of syncretism, which had already been in motion during the apartheid era. These preconceptions, and misconceptions, concerning the anticipated relations between elected councilors, traditional leaders, and communities framed the local government debate in the early 1990s and continue to be important for policy makers today (Keulder 1998).

For example, local government, and more specifically, the elected councilors, were described in the LG White Paper as the "representatives" of the community and were supposed to be primarily concerned with service delivery and development. Because these functions had "rarely been the prerogative of traditional authorities," it was not believed that these functions would overlap with the "traditional" functions of the chieftaincy (McIntosh 1995: 419). According to the LG White Paper, these "traditional" functions included land allocation, dispute resolution, and "cultural, ceremonial and religious" duties (LG White Paper 1998: 75; McIntosh 1995: 419). Those duties allocated to tribal and regional authorities during apartheid, mostly dealing with development issues, were now the sole responsibility of elected local government institutions.

In terms of situating the chieftaincy into the broader state-society framework, the LG White Paper clearly located it within civil society. In other words, rather than its taking part in actual governance, the chieftaincy was seen either as a facilitator of government policies or as an interest group for rural populations. For example, the LG White

Paper suggested that traditional leaders were to "assist[] members of the community in their dealings with the state, advis[e] government on traditional affairs, conven[e] meetings to consult with communities, mak[e] recommendations on land allocation . . . , lobb[y] government and other agencies for the development of their areas" (1998: 75–76). As we will see below, these themes were repeated in the TLGF Act that was passed in 2003.

At the same time, however, they were also seen as "the leaders" of "traditional communities." As "the leaders" of these communities, however, traditional leaders were expected to control those "traditional" aspects of daily life that fell outside the realm of the state. Again, according to the LG White Paper, these included the following: "[a]cting as head of the traditional authority, and as such exercising limited legislative powers and certain executive and administrative powers, presiding over customary law courts and maintaining law and order, protecting cultural values and providing a sense of community. . . . , being the spokespersons generally of their communities, *being symbols of unity in the community,* [and] being custodians and protectors of the community's customs and general welfare" (1998: 75–76; emphasis mine). As I have discussed previously, there is considerable evidence that local populations do indeed perceive the chieftaincy as a symbol of unity. The more critical question, however, is whether this responsibility can be dictated through state law—any more than the 1957 provision that demanded that people respect their chiefs or face the possibility of punishment.

In addition to performing its traditional functions, the chieftaincy was also expected to interact with the local government as crucial links, or gatekeepers, that would help facilitate the implementation of development projects (LG White Paper 1998; Poulnic 1997). The image of the chieftaincy as a gatekeeper is one that is prevalent in both the academic and policymaking communities (Rouveroy van Nieuwaal 1996). The image highlights how the chieftancy is both dependent upon the state and autonomous from it. In the role as gatekeeper, the chieftaincy will supposedly open up a previously closed community to other social forces (in this case local government), which will bring development and democracy to the area. One chief executive officer of a regional council explained the gatekeeper role in this manner: "You must understand that the tribal *amakhosi* is [*sic*] the king of that tribal authority and nothing happens in that area without permission. . . . [N]o project can get going if the *inkosi* has not approved it, [i]f you are just going to go in there and disrespect them, forget it. [Y]ou got to manage the process properly."[16] Obviously, if the state cannot effectively establish institutions in certain areas without the acquiescence of non-state social forces, the state building process is much more challenging. What this perspective misses, however, is the type of authority chiefs seek to exercise after his area is officially opened up.

The gatekeeper analogy also assumes that the different sources of legitimacy are always distinct and that there is no overlap between the two. While the legitimacy of traditional leaders is rooted in "tradition," the legitimacy of elected local councilors is supposedly situated in the significance of the electoral process (Peires 2000). In short, the LG White Paper assumed that elected councilors, as the "representatives of the community," would have authority and legitimacy independent from the rules, procedures, norms, and symbols attached to the chieftaincy.[17] Conflict could be avoided, and cooperation encouraged, once people understood that the authority of the chieftaincy and elected councilors emanated from distinctively different sources. But the process of making such distinctions at the local level has proven to be much more problematic as the contours of authority and legitimacy are much more fluid and contestable than was expected (Oomen 2005: 63–64; Goodenough 2002: 37–40).

The Making of Local Government: The Permanent Structures

The principles of the LG White Paper were molded into the legislative framework for the permanent local government institutions. These institutions, which were established in 2000, yet again changed the political landscape at the local level, which produced more confusion. Unlike the transitional institutions, these were designed to be more democratic and more efficient than the transitional institutions. For example, rather than over 800 local government institutions, the new legislation establishes only 299 (Lodge 2001: 21). In addition, the local, district, and municipal councils combine both proportional representation and single-member district, first-past-the-post representation to enable voters to hold individual councilors more accountable (21).

Traditional leaders secured the ability to attend and participate in local council meetings as non-voting members but were not allowed to exceed more than 10 percent of any one council (Municipal Structures Act 1998). Whereas in the transitional phase, provinces could manipulate the size of the councils to accommodate the traditional leaders, as was the case in KwaZulu-Natal, this was no longer possible after 2000.

The result of this rule was that not all of the traditional leaders would be able to participate in local government. In addition, the legislation also specifically delineated those functions that would be the responsibility of traditional leaders and local government. Similar to their complaints about the functions outlined in the LG White Paper, traditional leaders complained that the functions listed were "ceremonial" and "exotic" and did not give them real authority.[18] As they did in 1994 and in 1995–96, they threatened to boycott the election in 2000 if their demands were not met.

With the 2000 local government election on the horizon, and these threats made public, the ANC created a presidential-level Joint Technical Committee to address the traditional leaders' concerns. To allow time for these discussions, the elections were postponed until December 2000, and ultimately the legislation was amended to allow for 20 percent representation on the councils instead of 10 percent. Even with these concessions, traditional leaders still threatened to boycott the local government elections that would usher in the new local government dispensation. In October 2000, in the midst of negotiations with traditional leaders over their role within the new local government structures, former president Nelson Mandela entered the debate and remarked that "[t]he powers [chiefs] had before the whites came must be restored" (cited in Lodge 2001: 22–23). Despite such statements, and despite reassurances from President Mbeki and provincial and local government minister Sydney Mufamadi that the new municipal legislation would be reviewed, and that the constitution might be amended, to ensure that traditional leaders had real authority in the new dispensation, traditional leaders remained hostile to the reforms (Lodge 2001: 23). The traditional leaders agreed to participate in the elections only after they met with President Mbeki. At this meeting, Mbeki allegedly promised to make appropriate reforms, and thereby enhance the authority of the chieftaincy, after the elections.

After the elections in December, the ANC issued a Statement of Intent in which it promised the government would amend the constitution so that the powers of local government and traditional leaders were more clearly defined; but the government never sought the passage of the amendment. Instead, the ANC told traditional leaders that their functions would be addressed in more detail in the TLGF Act that was supposed to be passed in 2001, thereby delaying specific legislation on the role of the chieftaincy once again. In the end, it would not be until 2003 that the TLGF ACT was finally passed.

Following the implementation of the permanent local government institutions in 2000, the government focused on legislation that would deal with the chieftaincy more directly and more thoroughly than in the past. In April 2003, before the passage of the TLGF Act, President Mbeki stated, "[W]e cannot celebrate the 10th anniversary of liberation in a situation in which we have not met our constitutional obligation to resolve all matters attached to issues of the institution of the traditional system of government" (Mbeki 2003). The twin goals of the TLGF Act were to specify the roles and functions of the chieftaincy, which were left ambiguous in the 1996 constitution and subsequent legislation, and to "transform" it so that it could coexist with modern, democratic institutions. With these two goals in mind, the government could confidently state that the chieftaincy "has a place in our democracy, and has a potential to transform and contribute enormously towards the restoration of the moral fibre of our society and in the reconstruction and development of the country, especially the rural areas" (Republic of South Africa 2002, hereafter Draft WP on Traditional Leadership).

One of the most important features of this transformation was that the chieftaincy would become more representative and more accountable to those living in its jurisdiction. In addition, the legislation encouraged, and in some cases required, traditional leaders and local government officials to work together on development issues. With such goals in mind, the TLGF Act establishes the guidelines for the establishment of "traditional communities" as well as a set of new traditional institutions that govern these communities.

For example, the TLGF Act creates new traditional bodies, referred to as traditional councils, which are designed to meet the goals of broader representation, greater accountability, and coordination between local government institutions and the chieftaincy. These traditional councils replace the tribal authorities that were established under the Bantu Authorities Act of 1951. The TLGF Act also replaces the recognition of tribes, found in the 1927 Black Administration Act, with the establishment of traditional communities (Republic of South Africa 2003: chapter 2). According to the new rules, a community qualifies as a traditional community if it "is subject to a system of the chieftaincy in terms of that community's customs and observes a system of customary law" (Republic of South Africa 2003: chapter 2, section 2(1)). The premiers of each province have the discretion to recognize such traditional communities after consultation with the community, the provincial house of traditional leaders, and a king or queen, if the community is under the jurisdiction of a monarchy.

Traditional communities, however, are limited in the ways they can recognize their customary laws or practice their informal customs. For example, the TLGF Act states that traditional communities "must transform and adapt customary law and customs" so that they comply with constitutional principles. In particular, they must change their laws and practices so that they will "prevent[] unfair discrimination; promote[] equality; and seek[] to progressively advance gender representation in the succession to traditional leadership positions" (Republic of South Africa 2003: chapter 2, section 2(3)). How traditional communities are supposed to make these changes is not discussed, nor does the TLGF Act create an institutional body or process that will provide oversight on this matter. It is also unclear what sanctions a traditional community might face if it does not transform itself in this manner.

Unlike the previous traditional authorities, which consisted exclusively of traditional leaders, traditional councils must consist of no more than thirty members, of which one third must be women.[19] In addition, 40 percent of the council must be elected for five-year terms, and these elections were supposed to take place within one year of the signing of the TLGF Act, although this has varied throughout the provinces. Traditional leaders would appoint the remaining 60 percent of the members, but these appointments must keep in mind the one-third requirement for women.

Not surprisingly, these provisions were the topic of much discussion and debate within the Local Government and Provincial Affairs Portfolio Committee, which was the parliamentary committee charged with drafting the TLGF Act. During this process, the committee held numerous public hearings and invited interested parties to submit suggestions on the legislation. The Coalition of Traditional Leaders participated in this process, and they raised several concerns about the one-third requirement for women. A close reading of the Traditional Leadership and Governance Bill (TLGF Bill) and the final act shows that there was some compromise and negotiation concerning the composition of these councils. Indeed, unlike during apartheid, when chiefs and magistrates were the only actors involved with the definition of "customary law," this process was open to other civil society associations to participate, including various women's groups.[20]

For example, in committee, the TLGF Bill provided that only 25 percent of the council would be elected, and there was no stated term of office for those who would serve in this capacity. Interestingly, those traditional leaders who took part in the public hearings on the TLGF Bill never raised an objection to the election requirement. It was not clear whether this was because they had already accepted the reality of elections and understood how they could be managed at the local level or whether the ANC gave them no choice on this issue. They did, however, voice concern over the requirement that one third of the council must be women. At least publicly, they did not object to women serving on the councils in principle; rather, they suggested that in some communities there might not be a sufficient number of women who would want to participate and that they should not be forced to do so (Portfolio Committee Hearings, 9/17/2003). In the end, the final TLGF Act inserts a clause that takes into account this very concern. It reads as follows: "where it has been proved that an insufficient number of women are available to participate in a traditional council, the Premier concerned may, in accordance with a procedure provided for in provincial legislation, determine a lower threshold for the particular traditional council than that required" (Republic of South Africa 2003: chapter 2, section 2(d)). What type of evidence is needed to trigger this reduction is not clear, but it does ensure that the issue of the representation of women on these councils will continue in the future. For those involved in the fight for women's rights, this concession was yet another example that the ANC had sacrificed the principle of equality in order to placate traditional leaders (Walker 2005).

In addition to establishing traditional councils that consist of more elected members and women, the TLGF Act also attempts to make these councils nonpartisan. Allegations that political parties had utilized traditional leaders for political purposes were made during the apartheid period as well as in the post-apartheid period. In one of his frequent editorials, chief Patekile Holomisa, who is the president of CONTRALESA and an ANC member of parliament, argued that politicians should not make traditional leaders a "political football" before the 2004 elections.[21] Coincidentally, this editorial appeared only two days after South African newspapers reported that the province of Mpumalanga would spend R9.1 million to purchase vehicles for the province's fifty-four traditional leaders.[22] A few weeks after this announcement, Premier Mahlangu, who himself is a junior member of the Ndebele royal house, allocated another R1 million for the purchase of computers and other office supplies for traditional leaders.[23] Given the existence of such patron-client networks, the TLGF Act seeks to delineate the appropriate boundary between the chieftaincy and party politics. With respect to traditional councils, it states that they may "not be used to promote or prejudice the interest of any political party" (Republic of South Africa 2003: chapter 2, section 4(4)).[24] The extent to which political parties may seek to influence traditional leaders, however, is not mentioned.

Traditional councils are also expected to be accountable to their traditional communities. In one of the few clauses that uses the verb "must" rather than "may," section 4(2) of the act states that provincial legislation "must regulate the performance of functions by a traditional council by at least requiring a traditional council to keep proper records, have its financial statements audited, disclose the receipt of gifts and adhere to the code of conduct." Traditional councils must also meet at least once a year with their traditional community so that they can discuss their activities and finances (section 4(3)). These sections were substantively changed during the committee hearings. Finally, the earlier version did not require traditional councils to meet once a year. These provisions mark important changes from the procedures and rules that were in place during apartheid.[25]

The TLGF Act also mandates the establishment of local houses of traditional leaders, which replace regional authorities, in any district municipality where more than one traditional leader resides. These houses must have at least five traditional leaders and can have no more than ten. This number can be increased to twenty at the discretion of the minister if there is a district municipality where more than thirty-five traditional leaders reside. In addition, traditional leaders are chosen through an electoral college by their peers to serve on this body. As with the traditional councils, these local houses must also seek to promote the representation of women. The relevant clause states that "the electoral college. . . . must seek to elect a sufficient number of women to make the local house of traditional leaders representative of the traditional leaders within the area" (Republic of South Africa 2003: chapter 4, section 17(2)(c)). This clause was not in the original TLGF Bill but was added during the committee deliberations.

During the public hearings on the bill, the Coalition of Traditional Leaders argued that the preexisting regional authorities, which were established in 1951, should remain in place but simply be renamed as local houses. Ironically, the very authorities that traditional leaders resisted in the 1950s were now defended as the most appropriate institutions for their areas. While ironic, for traditional leaders to defend what was known, versus the unknown, was not surprising, and was in some ways predictable. They also did not want a limit on the number of traditional leaders that could serve on the local house. With regional authorities, all traditional leaders from the area of jurisdiction attend meetings and participate in the decision making. These arguments failed to persuade the committee, and the TLGF Act establishes a new institution that replaces the regional authorities.

In addition to creating new traditional institutions, the TLGF Act also specifies those functions that these institutions, as well as individual traditional leaders, are allowed to perform. What is most interesting about this list is that of the twelve separate responsibilities for traditional councils, seven refer explicitly to cooperation with local government on development issues. For example, traditional councils are required to "support[] municipalities in the identification of community needs" (Republic of South Africa 2003: chapter 2, section 4(c)) and to "participate[] in the development of policy and legislation at the local sphere" (Republic of South Africa 2003: chapter 2, section 4(g)). Only two provisions refer to "tradition" or "custom" (Republic of South Africa 2003: chapter 2, section 4(a) and (l)).

The TLGF Act makes clear that these functions are not subject to the discretion of government ministers or the traditional councils. In other words, traditional councils are expected to fulfill these responsibilities. It also states that the national or provincial governments *may* adopt additional laws "to support and strengthen the capacity of traditional councils" (Republic of South Africa 2003: chapter 2, section 5). The newly created local houses of traditional leaders are given a much more advisory role, and their responsibilities are subject to the discretion of government officials. Similarly, of the five responsibilities listed for the local houses of traditional leaders, four of them relate to local government and development and only one mentions "custom."

During the committee hearings, traditional leaders complained that these local houses were not given enough authority and that they should have more than an advisory role when it comes to development issues. In fact, traditional leaders argued that these local houses should be given the same responsibilities as regional authorities under apartheid. The problem with this argument, however, is that according to the 1951 Bantu Authorities Act regional authorities were empowered to handle many issues, such as education, infrastructure, hospitals, and agriculture, which are now under the purview of local and provincial government institutions. One of the consequences of the act is to shift power away from these regional bodies and to focus attention on traditional councils.

With respect to the duties of individual traditional leaders, the TLGF Act lists a variety of issues that the national or provincial government *may* assign to traditional leaders in subsequent legislation or regulations. These responsibilities range from "land administration," to the "administration of justice," to "tourism." In addition, in the case of any delegation of such authority, the national or provincial governments *must* "ensure that the allocation of a role or function is consistent with the Constitution and applicable legislation" (Republic of South Africa 2003: chapter 5, section 20(2)(c)). Further, "[w]here a traditional council does not perform an allocated function as envisaged in subsection (3), any resources given to a traditional council to perform that function may be withdrawn" (Republic of South Africa 2003: chapter 5, section 20(4)).

While mentioning the importance of cooperation between the chieftaincy and local governments throughout, the TLGF Act also makes this cooperation more explicit in two sections. For example in one section, it states that traditional councils "must co-operate with any relevant ward committee established" through the 1998 Municipal Structures Act (Republic of South Africa 2003: chapter 2, section 4(3)). Also, in a section that traditional leaders lobbied extensively for during committee, the act states that national and provincial governments "must promote partnerships" between traditional councils and local institutions. These partnerships "must be based on principles of mutual respect and recognition of the status and roles of the respective parties" and must "be guided by and based on principles of co-operative governance" (Republic of South Africa 2003: chapter 2, section 5). During the committee hearings, traditional leaders argued that this provision needed to be placed in the constitution itself in order to secure this assurance more permanently (Portfolio Committee Hearings, September 16, 2003). At the time of this writing, such a constitutional amendment has not been drafted.

THE POLICY OF INCREMENTALISM CONTINUES: THE LIMITS OF ACCOMMODATION AND TRANSFORMATION

It took well over a decade for the ANC to establish some semblance of the formal institutional character of its mixed polity. Not surprisingly, however, even after the passage of the TLGF Act, there are many unanswered questions concerning the authority of the chieftaincy, especially with the case of land allocation. In 2004, after years of acrimonious debates within the Department of Land Affairs, the Communal Land Rights Act was finally passed. This act provides that the newly created traditional councils play a central role in the allocation of land in the former Bantustan areas. Beall notes that the passage of the TLGF Act and the Communal Land Rights Act "significantly entrenches the authority of traditional leaders, and means, in effect, that legislation introduced in the 21st century will give perpetual life to a system of 'indirect rule' dating back to the colonial area and ossified under apartheid" (2005: 763). In a similar vein, Crais argues that these two pieces of legislation "indicate that, to the extent that the government is committed to building local institutions, it is casting its weight with traditional leaders . . . [and] is foreclosing other ways of thinking about history, politics and citizenship in post-apartheid South Africa" (2006: 735).

It does seem clear that the chieftaincy is likely to remain a powerful institution in the near future, and this is in part because the negotiators decided to recognize and protect its status in the early 1990s and to entrench its authority further in subsequent legislation. While some observers may disagree with these policy decisions (Ntsebeza 2005; Mamdani 1996), it is important to remember that a variety of external and internal factors constrained the ability of policymakers to simply abolish the chieftaincy outright. These factors included the rise of the global cultural rights movement, the pressure to adopt neo-liberal economic policies, the existence of weak or nonexistent institutions in the rural areas, the need to implement development projects, and the ability to mobilize voters. As was noted in the introductory chapter, given the trends throughout sub-Saharan Africa, the decision to incorporate the chieftaincy was seemingly more appropriate than not doing so.

What is perhaps more interesting is that given the amount of time and energy that was spent on determining the role of the chieftaincy in the post-apartheid order, in the end, these policies have failed to resolve some of the most fundamental issues concerning what constitutes "tradition" and what the proper relationship between the chieftaincy and democratic institutions should be in South Africa.[26] In the Draft White Paper on Traditional Leadership, the government argues that there is a clear distinction between the functions of modern government and the chieftaincy. While government is responsible for development issues, traditional leaders are expected to promote unity and preside over customary ceremonies. Only when these boundaries are established and maintained, argues the government, will the dignity of the chieftaincy be restored. This distinction between modern and traditional functions, as well as the notion that the transformation of the chieftaincy is necessary to restore its authenticity, is prevalent in the TLGF Act as well.

At the same time, of the functions listed in the TLGF Act, most of them relate to the role traditional leaders have with respect to development issues, while very few mention specific traditional functions that they have exclusive authority over. The fact that the government requires that traditional leaders provide support with development highlights the extent to which local institutions need the assistance of traditional leaders to successfully implement these projects. Both critics and proponents of the chieftaincy make the point that this institution, because it is close to the people and because it can ensure local government access to local communities, is crucial for this endeavor. Speaking on this issue at the opening of the Portfolio Committee Hearings on the TLGF Bill, acting provincial and local government minister Maduna stated that the "government believes that the envisaged partnerships will go a long way in accelerating service delivery in rural areas" (Portfolio Committee Hearings, September 16, 2003). Other national officials as well as provincial officials have repeated this sentiment over the years. Thus, while the colonial and apartheid regimes utilized traditional leaders to provide order, the post-apartheid regime appears to be stressing the principles of consultation (with the government and local populations), impartial decision making (non-political activities), and community welfare (development for the rural areas).

In terms of hierarchy, however, there is no question that the TLGF Act clearly reinforced the notion that elected local government institutions are the primary bodies for local governance and for leading local development implementation. Since the adoption of the Municipal Structures Act in 1998, traditional leaders have argued that they should be recognized as a fourth tier of government and that because they are closest to the people, they should have control over finances and development projects. Others have made historical arguments as well, arguing that policymakers have not taken into account the role the chieftaincy played during apartheid to safeguard and provide services to rural communities. For example, IFP MP Hlengwa, who is a chief in KwaZulu-Natal, commented that "I cannot be party to a law where the institution is buried alive. . . . As an institution, we were responsible for development in our areas [during apartheid]. When there were no municipalities in the country, who was doing all this? Traditional leaders looked after communities. In the new dispensation, why are we being left out?" (October 29, 2003).

Throughout this entire process, the debates surrounding the chieftaincy rarely focused on how the government might delineate more clearly the truly "traditional" functions of traditional leaders. The provisions in the TLGF Act that address custom and tradition appear just as ambiguous as the constitutional provisions. In one section, the TLGF Act simply states that "a traditional leader performs the functions provided for in terms of customary law and customs of the traditional community concerned, and in applicable legislation" (Republic of South Africa 2003: chapter 5, section 19). Yet during the lawmaking process, this is not where traditional leaders focused their arguments. Instead, they repeatedly requested that the government recognize their autonomy and independent political authority at the local level. For example, during the debate on the bill in the National Assembly, chief Hlengwa, IFP MP, framed the argument in the following way:

> The powers given to the traditional leadership by the Bill are virtually nonexistent and they almost smack of an insult to our intelligence. If one goes through a list of powers, one realises that what traditional leadership is empowered to do in terms of this Bill consists of activities which any NGO could conduct without any enabling statutory provision. None of the powers have anything to do with the governance of traditional communities. By implication, all the other traditional powers of traditional leadership have been excluded and, therefore, obliterated. Moreover, this Bill does not give any statutory power to traditional leaders but only to traditional councils. Leaders themselves have no statutory power nor function in terms of the Bill. Traditional councils are given all the pseudopowers, which are faculties that traditional leadership could exercise without any enabling legislation. (National Assembly Debate, November 11, 2003)

In the end, the substance of the debates over the constitutionalization of the chieftaincy, its relationship with local government, and the extent of its transformation were focused more on the extent to which the chieftaincy will maintain its autonomous rule-making and rule-enforcing functions and much less on the definition of "tradition" itself. In other words, it seems that the ANC recognizes the unique qualities of the chieftaincy and that it indeed occupies a space distinct from the state or civil society. The guiding principle through most of the policy discussions was how to accommodate the chieftaincy without allowing it to co-opt and transform those newly established state institutions (Migdal 1988). When seen in this light, the debates over the chieftaincy since 1994 can be appreciated for what they really were: how to utilize the chieftaincy to help facilitate the state formation process in post-apartheid South Africa.

It will become more obvious in subsequent chapters how the provisions of the TLFG Act, especially those that set forth institutional links between the chieftaincy and local governments with respect to development, are more reactive than transformative. An analysis of local level dynamics reveals that the TLFG Act simply rationalizes and formalizes linkages and boundaries that have developed since the early 1990s at the local level, and in the end, it is only at this level where we can begin to understand the nature and contours of the chieftaincy's legitimacy in South Africa (Oomen 2005; Williams 2004). This is, not surprisingly, one of the consequences of the policy of incrementalism, and indeed, might be one of the more general characteristics of policymaking in a mixed polity.

THE CONTESTED NATURE
OF POLITICS, DEMOCRACY, AND
RIGHTS IN RURAL SOUTH AFRICA

FOUR

Politics is bad for the community. . . . They [traditional leaders] will not be able to control us.

Now is democracy and people should do things being united.

[He] may be a traditional leader but [he does not have] more rights.

To understand the legitimation process in rural South Africa, it is important to recognize that these areas have not been immune from the broader sociopolitical changes that have occurred since the early 1990s. Indeed, it is one of the assumptions of the multiple-legitimacies framework that there are competing worldviews in the rural areas. In particular, the norms, rules, institutions, and symbols associated with the post-apartheid constitutional order raise expectations and influence authority relations in these areas. It is thus a mistake to believe that those living under traditional leaders, or the traditional leaders themselves, are somehow unaware of the fact that the new democratic dispensation provides opportunities for more political choice, participation, and accountability. At the same time, to expect people in South Africa, specifically those in the rural areas, to define and understand democratic norms in the same way as citizens do in the West is equally misguided (Schaffer 1998; Schatzberg 2001; Karlstrom 1996). Instead, it is important to focus on the ways in which preexisting and newly introduced notions of authority are blended together and mutually transformed, especially with respect to understandings of politics, democracy, and rights.

POLITICS, DEMOCRACY, AND RIGHTS IN RURAL SOUTH AFRICA

With the introduction of democratic discourse and practices into the rural areas since 1994, local populations are beginning to learn a new political vocabulary as well as new ways to interact with their leaders.

Obviously, the introduction of this discourse as well as the new electoral practices does not occur in a social or cultural vacuum. Instead, the rules and processes that make up the periodic ritual of elections are embedded in local understandings of authority. Specifically, the notions that traditional leaders are "the leaders" of the community and that the chieftaincy is a symbol of unity provide a lens to understand the changes occurring at the local level as well as a way to give meaning to politics, democracy, and rights. Make no mistake: questions concerning politics, democracy, and rights are salient to those living in rural areas. For many people these abstract principles take on considerable importance with respect to development, and there is a keen awareness that development issues are linked to the concepts of politics, democracy and rights.

More generally, there is a clear sense that the post-apartheid government's most important task is to improve the quality of life of its citizens. For example, in the three case studies, while only 30 percent believed that life was better since 1994, 56 percent of the informants stated that the most important job for local government was to bring development.[1] These changing expectations applied to traditional leaders as well. While most informants stated that traditional leaders were not involved with development issues before 1994, a majority believed that these leaders were now working on such issues. Perhaps of more importance was the attitude among most people that traditional leaders should be working on these issues as the leaders of the community.

Politics as Violence, Disunity, and Development

In Mvuzane, Kholweni, and Ximba, the idea of "politics" was rarely discussed openly, and questions about politics were oftentimes left unanswered. On numerous occasions, people would agree to share information only if the issue of politics was not raised. For example, even when the word "politics" was brought up during the course of a conversation— which in Zulu is simply *ipolitic*[2]—many individuals would be visibly disturbed and would change their demeanor. Such reactions were not surprising given the fifteen-year civil war in KwaZulu-Natal in the 1980s and 1990s between the Inkatha and African National Congress political forces, in which over twenty thousand people died. Over this period, there developed a deep fear of violence throughout the entire province, even in those areas that remained peaceful (Johnson and Zulu 1996: 189). What was surprising, however, were the distinctions made between politics and other community activities, which not only were accepted but were encouraged. For example, while it was difficult to discuss *ipolitic,* it was not difficult to have detailed conversations about the allocation of community resources, local government-chieftaincy interactions, chieftaincy-societal interactions, development, elections, and democracy more generally. In this way, people seemed to define politics quite narrowly as competition between political parties that resulted in violence.

This definition, while meaningful and coherent for local populations, contradicts common Western understandings of politics, which characterize it as a nonviolent mechanism to allocate resources, change rules, or debate ideas (Schaffer 1998; Karlstrom 1996). Instead, it was common to hear people define politics as promoting "different opinions" and fostering violence.[3] Because the maintenance of unity was considered one of the greatest social goods, the existence of different opinions through politics was perceived as dangerous for the community. One informant in Ximba stated that "politics is bad for the community. . . . They [traditional leaders] will not be able to control us."[4] Others were more specific and suggested that politics was equivalent to dividing the people or political parties fighting. Many suggested that politics leads to killing,[5] fighting,[6] and division.[7] For example, a traditional councilor from Kholweni noted that "politics is the opposite of democracy,"[8] and an *induna* from Mvuzane argued that it "brought hatred among people. . . . I hate it with all my heart."[9] Another person from Mvuzane simply stated that "politics can break us."[10] This type of virulent language concerning politics was common throughout rural KwaZulu-Natal. Defining it as the most dangerous threat to unity and security, most people considered politics as the community's greatest enemy.

Given these general perceptions of politics, it was not surprising that many people believed that chiefs or *izinduna* should not be involved in any "political activity." The reasons given for this, however, were different from those used to describe the dangers of politics more generally. While there was some fear that if these leaders were involved with politics there would be violence, most people suggested that their involvement would force them to take sides, and thus not be able to decide community matters fairly. It was often expressed that if this was the case, the community would lack peace, harmony, and unity. For example, informants in Mvuzane rejected the notion that chiefs or *izinduna* should be involved in politics as "there won't be peace in the community,"[11] "there is no harmony between people through this,"[12] and "before we were united, unlike now."[13] Fears that politics would result in biased decision making and the lack of unity were also common in Kholweni and

Ximba.[14] The chiefs from both Mvuzane and Ximba also agreed that they should not be involved in politics because it was inconsistent with their more important duties as community leaders. Chief Biyela from Mvuzane stated that "there is always no harmony [and] there is a lot of lies in politics,"[15] and chief Mlaba from Ximba, a member of Parliament in the KwaZulu-Natal Assembly, suggested that the national constitution should be amended to require chiefs to give up their title if they served as an elected member in a representative body.[16] A retired teacher from Kholweni perhaps summarized all these sentiments most clearly when he stated simply that the chief "must be the chief for all" and that this was not possible if he was involved in politics.[17]

Thus, when discussed in the abstract, "politics" was something that was feared, and most people did not believe their leaders should be involved in it.[18] Yet the boundaries between acceptable and unacceptable political activity were more complicated than these statements suggest. In particular, there were often important differences between what people claimed they believed in the abstract and what they accepted as "normal," "appropriate," or "beneficial" political practice. For example, even though a majority of people did not want their chiefs or *izinduna* involved with politics,[19] most people also suggested that these leaders *were not* engaging in political activity if they were ex-officio members of local government bodies or if they made community decisions concerning development. Such activities were not considered to be "political"; rather, they were perceived as behavior that was acceptable and desirable. In fact, community members often criticized chiefs and *izinduna* who did not have an active involvement with development or did not have good working relationships with elected councilors.

Even more striking were community attitudes concerning whether chiefs should run for elective office at the local, provincial, and national government levels. In many debates on this issue, it has often been assumed that both local communities and chiefs consider the process of choosing leaders, specifically through the election process, to be inconsistent with the nature of hereditary leadership and its so-called traditional basis of authority. Some leaders have even suggested that it would be undignified for chiefs, whose authority is sanctioned by tradition, to run for elective office, and thus allow ordinary people to choose whether they should lead or not (Butler 1997; CASE/AFRA 1998). These arguments persisted despite the fact that there were numerous examples of chiefs who had sought, and gained, elective office since 1994 (Koelble 2005).

The evidence in Ximba and Mvuzane contradicted these assumptions, as a majority of informants believed it would be beneficial if their chiefs ran for elective office.[20] In Ximba, where chief Mlaba was an ANC member of the provincial Parliament, most people stated that they were happy he was in this position. While very few people could explain exactly what he did in Parliament, most were convinced that one of the reasons for the implementation of development projects in the area was because of his influence at the provincial level.[21] Also, few believed that he was engaged in a type of political activity that was bad for the community or that it was undignified for him to be an elected member of Parliament. Indeed, unlike people in Mvuzane and Kholweni, most people in Ximba suggested that life was better for them since 1994, and many attributed this improvement to Mlaba's presence in the Parliament.

Perhaps even more interesting was that a large number of people in Mvuzane also believed that it would be good if chief Biyela ran for elected office. It was odd that very few people in this community equated running for elective office with political activity, even in this so-called traditional region of KwaZulu-Natal. Yet since he could best represent the needs of the community, it seemed only natural that he should do whatever was necessary to be close to those representative bodies that had access to resources. Given these concerns, it was not surprising that most people wanted him to run for office, because they thought it would help bring development to the community.[22] For example, one younger man in Mvuzane noted that it would be good if chief Biyela ran for office because he "will get a lot of information there and report back to us."[23] An older woman stated that "maybe development will come to our place" if he were to run.[24] Those who felt it would be a bad idea noted that there would be no one to "look after them" or that he did not have the education or skills to deal with people in Parliament.[25] In addition, while many people were not aware that chief Biyela was already an ex-officio member of local government, once they were told, most did not think that he was thereby engaged in politics. Finally, none of the informants voiced concern that it was possible for chiefs to run for elective office and lose. It was simply assumed that if they ran, they would win.

Still, perceptions of politics were not static, and they varied both within chieftaincy areas and between different chieftaincies. In fact, in some cases, informants did believe that politics was actually good for the community. While it is counterintuitive, these views were most frequently expressed in Ximba, which experienced an extraordinary amount of political violence in the 1980s and 1990s (Ntshangase 2003; Mathieson and Atwell 1998). Located approximately thirty miles from both Durban and Pietermaritzburg, the community was evenly divided in the 1980s and 1990s between both ANC and IFP supporters. The chieftaincies surrounding it, however, consisted mostly of IFP supporters, and during the fifteen-year civil war, there was considerable fighting within Ximba and between Ximba and its neighbors. In fact, in 1988 Inkatha supporters allegedly killed Ximba's chief Manzolwandle Mlaba (the present chief's brother), who was active in chieftaincy organizations that opposed Inkatha (most likely CONTRALESA or the United Democratic Front [UDF]) (Mathieson and Attwell 1998). The other areas in this study, Mvuzane and Kholweni, consisted overwhelmingly of IFP supporters, and there was relatively little political violence in these areas. Nonetheless, the idea of politics was accepted to a much greater extent in Ximba than in Mvuzane and Kholweni.

These seemingly contradictory findings make sense only in light of the linkages between politics, development, and democracy. In Ximba, people correlated politics, even party politics, with the implementation of development and other community benefits. One younger man said that it was a good thing that chief Mlaba "joined party politics" because "he is well known and it helps him to get funds from different people for his projects."[26] Another man noted that it was "easy for [chief Mlaba] to contact different departments. It is good because we got most of our needs. [It is] easy for [him] to get some things for the community."[27] Still, one traditional councilor asserted that "by politics we mean something which brings development. At first, we thought it was destroying the youth."[28] And finally, an older man who had served as an *iphoyisa* (a traditional security guard for ceremonies and celebrations) for many years saw in politics the possibility of actually *constructing and enabling unity:* "We can help the youth because we know the old and new things. Politics is good for the community. Politics means that people are doing things together though they have different opinions."[29] Thus, in Ximba, the positive view of politics was tied to the implementation of development projects as well as the ability for people to do "things together though they have different opinions."

Even though people in Ximba were more comfortable with party politics than in Kholweni or Mvuzane, the situation should not be exaggerated. The area was still overwhelmingly ANC controlled, and ANC committee structures were present throughout. While the level of tolerance seemed greater in Ximba, there was still a sense that it was an "ANC area" and it was difficult for IFP members to influence local-level decision making. One informant recalled that before 1994, many members of the community were IFP supporters until the chief called a meeting and "told them to be ANC." He said this did not cause any problems and that "people did not know that chief Mlaba liked the ANC before."[30] I heard similar admissions in Mvuzane, where ANC supporters stated that they were unable to organize in the community because it was well known the chief was an IFP supporter and that it was an "IFP area" (Aitchison 1989; Mare and Ncube 1989). Thus, while most people believed that chiefs and *izinduna* should not be involved with "party politics," most were also aware that these leaders were members of specific political parties and in some cases suggested that they were the local leaders of these parties in their area. Whereas people in Mvuzane and Kholweni feared that if members of the chieftaincy were involved in party politics, the community would become divided and would not have access to development resources, in Ximba, the experience was such that these fears were not as great.

These observations suggest that understandings of politics were not static and that they were influenced through concrete experiences—both positive and negative. Further, ideas about politics were intricately linked with other community goals and values. Simply put, at its worst, "politics" in KwaZulu-Natal referred to fighting between the ANC and the IFP. In this way, the fear of politics was specific and precise: fighting and killing between rival political parties. At its best, politics was seen as a way to access resources and resolve disputes. In the three case studies examined here, only Ximba approximated this latter scenario, and it seemed to have occurred here only after the community experienced relatively peaceful party politics and perceived there was a correlation between politics and acquiring development resources. Yet all three demonstrated the important linkage between understandings of politics and notions of peace, harmony, neutrality, and unity. For many community members, chiefs, and *izinduna* there was an initial fear that party politics would lead to disunity and biased decision making. At the same time, the allocation of scarce resources such as development projects, the presence on a representative body outside of the area, and even chiefs competing in electoral contests were understood as something different from politics.

Democracy as Development and Unity

Over the last decade, public surveys in South Africa reveal that South Africans have a mixed perception of their democratic government (Mattes 2002).[31] While 60 percent of South Africans state that democracy "is preferable to any other kind of government," and 55 percent state that democracy is always the best form of government "even if things are not working," only 30 percent respond that they are unwilling to live under a non-elected government (Mattes 2002: 30). Rather than increasing, levels of support for democracy have stagnated since 1995, and South Africans' support for democracy is actually lower than what we find in Botswana, Malawi, Tanzania, Zambia, and Zimbabwe (ibid.).[32] In addition, trust in elected institutions has steadily declined since 1994, as South Africans are likely to believe that national, provincial, and local representatives do not care about their welfare (Bratton, Mattes, and Gyimah-Boadi 2005).

Given the extraordinary transition to democracy in the early 1990s, it is not surprising that these surveys also find that most South Africans are familiar with the idea of democracy and can give a definition when asked. Interestingly, when asked to define democracy, many South Africans associate it with substantive issues such as economic benefits and access to basic infrastructure. More than any other country in the region, South Africans attach less significance to the procedural aspects of democracy and more importance to economic and substantive attributes (Koelble 2005: 23; Mattes and Thiel 1997; Mattes 2002: 31; Africa and Mattes 1996: 6). There is also evidence that many South Africans believe in a much more consensual understanding of democracy as opposed to one based exclusively on majority rule. For example, of the 140 respondents who were asked to give their own definition of democracy in Mvuzane, Kholweni, and Ximba, approximately 50 percent stated that it means majority rules or freedom and rights, but another 40 percent asserted that it means "unity," "share the same views," "equality," or "have a say in government." These results are consistent with other research conducted in chieftaincies throughout South Africa (Oomen 2000; Goodenough 2002).

Unlike politics, many people considered the idea of "democracy" to be an important aspect of local life and beneficial to the community rather than a threat. At the same time, there was some confusion as to how democracy should operate in the community while maintaining the principle of unity. For example, as noted above, when asked about democracy in the abstract, a majority of people defined democracy as either majority rules, the ability to exercise freedom and basic rights, or equality. When asked more specific questions, however, or why they thought voting was important, most informants linked the idea of democracy with development projects. These findings are also consistent with what opinion polls have found throughout South Africa (Bratton and Mattes 1999).

In some cases, the introduction of democracy was linked with the ability to express oneself without any official constraints or limits. A member of a development committee in Mvuzane stated that democracy was the "freedom of doing anything you like . . . no restrictions on what you are doing."[33] A traditional councilor linked democracy directly to party politics and said that "it means that everyone has a right to say what he wants to, to do whatever he wants, to join any party he likes—freedom."[34] For most people, however, there was recognition that such freedoms needed boundaries. In most cases, people looked to the chieftaincy to provide these boundaries or at least to control the process so that it did not lead to chaos.

One of the ways this revealed itself was through the definition of democracy itself. For example, while the ideas of majority rules, freedom and rights, and equality were important in these communities, democracy was also equated with the idea of unity and the ability of the community to come together and share the same ideas. For an outsider, one of the most challenging aspects of understanding the penetration of liberal democratic ideas in local areas was grasping how the meta-concepts of democracy and unity were expected to coexist. In most cases, however, local populations were unaware of any inconsistencies between these two principles. In other words, for many living in the rural areas the principles of democracy and unity were not inversely related. For example, in Mvuzane, democracy and unity were perceived as complementary and compatible ideas: "Now is democracy and people should do things being united";[35] "Democracy is being united";[36] "[Democracy is] different opinions which will make one thing."[37] Chief Biyela shared these sentiments and stated that democracy existed when there were "people who are united and have freedom."[38]

In Kholweni, much of the frustration with chief Mtembu, and the way he conducted affairs in the area, surfaced when the topic of democracy was discussed. Many informants noted that there was no democracy in the area because "there is no unity"[39] or because "we do not [share] the same ideas."[40] What was interesting here was that not only was unity conceptualized as something that should coexist with democracy, but it was actually one of the necessary preconditions that enabled the existence of democracy. On the other hand, in Ximba, where there was a general impression that the chieftaincy was functioning as a democracy, the concept of unity was important as well: "Because we all voted that is why we call ourselves democracy. We are unified and we have equal rights. We do have democracy here. The only problem is that we still do not understand [it]";[41] "[There is democracy here because] there is no disagreement";[42] "There is democracy in this place though people do not share the same ideas."[43] Thus, when people articulated ideas about democracy and were asked to evaluate whether democracy existed in their area, the concept of unity, as well as majority rules, freedom, and rights, were the key barometers for their opinions.[44]

Still, there existed significant tensions between these different ideas. In many cases, the desire to formulate consensus, to share the same ideas, or to avoid disagreement concerning decision making was more difficult when people exercised their right to express themselves in ways not acceptable in the past. In most cases, debates over these types of issues took place during community meetings, which were a regular feature of daily life in the rural areas. There were usually no set times for meetings to occur; rather, they were called when there was a need. Attendance varied depending on when the meeting was called and what types of issues were to be discussed. In most cases, meetings were called to discuss development issues, but other issues or conflicts were often raised and discussed as well.

When people discussed whether democracy was actually practiced in their community, most referred to meetings and the process of decision making at these meetings.[45] For some, democracy was equivalent to the ability to be "given a chance to voice their opinions."[46] Even though it was important for people to be afforded a public space to voice their opinions, there was little indication as to whether they expected this access to influence the decision-making process itself. While there was little dispute that chiefs, *izinduna,* and traditional councilors should consult with the community before making decisions, the precise nature of this consultation varied according to issue, the area involved, or the individual leaders involved.

The chieftaincy was the central social, political, and cultural aspect of the community, and many community members believed they were required to respect the decisions of these leaders as long as the decisions promoted unity, were made in an unbiased fashion, were made after consultation, and were in the interest of the entire community. While such evaluations were open to contestation, in many cases people trusted the judgment of their leaders until they were given a reason to believe otherwise. There was never a case where decisions were put to a formal "vote" in the meeting; rather, all interested parties at the meeting were allowed to voice their opinion and interact with others, and eventually a consensus would emerge. As long as chiefs, *izinduna*, and traditional councilors provided some points of access for people to voice their concerns, and invoked common values and beliefs to justify their opinions (the promotion of unity), they were usually able to use these gatherings to promote their own positions, and in most cases, the community ended up accepting these positions. Thus, as long as debate and consultation proceeded in this fashion, the contradictory values of allowing for different opinions and seeking unity could be achieved.

One of the key components to this process of decision making was the extent to which these public forums were open to the entire community and allowed for all opinions, even those critical of the chieftaincy, to be expressed. Yet there was evidence that "consultation" was limited in terms of gender, age, family, and viewpoint. One way this manifested itself was that some opinions were valued more than others, based on the identity of the person rather than the content of the advice. One younger woman from Mvuzane described how "democratic" practice excluded certain groups in the rural areas:

> I do not know [whether the chieftaincy practices democracy] and I don't think so. If there were people like you who have open minds between *amakhosi* maybe there will be democracy. The problem is maybe you are young or you have a surname, which is not liked by *inkosi* or you are a female. You find that your opinion will not be taken seriously, but after you have left they will start saying it was a good point. *Inkosi* and *induna*'s opinions are always taken as the good ones. Like it or not what they have said must be done.[47]

In many instances, women were influential political actors with respect to development and local government issues even though they faced overt and covert forms of discrimination and were rarely allowed to hold positions of authority within the chieftaincy structures. For example, in my three case studies no women were formally part of the all-important *isigungu*—the chief's advisory group—that would meet regularly in a small room separate from the community hall before most community meetings. These small meetings were where the chief shared his opinions, if they were not already known, and discussed what matters should be discussed at the general meeting. In this way, the *isigungu* served an important agenda-setting body, and the most notable local elites were usually invited to attend and to participate in the discussions.

Despite these constraints, women were often in the majority at community meetings and frequently raised questions and discussed issues. There was also evidence that the attitudes concerning the role of women with respect to the chieftaincy were changing. When asked if the chiefs and *izinduna* actually seek out the advice of women, an overwhelming majority of people claimed that they did (91 percent). Equally important, many people in Mvuzane and Ximba claimed that interacting with women in this way was a "new thing" (i.e., since 1994). It was only in Kholweni that a vast majority of the people claimed that the chiefs and *izinduna* were actually taking the advice of women before 1994.

Yet there were limits to their participation and their influence in community matters. While there was one traditional councilor in both Mvuzane and Kholweni who was a woman in 1998 and 1999, in none of the three case study areas were women chosen to be *izinduna*. In terms of attitudes, however, there were some indications that those living in Mvuzane, Ximba, and Kholweni were ready for a woman to be a chief, an *izinduna,* or a traditional councilor. When asked if a woman could hold any of these positions, a vast majority claimed that she could, and another solid majority believed that if a woman were to occupy such a position that it would be good for the community.[48] In fact, in Kholweni, the community actually chose a woman to be their chief in 2003.

Finally, despite changing attitudes, in many cases situation and context tended to determine whether women could participate in community meetings. For example, in Mvuzane, chief Biyela was explicit that he wanted women to participate in the decision-making process and often threatened some *izinduna* that if they did not do their job properly—which in most cases referred to helping with development—that he would replace them with a woman who would work harder. Chief Biyela also "allowed" one ward in the area to elect a woman as a traditional councilor, and he would often seek out her advice and give her important responsibilities concerning development, local government, and the elections.[49] Still, there were times when there was open hostility to women who had achieved positions of power within the chieftaincy. On one occasion a woman stood at a meeting to read a letter she received from a development nongovernmental organization. The man sitting next to her made a remark and promptly left the meeting. She sat in her chair and gave the letter to the elected councilor—a male—to read aloud. It was only after the meeting that I learned that many in the community considered it "rude" for women to stand and read such things in the manner she did at this meeting. While the chief publicly ridiculed this man for his behavior, most people after the meeting believed his reactions were acceptable.

Also, there was a noticeable difference between community meetings within the tribal authority areas and regional authority meetings that were held outside of the community, usually in the nearest town. The regional authority met four to five times a year, and it consisted of all of the chiefs from the area. These meetings were much more "male-centered," and women were much less likely to ask questions or raise concerns at this forum. In addition, while women were often in the majority at tribal authority meetings, at the regional authority meetings they were often in the minority. At the same time, there was generally less opportunity for anyone—male or female—to participate in the decision-making process at regional council meetings than at tribal council meetings. Thus, while women have struggled in the rural areas, the attitudes concerning their appropriate place in public affairs appear to be changing—but these changes have been slow and have been dependent upon a variety of factors, including the attitudes of individual chiefs and the sociopolitical context.

Another aspect of political life that was in a state of flux concerned the practice of consultation. Many people in the rural areas frequently mentioned the importance of consultation when describing democracy, but in practice, consultation has been limited. More specifically, when disagreement did occur between community members and the chieftaincy, there were often no other actions that could be taken other than to continue to voice disapproval. In other words, there were no institutional mechanisms that allowed the community to overrule the chief's decisions. While individuals were able to appeal "customary law" decisions made in the chief's court, this same appeal process did not apply to those ordinary and daily decisions made outside of court. There were many instances where community members suggested they disagreed with a particular decision but did not feel they had any way to change it. One woman in Kholweni suggested that the community would simply defy the chief if he decided against community consensus—"[i]f he does not want to change it we just do not do what he wants us to do."[50] Many simply stated that they voiced their concerns at the meeting, but unfortunately, the consensus was against them.[51] In both Mvuzane and Ximba, these attitudes were reflected in that most people stated that they could not disagree with the decision of traditional leaders or that the community "never" experienced disagreements. Only a minority suggested that disagreements led to more consultation and a changed decision.

It is also worth noting those ideas and practices people did not mention as important with respect to democracy. Given the experiences of apartheid, and the discourse of the liberation movement that focused on voting, the rule of law, and protection of rights, it was surprising that few people mentioned regular elections, the rule of law, or protection of rights as important aspects of democracy. While the ability to choose leaders was important in rural areas, this was usually linked to the prospect of receiving development more than an abstract appreciation of elections. Also, for most people, the introduction of elections in 1994 had not positively changed their lives, and many believed that it had not really changed local political dynamics. In this way, chiefs and *izinduna* have been able to encourage the electoral process in their areas without ceding much of their own authority. More specifically, many people voted because they believed it was another way to acquire their "needs"; it was not symbolic of the intrinsic worth of the electoral process itself (Bratton and Mattes 2001).

Rights as Equality and Development

Finally, in each of the three case studies, there was widespread agreement that one of the most important aspects of the 1994 elections was that it afforded every community, as well as each individual, specific rights.[52] The most important of these newly acquired rights was the ability to get basic needs. While most people in the rural areas had never seen a copy of the new constitution, they did know that this document required the government to provide specific necessities such as water, roads, schools, and electricity.

In most cases, when asked to define the term "rights," informants stated it referred to "something we must get." Further, the specific right that was considered most important was the right to development projects. In other words, there was a conception that positive rights, or the right to something, took priority over negative rights, or the right from something. These understandings were crucial with respect to how community members evaluated the success of democracy since 1994 and the efficiency of local government institutions. In the vast majority of cases, community members concluded the government had failed to deliver on its promises, and thus they did not trust the government and they believed the government did not respect them. Opposition politicians have continuously sought to exploit this theme as a way to distinguish themselves from the ruling ANC. For example, chief Buthelezi has remarked that the ANC government had failed to deliver services, and instead, continued to offer promises: "Promises give no shelter when it rains, promises do not keep us employed. We leave promises to others and simply get the job done" (South African Press Association, December 16, 2000). In addition, these negative evaluations of government enabled chiefs and *izinduna* to argue that they would be better service deliverers than government.

But the issue of rights also poses interesting questions concerning chieftaincy-societal relations more generally. That is, are chiefs, *izinduna,* and traditional councilors able to claim *more* rights in the community because of their status and leadership positions? Given the centrality of the chieftaincy to the decision making and cultural aspects of daily life, it would not be surprising to find people willing to allow their leaders to claim special privileges. This, however, was not the case. Most people believed that these leaders should not receive development before the rest of the community, and in fact, many felt they should receive it last. One Kholweni resident, who echoed the sentiment of many others, argued that chiefs, *izinduna,* and traditional councilors should not receive development first because all "people are equal."[53] Others were more specific and stated that "when it comes to development we are equal."[54] Another reason often given was that these leaders "were working for the people," and thus, should not receive special treatment.[55] Still others noted that such a matter was one that the community should decide together after consultation.[56] Finally, some community members believed that such decisions should be made by the elected councilor because "development is for the whole community."[57] These views were shared not only by community members, but also by chiefs, *izinduna,* and traditional councilors as well. As I explained in chapter 2, such attitudes about the nature of equality are at odds with many historical accounts of the chieftaincy in the pre-colonial period, when a strict sociopolitical hierarchy was expected.

Nonetheless, the distribution of development projects within tribal authority areas suggested a different political reality. In both Ximba and Kholweni, the chiefs occupied homes that were equipped with running water, electricity, and telephone service. The chiefs in these areas managed to get these things in the 1980s, while the rest of the community were not given similar opportunities. In many conversations, informants complained about this situation and expressed frustration that "their side," meaning their particular tribal ward, was neglected. In Mvuzane, even though the chief's homestead was not equipped with electricity or phone service, he did have running water, which was put in the early 1990s. In a community where most people walked long distances for water, many people resented the fact that the chief had access to his own water.

Without fail, in Mvuzane, Ximba, and Kholweni, the chiefs' tribal ward was the most developed, and these complaints increased in those wards that were farthest from the chiefs' homesteads. For example, one person in Ximba complained about this situation and argued that chiefs and *izinduna* "were not elected so that they can get their needs first."[58] While in some cases community members were reluctant to criticize individual behavior of their leaders, when I raised the topics of rights and development, people were much more willing to be critical. One retired teacher in Kholweni stated that if the chief gets development first the community would "scold" him.[59] Others responded with equal apprehension and said such things as "they [the chiefs, *izinduna,* and traditional councilors] must not eat the money. [We] need development for others,"[60] "we might end up getting nothing,"[61] "[we] can't accept a thing like that. [He] may be a traditional leader but [he does not have] more rights,"[62] and "it is not good though as leaders this may happen. If they have these things first, they will not think of the people."[63]

Despite these misgivings, however, most informants admitted there was nothing that could be done to stop this allocation of resources other than prohibit the chief from becoming involved in the development process.[64] Many people, however, considered such a "solution" to be beyond the realm of the possible, as the chief represented the unity of the community and no development could happen in the area without the approval of the chief. In most communities, it was the youth who were most critical of this situation and who were most likely to confront their leaders. In Ximba, the youth formed separate development committees to address this issue but were often unable to affect the decision making, as the older people were hesitant to voice their concerns publicly. One younger person suggested that while the youth were trying to take proactive actions, the older people simply chose to "talk amongst themselves" and do nothing.[65] In the end, without the cooperation of older members of the community, it was difficult to change the decision-making process.

Given such attitudes, it was not surprising that in those cases where chiefs and *izinduna* were forced to resign, one of the central issues was how they handled development issues, and specifically, whether the community believed the traditional leader was more concerned with his own individual gain rather than the community welfare. Unlike the issues of politics and democracy, where the boundaries between acceptable and unacceptable behavior were somewhat ambiguous and open to contestation, with respect to individual and community rights to development, the boundaries were unequivocal. Even though the process of consultation was such that people were unable to actively disagree with the chieftaincy, there were examples that demonstrated how the community was not always helpless against such decision making.[66]

Such an understanding of rights with respect to chieftaincy-societal relations demonstrates how the idea of unity can be used as a way to limit power as well as to enable it. While in many cases chiefs and *izinduna* used the notion of unity to expand their authority, to reinterpret understandings of democracy, and to justify particular community sacrifices, the boundaries were understood differently here and actually seemed to limit the authority of traditional leaders. In most cases, however, it was still difficult for members of the community to translate these perceptions into meaningful political action because of the lack of institutional mechanisms to do so, although this has been changing as well. Still, the issue of rights and its relation to development demonstrates that these leaders must take seriously the principles of unity, neutrality, and community welfare if they want to maintain their legitimacy.

THE SPECTACLE OF DEMOCRATIC CHOICE: THE 1999 ELECTION IN RURAL SOUTH AFRICA

Over the last eight years, government-sponsored elections have become a regular feature of rural political life. Since 1994, there have been seven elections held in the rural areas—four national/provincial elections (1994, 1999, 2004, and 2009) and three local government elections (1996, 2000, and 2006). As was expected, the voter turnout in 1999 (68 percent) was lower than in 1994 (87 percent) (Reynolds 1999: 178). Nonetheless, the election was much more efficient in 1999, and unlike 1994, there was very little political violence. Thus, most commentators suggested the 1999 election was more successful than previous elections (Reynolds 1999). While there are numerous studies on elections in South Africa, few examine how the process occurred in the rural areas. In this section, I will focus on how a particular election unfolded in the Mvuzane Tribal Authority.

The 1999 election in Mvuzane was both an exciting and a confusing process for the community. While people were generally excited about the elections, very few people who lived in Mvuzane believed that any of the previous elections had changed their lives for the better, and they approached the 1999 election with guarded optimism.[67] Even though the elections were held on June 2, 1999, the registration period began in late 1998 and proved to be a time-consuming and confusing process for many voters. In both the 1994 national elections and the 1996 local government elections, the government had yet to establish a formal registration process. In 1994, for example, people were allowed to vote at any voting station, and it was possible, although illegal, for people to vote more than once without raising suspicions. For the 1999 elections, however, the government required that every eligible voter register prior to Election Day. To facilitate this process, the government set aside two days when registration would occur in December 1998.

For this process to be successful in the rural areas, the government relied upon the chieftaincy structures to communicate the necessary rules and guidelines to those living in their areas and to help mobilize people to register and then to vote. Unlike the previous elections, chiefs at the national level did not threaten to boycott the 1999 elections. Instead, the mood was much more cooperative. This was especially the case at the local level, where chiefs, *izinduna,* and traditional councilors were focused on helping those living in their areas to understand the voting procedures and to exercise their right to vote.

In many ways, registration weekend in Mvuzane was more confusing and frustrating than Election Day—which also had its share of problems. Chief Biyela was actively involved in the period leading up to the registration period, and he held several meetings to inform people about the process. For the most part, however, he relied upon the elected councilor, and one of his closest advisors, Vusi Chamane, to gather the necessary information from government sources. With the registration weekend scheduled for December 4–5, 1998, it was not until November 29 that Vusi received the necessary information from government officials concerning where people should register. This information was crucial because the government wanted people to register in the same places where they would vote on Election Day. Vusi was hesitant to tell people where he thought these places were going to be because he did not want to be wrong and have people accuse him of lying to them.

Vusi's concerns about the registration and voting sites were mostly focused on how many would be allocated for the area and where they would be located. Obviously, he and chief Biyela wanted these sites close to where people lived, and they wanted as many as possible so that people would not have to travel long distances to register and vote. As it turned out, the government established three registration sites in Mvuzane despite the fact that Vusi had made a formal request to the Independent Electoral Commission (IEC) for five. Vusi and chief Biyela were frustrated that this process was controlled by what they called "city boys," who did not have any idea how far people's homes were from the sites or the distance people would have to travel. Vusi estimated that people would have to travel—most often on foot—an average of 15 kilometers (9.3 miles) on at least three separate occasions to exercise their right to vote—in December to register, in February to check the registration lists and receive their identification cards, and in June to vote. As an IFP elected councilor, in an area largely controlled by the IFP, Vusi suggested numerous times that "the government" probably did not mind these obstacles in the rural areas because "other parties" (i.e., the ANC) had little support in these areas, and the government was probably making it harder for people to vote in order to keep power.

The belief that elections were under the control of outsiders was a constant theme in Mvuzane. As the registration period approached, Vusi had hoped that members of the community would be in charge of the process and perhaps even create some temporary jobs and some income for the area. Due to a lack of funds, however, the IEC utilized civil servants, mostly teachers, to help with the registration process and volunteer their time. Most of the people in charge of the registration process in Mvuzane were teachers from the neighboring town of Eshowe who were not known to the community. Vusi and chief Biyela, both before and during the registration, assured people that these workers could be trusted to conduct the registration fairly even though they were not from the area.

At a community meeting two days before the registration, chief Biyela encouraged everyone to register. He instructed the *izinduna* to tell the people in their areas to register and to help them in any way possible to get to the sites. Chief Biyela also announced that people should not worry about party politics or the registration. He said that this was not the actual election and that parties were barred from doing "political things" at registration. Most of the questions, however, focused more on process than on party politics issues. There was a great deal of confusion about the specific dates, times, and places for registration. In many cases, people could not understand why they had to travel such long distances to designated registration sites when there was a school or store closer to their homesteads. While Vusi and chief Biyela tried to explain the reasoning underlying the IEC's decisions on sites, many people were outwardly frustrated. Some asked specific questions about how the elderly or infirm were supposed to get to these sites and whether the IEC would allow relatives to register for them. Chief Biyela explained this was not allowed. The community was also told that all the registration sites would be at schools and that the tribal court would not be used as there was a fear this would not be considered a neutral site.

Others were concerned about outsiders coming into the area to help with the process. One *induna* complained that he and some other people from Mvuzane had gone to Eshowe to volunteer their services but had been turned away. Again, it was explained that teachers, principals, and other volunteers were in charge of this process and that there might be other, informal, ways the local community members could assist on registration day. Chief Biyela also forewarned those at the meeting that members of the South African Defense Force (SADF) would be at the sites to make sure there was no violence, but that this was a precautionary measure and that he was not expecting any problems.

While the community was told that the tribal court would not be used as a registration site, as it turned out, it was.[68] Throughout the day, people gathered at the court, and chief Biyela spoke to groups of people, telling them where to line up and what to do. He stayed at the site most of the day, casually walking among the people and answering questions. Teachers from Eshowe who were there helping with the process noted that it was encouraging to see the chief so active in the process and that he had been successful with mobilizing those in this area. In addition, there were three to four SADF officers at the court with automatic weapons hanging off their shoulders to provide security if there were any problems. On the side of the court, near the entrance where the registration was conducted, was an IFP placard urging people to register and vote.

Inside the court, the process was orderly as people waited to have their identification cards scanned into the computer. Shortly after noon, the batteries in the scanning machine failed and the registration process stopped. The principal IEC officer in charge of the site had left, and his assistant did not have a car to go and retrieve another battery. Chief Biyela was meeting with some *izinduna,* traditional councilors, and others, both men and women, in a small office space connected to the main room of the tribal court when he learned about the battery problem. The chief and his *isigungu* often met in this space before and after community meetings. He asked those in the room what they might be able to do. He was concerned that the people waiting in line would not be able to register, and he did not want this to happen. After some discussion about possible options, they found a volunteer who drove to the town, Gingindlovu, approximately 70 kilometers (45 miles) to get the battery so they might be able to continue the registration process later in the afternoon or the next day.[69]

Over the next six months, until the June elections, there continued to be minor problems as people who were registered could not find themselves on the voter's rolls. When the elections were held, however, the area of Mvuzane ended up voting overwhelmingly for the IFP, just as it had done in 1994 and 1996. Voting day in Mvuzane was less confusing than the registration weekend. As was the case in many rural areas, people in Mvuzane began lining up to vote as early as 4:00 AM. While the voting was supposed to begin at 9:00 AM, the ballots arrived late, and the actual voting did not begin in some places until 11:00 AM.

Chief Biyela and most of the *izinduna* were present at various voting sites throughout the entire day. At the voting site closest to his homestead (unlike with registration, voting occurred at the high school across the dirt path from the tribal court but not in the court itself), chief Biyela walked up and down the line of people to assure them that the voting would happen soon. Whenever he saw elderly people in line who were either disabled or obviously weak, he brought them up to the front. He told all those waiting that he wanted the elderly and weak to vote first. When the school door opened and voting was to begin, everyone quickly gathered at the entrance and what was once one line became a crowd of people. Chief Biyela repeatedly told everyone to stand back, but his requests were largely ignored. He then started swinging his walking stick in the direction of people's legs and they quickly started to move and got back into line. Some people laughed as they saw chief Biyela do this, and he almost immediately began to joke with people as soon as they were in line. No one was hurt, or even hit, during this scene, but a clear message was sent that this process would proceed in an orderly fashion. The white SADF personnel who were present did not interfere and stood silent against the side of the school building. The elderly and disabled were then brought to the front, and the voting began.

After the polls had been open approximately ten minutes, chief Biyela asked to see Vusi, and they had a brief discussion. Apparently, some people felt intimidated that there were IEC and political party observers watching them mark the ballot, and this was causing some problems.

This arrangement was part of the negotiations that occurred between the political parties and the IEC before the election. To assist those who were illiterate, without threatening the fairness of the electoral process, the ANC and IFP agreed that if someone needed help marking their ballot in KwaZulu-Natal an ANC and an IFP representative, as well as a "neutral" IEC observer, would be present as advice was given. This was to make sure that if a person requested to vote for one party that the person assisting did not mark another party instead. This arrangement was used in places other than KwaZulu-Natal as well, but usually only in places where it was suspected two or more parties would be in competition. Chief Biyela asked Vusi to explain the people waiting in line that if they needed help to vote, they needed to ask, and that if they did so, these representatives would all help them mark their ballots.

For the next hour, Vusi told groups of people waiting in line what was happening. He then asked one of the ANC representatives to join him as they went down the line. He told people not to be afraid that there were both ANC and IFP representatives watching them. He emphasized that they were only there to help and to make sure the voting was fair. He and the ANC representative stressed that they should vote for whichever party they wanted. Many people in line did not like the idea of an ANC representative in the voting area, but the voting continued without incident. This was not the case in some areas outside of Mvuzane, where many people alleged voting fraud because only an IFP representative was present at the voting stations. In the end, the IFP carried Mvuzane with over 70 percent of the vote.[70]

DEMOCRATIZATION FROM WITHIN: "ELECTING" TRADITIONAL LEADERS

As the previous discussion of the 1999 election suggests, despite the centrality of the chieftaincy at the local level, elections are perceived as a legitimate and necessary mechanism to transfer and distribute political power. It would be a mistake to assume, however, that people consider elections to be "the only game in town." Rather, many understand elections to be simply "another game" that can be utilized to acquire desired resources. This is the case not only with state-sponsored elections for local, provincial, and national government, but within the chieftaincy as well. Beginning in the early 1990s, chiefs began to allow their communities to "elect" *izinduna* and traditional councilors. In the past, the chief either appointed people to these positions or recognized the existence of a valid hereditary claim. The reasons for these changes were twofold. First, communities pressured their chiefs to allow elections as they sought to put more qualified leaders into these positions. Because communities wanted to attract as many development projects as possible, there was an incentive to choose local leaders who had the education to best perform this function. It also seemed possible that there was some "demonstration effect" caused from the state-sponsored elections as well and that local communities sought to transfer national electoral practices to the tribal authority level. The second reason for this change was that chiefs saw this as an opportunity to lead the democratization movement in their areas, rather than become consumed by it. Unlike the situation with state-sponsored elections, where the chieftaincy acted as a mediator between the government and the people, the incorporation of elections was something the chieftaincy could control with much more autonomy.

Throughout South Africa, the chieftaincy structures are decentralized, and until the passage of the TLGF Act, the main bodies in the rural areas were the tribal authorities and regional authorities. While a chief, along with his *isigungu,* is in charge of each tribal authority, the tribal authority is itself divided into distinct tribal wards that are under the control of *izinduna* and traditional councilors. Even though the chief and his *isigungu* are at the apex, these men would be unable to effectively rule the area without the assistance of the *izinduna* and traditional councilors. In each ward, there is usually one *induna.* The *izinduna* hear cases, solve problems, and report directly to the chief. Many of the *izinduna* are also part of the *isigungu,* although this is not always the case. While the number varies, in most cases each ward has one to two traditional councilors who are supposed to report to the *induna* in his area. Traditional councilors solve "community problems," and in some instances they were allowed to hear cases.

While it is difficult to pinpoint an exact date, it seems that until the early 1990s, the chief and his *isigungu* would choose the *izinduna* and traditional councilors and announce their appointments at meetings. In some cases, the position of *induna* was considered hereditary, and this position was passed to the eldest son of a particular family.

By most accounts, this process changed around 1994. In Mvuzane and Kholweni, for example, many of the *izinduna* and traditional councilors had been chosen since 1994, and most people commented that the community "elected" these leaders. At the same time, it was much easier for people within a particular ward to choose a traditional councilor than it was for them to choose an *induna.*

One reason that this was the case was that the duties of the traditional councilor changed dramatically since the early 1990s. While in the past the traditional councilor was supposed to assist the *induna* and help resolve community disputes, this position had become much more focused on development issues. Traditional councilors were often responsible for holding ward-level development meetings, and many served on the ward development committees. Indeed, when asked about their duties, most traditional councilors responded that they were responsible for making connections and bringing development projects.[71]

Of course, the ability for community members to choose traditional councilors or *izinduna* was dependent upon these positions becoming vacant, and this was occurring more often in Mvuzane, Ximba, and Kholweni. With a new stress on the importance of development, many positions in these areas have been filled since 1994 with people who are often younger and who have more formal education, and thus, have a better opportunity to access development resources.

For example, in Mvuzane, there were fifteen separate wards and a total of sixteen *izinduna*. As of July 1999, of these sixteen, only six had served for more than eight years. There were six who have served for less than six years and four who had served less than eight years.[72] Most importantly, of the sixteen *izinduna* in Mvuzane, approximately ten had acquired their position through the process of elections rather than appointment. Of the approximately twelve traditional councilors, a majority were chosen after 1994. In Kholweni, there were only three wards with two *izinduna*. The two *izinduna* had each served less than five years, and the other *induna* was forced to resign in June 1999 for misappropriating development funds. In both Mvuzane and Kholweni, most people suggested that those *izinduna* and traditional councilors chosen after 1994 were elected by the community and were not appointed by the chief.

It was only in Kholweni, however, that I witnessed this process as it unfolded. In this case, the *induna* was forced to resign because of complaints from the community, and the chief did not take an active role in his dismissal. In addition, after his dismissal, the community organized the election of a new *induna* on their own with little guidance from chief Mtembu. With these new electoral practices, however, there was confusion in both Mvuzane and Kholweni as to whether the newly elected *izinduna* and traditional councilors had fixed terms of office or whether the term was indefinite. Many people assumed the traditional councilors were to serve a fixed term, but there was more disagreement as to whether the same rule applied to *izinduna*. As with many issues in the rural areas, the election of *izinduna* is one that has developed based on local circumstances.

IMAGINING DEMOCRACY IN A MIXED POLITY

Understanding the ways in which preexisting notions of authority and new notions of authority intersect must start with an examination of how people in rural South Africa imagine their political universe. This chapter demonstrates that the notion of unity and harmony permeate local understandings of the chieftaincy as well as politics and democracy. As a lens to understand politics and democracy, the chieftaincy has managed to continue to shape local-level politics even with the introduction of new norms, institutions, and practices. At the same time, it is also the case that the desire for development and the perception that development is a right is a powerful notion in the rural areas. In fact, when it comes to the right to development, the notion that the "chief is a chief through the people" is interpreted to limit the influence of traditional leaders, and there is an expectation that an egalitarian ethic will constrain their behavior. In short, chieftaincy-societal relations are marked with both continuity and change—both in terms of attitudes and practice.

What is clear is that people living in rural areas do desire more opportunities to choose their leaders, and they have been pleased with introduction of mechanisms that hold them accountable. At the same time, while there is a general acceptance of new norms and institutions, there is also the perception that too much democracy is dangerous, undesirable, and even destructive because it threatens the unity and security of the area. What may be difficult for some to appreciate is that for those living in the rural areas, it is commonsensical that the institution of the chieftaincy and democratic elections can, and should, coexist. Such a "double-mindedness" is something that observers of African politics have long noted, but it is rarely incorporated into analyses of the process of democratic consolidation (Whitaker 1970). While the rules, processes, and values associated with elections are definitely not "the only game in town," they are nonetheless important and have affected local-level political dynamics in unanticipated ways. Specifically, local communities encourage their chief, *izinduna,* and traditional councilors to take part in the electoral process and adopt internal reforms that allow for more participation and choice. At the same time, however, under pressure from local communities, some democratic ideas and institutions were incorporated into the chieftaincy structures long before the passage of the TLGF Act in 2003.

These dynamics suggest that, at least in the short term, it is incorrect to assume that people believe they must make a choice between the chieftaincy and democratic institutions. Instead, these two institutions are blending together in complex ways to create new types of norms, rules, and processes that are distinct and unique. For example, the relationship between Vusi and chief Biyela in Mvuzane is not uncommon. In many rural communities, the elected councilor and chief work together on local matters (Oomen 2000; Goodenough 2002; Keulder 1998: 287–324). In addition, there are many examples where the elected councilor serves as part of the chief's *isigungu* as well. While the chief needs the elected councilors to acquire resources and information (i.e., where and when the elections will take place), the elected councilor needs the permission of the chief to carry out his duties.

As the narrative on the 1999 election reveals, while the chief relied upon the elected councilor for information, the chief was still the spokesperson for the community and directed the elected councilor to undertake specific tasks. The example of Mvuzane also highlights how the actual success or failure of the electoral process depends to a great extent on the ability of the chiefs, *izinduna,* and traditional councilors involved. In this way, these leaders often serve as the main source of information for communities. It is important to recall that just days before the registration process the exact registration sites were still unknown. Vusi had hoped to learn this information so that it could be announced on the radio before registration, but this did not happen. Instead, this information was given at a meeting just days before the registration, and *izinduna* were told to share this information with those in their wards who were not at the meeting.

In addition, the presence of chiefs, *izinduna,* and traditional councilors during the course of both registration and voting provided a sense of order to the process. They were expected to maintain order and peace in the area, and it was not surprising that chief Biyela and his *izinduna* took these responsibilities seriously. This was especially the case on Election Day when there was a rush to enter the school once the site had been opened. While the government believed the presence of SADF officers was necessary to ensure peaceful elections, it was chief Biyela who helped with crowd control when people crowded the doorway of the school. It is doubtful whether those standing in line would have behaved the same way if it were the SADF officers who attempted to clear the area.

Another important function of the chieftaincy during this electoral process was its ability to reassure the community that those who were outsiders—whether they were teachers from Eshowe, SADF officers, or ANC and IEC representatives—should not be considered a threat. In some cases, the concept of "stranger," as it relates to chieftaincy areas, tends to overestimate the exclusiveness of these rural communities and underestimate the fluidness of boundaries and the many interconnections between the rural and urban areas. With respect to the election process, however, the boundaries between insiders and outsiders were definitely important. On each occasion where the presence of "strangers" was questioned, chief Biyela or Vusi told the community that there was nothing to fear—that unity and harmony would prevail.

This concern over strangers, or what Vusi called "city boys," highlights the inherent tension between the process of democratization, which in the very least anticipates the diversity of ideas and the importance of individual choice, and the value of unity, which encourages oneness, and in some cases exclusiveness. In Mvuzane, chief Biyela and his assistants attempted to balance these competing pressures during the electoral process in 1999. While the chief publicly encouraged people to vote freely, and to not be fearful of party politics, his physical presence during this process was a reminder of the central role the chieftaincy plays in the daily lives of the people and the fact that after the spectacle of the elections was over, the leaders of the community would still be the chief and his assistants. Nonetheless, the chieftaincy has not been unaffected by the introduction of electoral rules, processes, and values. Since the early 1990s, people have demanded internal reforms to make the chieftaincy more representative and accountable. In many communities, chiefs have decided to respond to these demands and have allowed for more participation within chieftaincy areas (Oomen 2000).

Even though it is debatable how much actual choice these new procedures allow, there is no question that they have enabled certain groups more access to the local power structure. In particular, women and younger men are much more involved with community issues than in the past. Also, there are changes concerning the functions of *izinduna* and traditional councilors. In this way, there is flux in terms of who can participate at the local level and the duties of those who are community leaders. These changes have caused some tensions, especially concerning the role of women, and some chiefs are better suited than others to handle these conflicts. Still, the ability of the chieftaincy to make these changes demonstrates the dynamic nature, and adaptability, of the institution.

While it is too soon to evaluate whether changes concerning how the community selects their leaders will lead to the adoption of other democratic values, there is no question that communities in many rural areas want such changes even though they also continue to believe the chieftaincy must not be abolished. There is also reason to believe that these internal experiences with "democratic reform" are in many ways more meaningful and important than the process of participating in government-controlled elections. These internal experiences provide an opportunity for people to understand how elections work, and because these elected officeholders live in the community, there is a better likelihood that they will be held accountable. In addition, people are able to create inventive ways to combine their simultaneous desires for more democracy and development as well as for the security of the chieftaincy and the maintenance of unity. Government-sponsored elections, on the other hand, are isolated events that are sometimes difficult to understand or situate into broader sociopolitical contexts at the local level. In other words, the spectacle of elections leaves people with renewed hope but with little understanding of how government makes decisions or how to hold governmental bodies accountable for their actions, while internal reforms are experienced on a daily basis that allows members of the community to more actively participate with governance issues.

These examples suggest that the Western conception of liberal democracy, which highlights the importance of free and fair elections, is contested in the rural areas (Koelble 2005; Schaffer 1998). While elections are important, so are chieftaincy institutions, and it is doubtful that people in these areas are likely to conceptualize democracy as "the only game in town." Instead, one of the consequences of a mixed polity is that people seek to blend together different sources of legitimacy. For the reasons discussed above, in many ways, chiefs, *izinduna,* and traditional councilors must at least appear as if they are embracing some aspects of the democratic process to maintain their authority. Whether this includes allowing communities more choice in choosing *izinduna* or traditional councilors, or providing information about the registration and voting process, local leaders cannot afford to ignore democratic pressures or they risk being overcome by them.

The difficulty, however, is how the chieftaincy is able to maintain community unity as alternative ideas and institutions become more embedded in the community. The results of this process will vary from community to community as different leaders employ different strategies and techniques. As the findings from the three communities in KwaZulu-Natal suggest, the ways in which communities and the chieftaincy incorporate democratic ideas and institutions will vary, and it is dangerous to assume these processes will be uniform throughout the country.

What is certain, however, is that the introduction of elections in rural areas has undoubtedly altered chieftaincy-societal relations. Yet rather than leading to the end of the chieftaincy, these changes have produced more mixed results. Chiefs, *izinduna,* and traditional councilors, and those who live in their areas, all have found ways to situate newly introduced electoral procedures into the preexisting institutional and ideological frameworks. More importantly, they have attempted to find ways to utilize these new practices to enhance their own authority.

THE CHIEFTAINCY AND THE ESTABLISHMENT OF LOCAL GOVERNMENT

Multiple Boundaries and the Ambiguities of Representation

It [local government] provides people with their needs—it is about development.

I think if our inkosi had dignity we could be helped because you find that in some other areas the [local government] is helping but not in our area.

We will understand [local government] more easily because we know him [the chief].

One of the central premises of the LG White Paper in 1998 was that the sources of authority for the chieftaincy and local government would be distinct. In this way, the ANC hoped that it could accommodate the chieftaincy while simultaneously creating democratic government at the local level. This has proven to be a difficult task as the establishment of local government institutions has altered the legitimation process in rural areas. In particular, the "official" boundaries between the authority of local government institutions and the chieftaincy at the local level that existed 1996–2000 were not as unambiguous as the ANC anticipated. Rather than providing clarity, the establishment of rural local government in 1995–96 was a process that superimposed a new set of norms and rules onto a sociopolitical context where the chieftaincy remained dominant. One of the results is that the authority of each overlaps the other in ways that tend to obscure, rather than reinforce, the boundaries that exist between the chieftaincy and local government institutions. An analysis of how and why these boundaries become blurred highlights the ways in which local populations give meaning to the newly established democratic institutions and their experiences with these institutions.

One of the more significant legacies of colonialism and apartheid is the multiple political boundaries that exist at the local level, especially in the rural areas. As government officials sought to implement local government institutions throughout South Africa, they had to come to grips with apartheid-era boundaries that remained meaningful to local residents. More specifically, in 1995–96, when the first local government institutions were established, the preexisting tribal authorities and regional authorities remained intact. Until the passage of the TLGF Act in 2003, there were 280 tribal authorities and 24 regional authorities in KwaZulu-Natal that continued to function as they had during apartheid. Even with the passage and implementation of the TLGF Act, these boundaries have not disappeared, as tribal and regional authorities were simply replaced with traditional councils and district houses of traditional leaders. For the most part, these new bodies have jurisdiction over the same boundaries and have kept the same names (i.e., Mvuzane Tribal Authority was renamed Mvuzane Traditional Council).

Indeed, the institutional changes that occurred in 1996 were in some ways even more important than those adopted in 2003 with the TLGF Act. What changed in 1996 was that the chieftaincy was forced to compete with the newly established local government institutions, and more specifically, with elected local government representatives. This posed a number of challenges for the chieftaincy.

First, unlike the members of the tribal and regional authorities that chiefs were able to appoint, local government institutions consisted of elected representatives who based their authority on the electoral process. For many in the rural areas, the presence of elected representatives tended to complicate the idea of "representation," especially as both traditional leaders and elected councilors competed for the respect and loyalty of the people.

Second, under the constitution, local government institutions were responsible for a range of development issues that had been under the jurisdiction of the tribal and regional authorities during apartheid. Pressures for both conflict and cooperation have developed as the chieftaincy and elected councilors have attempted to secure their autonomy, even though local populations expected that traditional leaders should work with local government to facilitate the development process and to maintain the unity and harmony of the area. The next chapter examines in much more detail the implementation of development projects in the rural areas, but the issue of development is also intricately bound up with perceptions of local government.

Third, the fact that traditional leaders were ex-officio members of local government meant that they were forced to interact with elected officials in an entirely new political space that was fundamentally different from the tribal and regional authorities. Many traditional leaders used their ex-officio status to monitor the decisions of local government as much as possible. In most cases, they did not perceive elected councilors as their equals and preferred to interact with elected councils through tribal and regional authorities rather than through local government institutions.

And fourth, the existence of a "strong" local government influences the ways in which people perceive the chieftaincy. The weak-state thesis assumes that the chieftaincy's legitimacy is based on the fact that many citizens in the rural areas are forced to rely upon traditional leaders because state institutions are unable to effectively respond to their needs. While local government institutions in Mvuzane and Kholweni have been unable to broadcast their authority since 1996, the Durban Metro Municipality, where Ximba Tribal Authority was located, has been much more effective. Thus, the traditional leaders in Ximba encountered the possibility that a more capable local government institution would expand its authority at the expense of the chieftaincy.

It is important not to underestimate the extent to which the preexisting tribal and regional authority boundaries and institutions affected the process of decentralization and the ability of the state to broadcast its authority in the rural areas (Wunsch 2000; Herbst 2000). These preexisting boundaries afforded the chieftaincy a distinct advantage in terms of the legitimation process because the boundaries of its authority are much more certain than those of the newly introduced local government institutions. In addition, it is a mistake to assume that before the establishment of the local government institutions in 1996 there were no governance structures at the local level. While there is no doubt that during apartheid the tribal and regional authorities lacked the capacity to respond to the needs of the people, those living in the rural areas nonetheless depended on traditional leaders for many of their basic needs. While they never had complete autonomy from the apartheid state, and while they shared authority with local magistrates, traditional leaders did have some discretion over many daily decisions. In fact, one of the central features of the chieftaincy, both during and after apartheid, is that it often functioned as a "mini-state" within its demarcated area (Koelble and LiPuma 2005). Moreover, the apartheid regime empowered the chieftaincy to fulfill duties that are normally allocated to local government institutions. Given this reality, it is not surprising that there remains a widespread belief that traditional leaders must play some role in the local governance process. Even with the introduction of official local government institutions since 1995, this belief is still prevalent in many areas, and it continues to shape the interactions between the local government and the chieftaincy.

THE MAKING OF LOCAL GOVERNMENT: EXPECTATIONS AND REALITIES

For the post-apartheid state, the establishment of effective, efficient, and accountable local government institutions is critical for its political legitimacy, as it is the level of the state that is most likely to have frequent interactions with society (Atkinson 2002; Tapscott 2005). In particular, the success or failure of local government is directly linked to the delivery of development projects. For example, in Mvuzane, Ximba, and Kholweni, a vast majority of the people associated local government with the delivery of development and nothing else.[1] Indeed, President Mbeki stressed this very point at the fifth annual conference of the South African Local Government Association (SALGA) when he stated that

> [i]n a large measure, the future of this country regarding the major problems it faces, rests in the hands of the people who lead us in local government. . . . We can vote as much money at the national level to do all sorts of things, but if local government is unable to use that money properly, nothing will change. Our future depends on yourselves. . . . We must be able to say at some point that we have succeeded in reducing poverty levels, that we have created new infrastructure and that these places are now better than they were before. (South African Press Association, "Municipalities Have To Overcome Vestiges of Apartheid: Mbeki," April 5, 2001)

Despite the importance the ANC attaches to the development of local government, the reality is that it has so miserably failed to deliver basic services that it has been described by local government MEC (member of Executive Committee) Mike Mabuyakhulu as in a state of "total collapse,"[2] and by United Democratic Movement leader Bantu Holomisa as "nauseating."[3] Even President Mbeki has warned elected local government officials that poor performance will no longer be tolerated.[4] There is ample evidence to support the failure of local government as well as the negative assessments that many citizens have of local government. For example, as of 2006, 136 of the 284 municipalities were under the jurisdiction of Project Consolidate—a central government program initiated in 2004 to help struggling local governments.[5] Of the 136, rural municipalities make up the majority. In addition, after over a decade of local government, most public opinion polls reflect growing dissatisfaction. One poll before the 2006 local government elections found that 60 percent of urban voters did not believe voting was an effective way of ensuring good government, and another found that 53 percent of those in the urban areas were not satisfied with local government performance.[6] Similarly, in its 2006 survey, Afrobarometer found that attitudes about local government councilors had declined significantly from 2004, when 51 percent either approved or strongly approved of their performance, to 2006, when only 38 percent gave this mark.[7] Another analysis has found that South Africans living in the rural areas are less satisfied with local government than those living in the urban areas and that the most dissatisfied citizens are those who live in the poorest provinces (Bratton and Sibanyoni 2006). These surveys suggest that there is a serious disconnect between the expectations that South Africans have about local government and the reality of local government performance. Obviously, such a gap has negative implications with respect to the state's ability to generate legitimacy at the local level.

These more recent surveys are consistent with the attitudes that existed in the late 1990s in Mvuzane and Kholweni with respect to the Uthungulu Regional Council (URC), which was the local government institution introduced in these areas in 1996. In short, a vast majority of those people interviewed in Mvuzane and Kholweni stated that the URC had not done anything to help their communities.[8] In those cases where citizens were not outright negative about local government, they were usually ambivalent, uninformed, or apathetic. Many reported that they did not know their elected local councilor and that they did not attend local government meetings. It was common for people in the rural areas to admit that they were confused with the way local government worked and that they rarely heard from their elected representatives. For example, one person complained that the "Uthungulu Regional Council has never done anything for us here. We have a problem. These are the people who have been promising us funds, but nothing has happened."[9] These findings are consistent with other studies, such as Oomen's on the chieftaincy in the Northern Province, where she found that, "[i]n general, the people we spoke to had no strongly held ideas about which authorities should do what, but just hoped that things would get done in their area" (2005: 173).

Another indicator of ambivalence about local government is the voter turnout for these elections, which failed to reach 50 percent in the three local government elections (Independent Electoral Commission website). While there are various explanations as to why voter turnout has decreased with local government elections, none of them are particularly positive. Whether people do not vote because of they are apathetic or because disappointed citizens choose to abstain from voting altogether rather than vote against the ANC, there is no question that people are losing faith in local government.[10] Thus, it is common to find many complaints concerning local government, such as that "no matter who you vote for, nothing ever changes" and that voting was a waste of time "because local councilors don't help us."[11] Even though there is general dissatisfaction with local government and voter turnout in local elections has been lower than national elections, this has not resulted in dramatic shifts in the composition of local councils. Nationwide, the ANC dominates local government structures and secured a majority on 203 of the 237 councils in 2006 (Independent Electoral Commission 2006). The only competition it faces is from the Democratic Alliance (DA) in the Western Cape and the IFP in KwaZulu-Natal. Given these stable voting patterns, it is not surprising that the IFP has remained in control of the local municipality where Mvuzane and Kholweni are located and that the ANC has controlled the Durban Metro Municipality, where Ximba is located, since 1996.

At the same time, to expect people to have a positive opinion about local government and to take elections seriously presupposes that they have actually interacted with it in the first place. For many in the rural areas, that is not the case, because local government lacks a physical presence and is barely visible. In many cases, local government officials do not have offices in the rural areas, and when they do conduct business, it is usually done at the tribal court, which may only hasten their confusion concerning the boundaries of authority. This was definitely the case in both Mvuzane and Kholweni, where elected officials had no offices in the area. In addition, it was not until 2004 that there were any symbols of local government authority, such as signs designating which jurisdiction one is entering or development projects with the name of local government associated with it. Because many local residents rarely met with their elected representatives, except when there were elections, there were few opportunities for dialogue (Bratton and Sibanyoni 2006).

There is no question that South Africa has struggled to establish strong and effective local government institutions in the rural areas. This political reality provides the context to examine how the introduction of these institutions affects the legitimation process in the rural areas. Specifically, it is important to consider the ways in which people evaluate the chieftaincy and the interactions between the chieftaincy and local government institutions, and more specifically, elected councilors.

FROM THEORY TO PRACTICE: CHIEFTAINCY-STATE RELATIONS AT THE LOCAL LEVEL, 1995–2000

Even though most rural local government institutions have underperformed and lacked capacity, the extent to which traditional leaders perceived them as a threat to their authority, especially when they were first established in 1995–96, should not be minimized. It is quite right that the establishment of these local government institutions was an attempt by the post-apartheid state to create a new set of boundaries in the rural areas that would establish a social space that was autonomous from the authority of the chieftaincy. To accomplish this, local government institutions have sought to define, and redefine, the political and social space in rural areas to enforce a new set of norms, rules, and symbols that are crucial for establishing its social control (Migdal 1994; Wunsch and Olowu 2004). For their part, after losing the battle as to whether local government institutions would be established, traditional leaders have sought to establish accommodations with local government institutions, with the goal of controlling them as much as possible. To better understand how the chieftaincy has managed to co-opt and alter these institutions, it is important to examine more closely the attitudes that people have about the authority of each at the local level.

Perceptions of Local Government and Chieftaincy Authority

With the establishment of local government institutions in 1995–96, it was not known exactly how traditional leaders, elected representatives, and local populations would interact with one another. As I have already mentioned, one of the characteristics of the policy of incrementalism was that the ANC was slow to define the specific duties and functions of the chieftaincy and local government (Republic of South Africa 1998a; Polunic 1997; McIntosh 1995). The government seemed to have assumed, incorrectly, that the chieftaincy and local government could coexist in such a way that each would draw support from its separate base of legitimacy. There was little recognition that local populations would expect traditional leaders to actively participate with local government institutions, and even more importantly, that the leaders risked losing support if they did not work with local government to get access to resources. In addition, there was faint acknowledgment that the authority of the elected councilors who represented the rural areas, no matter their political affiliation, would be linked to the chieftaincy in complex and subtle ways that defied the existence of precise boundaries.

This is not to say that there were not attempts to construct the appropriate boundaries between the two. In fact, both before and after the establishment of local government in 1995–96, traditional leaders, elected councilors, and members of rural communities were taught that traditional leaders and elected councilors were distinct types of representatives with different bases of authority. This was mostly accomplished through workshops, conferences, and radio broadcasts, but it also took place within local communities more informally as well.[12] The goal was to teach people the appropriate role of local government, elected councilors, and the chieftaincy in the new South Africa.[13] All "stakeholders" were brought together and told that local government was legally responsible for delivering resources such as potable water, electricity, and clinics. They were also told that while the elected councilors were the ones most responsible for development, the chieftaincy would be adequately consulted on all matters and that it would be a crucial link to connect the elected councilor to the larger community, thereby fulfilling its gatekeeper status.

These conferences and workshops continued as the government prepared rural communities for the implementation of the permanent local government institutions in December 2000. The amount of time and resources dedicated to these gatherings led one elected councilor to suggest the Mandela regime should be labeled the "government of learning" rather than a "government of transformation," indicating that far too much time was spent on discussing the roles of the different actors and far too little spent on addressing the problems in the community.[14] Another government official suggested that this period was essentially about "looking inward" as the state was seeking to build up its own capacities and merge together the preexisting apartheid institutions with the post-apartheid ones. He hoped that in subsequent years the government would begin to "look outward" to those people it was supposed to serve.[15] Even though the first five years of local government had been formally designated as a "transition period," we should not underestimate the degree to which this period affected the present local political landscape. Indeed, there is evidence that relationships and networks forged during these first five years will most definitely prove difficult to undo in the future (Crais 2006; Beall, Mkhize, and Vawda 2005; Oomen 2005; Williams 2004; Goodenough 2002).

After spending time in the rural areas, however, it did not take long to recognize that the distinctions between elected local government and the chieftaincy set forth in the LG White Paper in 1998 were oftentimes more ambiguous, nuanced, and contradictory at the local level than this document assumed. On the one hand, there was some evidence that the distinctions set out in official government discourse, such as in the LG White Paper, did resonate at a superficial level with rural communities (Keulder 1998; Republic of South Africa 1998a). For example, in Mvuzane, Kholweni, and Ximba there were occasions when people tended to differentiate between the duties of traditional leaders and elected councilors in a manner consistent with official policy. This, however, occurred only at the most theoretical and abstract levels. In other words, when people discussed the differences between the functions of elected councilors and traditional leaders in the abstract, and without any connection to their own traditional leaders specifically, they tended to associate the elected councilor with the person responsible for development issues and chiefs with those who "deal with social problems of the community."[16] In addition, when asked what was local government's most important responsibility, 58 percent of those living in Mvuzane, Kholweni, and Ximba specifically mentioned development.

These findings seem to be consistent with other research in a variety of rural areas as well. For example, Goodenough finds similar dynamics in her research in KwaZulu-Natal, as does Oomen in the Northern Province (Goodenough 2002; Oomen 2005). In particular, Oomen notes that when asked about specific governmental functions, such as water, electricity, and clinics, most people believed that these were the responsibility of local government and not traditional leaders (2005: 174). Thus, at one level at least, community perceptions as to the differences between elected councilors and traditional leaders roughly mirror the distinctions set forth in the LG White Paper and other policy documents.

Interestingly, however, the degree to which people associated elected councilors and traditional leaders in this manner differed in significant ways between different tribal authority areas as well as within particular tribal authority boundaries. For most citizens, the sentiment was that both elected councilors and the chiefs should be working with local government to try to get development projects. Yet there were differing attitudes in each of the case studies concerning whether chiefs were actually engaged in this process. Perhaps the most significant finding here was that in Mvuzane and Ximba, where the community was most positive about the overall performance of the chieftaincy with respect to development, there were more respondents who suggested there was "no difference" between the elected councilors and traditional leaders. In this way, in those cases where chiefs were perceived as "working for development," there was a blurring of boundaries between the chieftaincy and elected local government. In Kholweni, however, where the chief was accused of ineffective leadership, most informants believed that it was the elected councilor who was most responsible for development and the chief who was most responsible for "solving problems."[17] This suggests that the more the traditional leaders have been able to expand their authority over development issues, the more difficult it has been for people to distinguish these leaders from elected councilors.[18]

Whereas at a more abstract level there was some agreement on the different responsibilities for elected councilors and traditional leaders, these distinctions became more ambiguous and fluid when there were real issues raised in the community that demanded resolution, especially those related to development. More specifically, traditional leaders have proven quite capable of redefining the notion of "community problem" to include development issues, and communities are beginning to expect their traditional leaders to actively engage local government to get access to development services.[19] In this way, traditional leaders have extended their authority over an issue that, according to the LG White Paper, is not one of their traditional responsibilities and should therefore be left to elected councilors. Echoing what many people said on this issue, a woman in Mvuzane said that "*inkosi* is trying. The government is doing nothing. Yes [traditional leaders should be involved with development], though nothing is happening. We depend on the *inkosi* for all our needs."[20] Such sentiments, which combine frustration, desperation, and an enduring faith in the chief, were common in Mvuzane, Kholweni, and Ximba.

There was less confusion, however, concerning the more fundamental issue of whether traditional leaders or elected councilors exercised more authority in the area. When conversations turned to the exercise of authority between traditional leaders and elected councilors, as opposed to a discussion about the different responsibilities each has, the distinction drawn between "community problems" and development was not as important. For example, one traditional councilor suggested that "the *ubukhosi* [the chieftaincy] is to rule over the people. To keep law and order. The elected councilor deals only with development."[21] A member of a development committee in Mvuzane made it even clearer when he said that "*induna* and *inkosi* deal with social problems while the councilor deals with Uthungulu Regional Council and development. But *inkosi* is more powerful."[22]

In Mvuzane, chief Biyela articulated the difference between himself and the elected councilor in that "the elected councilor deals with development. He does not deal with the cases."[23] What was most interesting about the manner in which chief Biyela made this distinction was that he suggested limits to the elected councilor's authority but did not suggest limits to his own authority. Later in that same discussion, he noted that bringing development to the community has been his most important duty since 1994, when he and his community first learned about development. Similarly, even though elected councilors claimed they did have decision-making power with respect to development, they also admitted that they were still under the chief even with their position and must ultimately follow his decision.[24]

Similar sentiments were echoed in Kholweni and Ximba despite the fact that in the former the chief was incredibly unpopular and in the latter the local government had a much greater presence. Thus, unlike in Mvuzane, while a majority of informants in Kholweni suggested that the chief not be able to overrule a decision of local government, nearly 90 percent believed that the chief should have a say in local government decisions,[25] and over 90 percent mentioned either the chief, the *izinduna,* or traditional councilors as "the leaders" of the community.[26] Likewise, in Ximba, despite the relative success of local government, over 95 percent stated that the traditional leaders were "the leaders" of the community.[27]

All Local Politics Is Personal: Relationships between Elected Councilors and Chiefs

While much of the national debate over the relationship between the chieftaincy and local government was focused on whether the chieftaincy was "under" the local government or vice versa, there were different concerns at the local level. Most people believed that the only way to get development to their areas was if the chief and the elected councilor cooperated and maintained "unity" with one another.[28] From its policy pronouncements in the LG White Paper and the TLGF Act, it appears as if the ANC recognized the importance of cooperation as well. For many in the ANC, however, the reason for cooperation is based more on pragmatic concerns than on the principle that the chieftaincy deserves to be consulted because of their status in the community. Given this reasoning, it was not surprising that after the ANC defeated the IFP in provincial elections to become the majority party in KwaZulu-Natal in 2004 for the first time in the post-apartheid era, it continued to promote the importance of cooperation. Thus, even though the IFP has the reputation of supporting the chieftaincy more than the ANC, there has been no noticeable shift in public policy in KwaZulu-Natal since 2004. In fact, at a conference on local government in 2005, KZN local government MEC Mike Mabuyakhulu, a member of the ANC, commented specifically on the government's desire to utilize traditional leaders to help with state building and development.[29] One of the resolutions at the end of the conference was to create "synergistic partnerships between traditional institutions and municipalities . . . given the service delivery backlogs in the traditional community area."[30] Thus, to enhance the authority of local government, the ANC has adopted a set of policies that promote cooperation with the chieftaincy.

Long before such pronouncements, however, as early as 1998–99, those living in the rural areas had already recognized the importance of cooperation and were quite willing to articulate the reasons why this was the case. For example, many people recognized that tribal authorities lacked the capacity to fund or implement development projects without the assistance of local government, and thus, they believed that cooperation was necessary to get access to necessary resources. While the ability of elected councilors to make decisions independent of traditional leaders was quite rare, many people in Mvuzane, Ximba, and Kholweni maintained that the elected councilors should be allowed to use their connections to bring resources to the community. In most communities, the elected councilor, for all practical purposes, was the local government, as there was little physical presence of local government in the rural areas. Even though most people did not yet understand how local government worked as an institution, there was a prevalent perception that local government was the main source of scarce funds. Accordingly, the main responsibility of the elected councilor was to access these newly established "channels" for the benefit of the community. In many cases, however, elected councilors knew as little about how to access these "channels" as ordinary local residents. As for traditional leaders, they were expected to work with elected councilors to assure that resources were actually delivered to their specific areas and to resolve conflicts that might arise over development projects.

While the belief in cooperation was partly based on the desire to secure development resources, another reason why local populations expected cooperation had to do with the moral authority of the chieftaincy itself. Indeed, the notion that "nothing can be done without the cooperation between the elected councilor and *inkosi*" was a common refrain throughout rural South Africa.[31] An equally common refrain was one that directly relates to the authority of the chieftaincy itself—that the elected councilor "will not do anything without *inkosi*."[32] Other research has found similar sentiments throughout the province, such as, "We as a community should talk to the councilors and we must use the *inkosi* and *induna*. This unity solves the problem. . . . Then there will be progress" (Republic of South Africa 1998a: 27) and "in this area we are living in peace and harmony . . . the reason for that is that people in Nzimakwe [Tribal Authority] area work through cooperation" (Goodenough 2002: 154; see also Beall 2006: 469; Oomen 2005). Thus, it seems that the belief in cooperation is based on the fact that as the leaders of the area, traditional leaders should be involved in the local government process, and more specifically, that the chieftaincy remains at the center of the community and that for the sake of unity, cooperation must ensue.

This sentiment that cooperation must exist in order to get development projects and to maintain unity has put pressure on both traditional leaders and elected councilors to forge working relationships. One of the unintended consequences of such cooperation, however, has been that local communities have blamed both traditional leaders and elected councilors when development did not occur. The longer people have waited for development, the more intense the criticism has become. For example, throughout KZN, there was a sense in the rural areas that life should be getting better with the new government but that conditions have only gotten worse since 1994 (IDASA 1996). Indeed, in both Mvuzane and Kholweni only one in five respondents believed that their lives were better since 1994, while just over half of the respondents in Ximba considered this to be the case.[33] One woman aptly described this frustrating situation as one where "[t]hings are starting to change now though nothing has changed."[34] Even though few rural communities had seen the changes promised in 1994, there was still a sense that the government would help in the future. With such high expectations for change, both traditional leaders and elected councilors were often in a position where they had to explain to their communities why so little had been achieved. This was difficult and unfamiliar territory for both sets of leaders.

For many in the community, the lack of development indicated that the chief was not fulfilling his duty to forge the proper relationship with local government. In the past, traditional leaders had not faced these types of pressures because there were much lower expectations for development. There was a clear sentiment in Mvuzane, Kholweni, and Ximba that traditional leaders had not sought development projects before 1994—largely because the resources were not available to them. With the end of apartheid, however, attitudes have changed, and people were not afraid to suggest that the lack of change since 1994 was because their traditional leaders lacked "dignity" and that other areas with more "dignified" traditional leaders were receiving resources.[35] In fact, in Mvuzane, one of the fifteen wards was threatening to join the neighboring chieftaincy, as they believed the other area received more resources because their chief and elected councilors were working harder for the community. In this case, the establishment of local government, and the desire to secure development projects, challenged the preexisting traditional boundaries and seemed to reintroduce the possibility of exit as a response to poor leadership. This process is even more prevalent within tribal authority boundaries as new jealousies and conflicts have arisen between different wards over the allocation of development projects.[36]

For example, from 1996 to 2000, Ximba was part of the Durban Metropolitan Council local government, but a large number of other tribal authorities near Ximba were not. One of the reasons why many of these other tribal authorities were not included in the Durban Metro was because the ANC dominated this structure and many of the tribal authorities near Ximba were dominated by the IFP. Thus, when the boundaries were drawn for the transitional local government institutions, many IFP areas lobbied to join other local government councils, where the IFP was in control. By 2000, however, it was clear that those tribal authorities in the Durban Metropolitan Council, including Ximba, had access to more development resources and more development projects. Not surprisingly, many of the tribal authorities that were not part of the Durban Metropolitan Council lobbied the local government demarcation commission to draw the boundaries for the new Durban Metropolitan Council in a way that included their areas. While there were only a few tribal authorities in the Durban Metropolitan Council, with the establishment of the eThekweni Municipality in 2000 there are now fifteen tribal authorities within its jurisdiction, a vast majority of which were under another local government jurisdiction from 1996 to 2000 (Beall, Gelb, and Hassim 2005).

At the same time, elected councilors were oftentimes blamed for the lack of change. In fact, they were sometimes criticized because they had become *too close* to traditional leaders and that elected councilors were showing *too much* favoritism to the leaders. In many cases, people complained that development projects occurred only "close to the chief's homestead" or that the elected councilor was personally benefiting from his position.[37] There were always lively rumors that accused the chieftaincy and elected councilors of corruption and asserted that money was "lost" after it was approved. Not surprisingly, the people making such claims were usually those local elites who believed they had lost access to important patronage networks as new channels had been forged between the chieftaincy, elected councilors, and local governments.[38] Just as pre-existing structures and norms have proven important for elected councilors and traditional leaders to maintain authority, new structures and norms have also emerged from which not all elites have been able to benefit. What was striking was that the same people who made these types of complaints were likely to insist that elected councilors must not disrespect traditional leaders because they were the leaders of the community.

In response to complaints concerning the lack of development, both traditional leaders and elected councilors were more likely to blame "government" rather than blame each other. There was also a tendency for traditional leaders to make a "do-it-ourselves" argument. Chief Mkwanazi in northern KwaZulu-Natal argued that his people "must avoid waiting for the government" and that "we must make decisions and do things for ourselves, so that our children can improve economically" (Goodenough 2002: 149). In a similar vein, chief Mzimela has stated, "[W]e are born administrators. It is our responsibility to bring development to the people. We do not want to lose our power as *amakhosi*."[39] Many chiefs argued that all funds should be deposited directly into their tribal authority accounts, and elected councilors suggested that local government was not structured to facilitate real debate and to solve community problems.[40] Obviously, it is extremely unlikely that traditional leaders will secure this much official autonomy at the local level. What is also clear, however, is that the pressure for development has created a situation in which elected councilors and traditional leaders are likely to continue to forge mutually dependent relationships in the future.

Of course, the ability of the chiefs to forge close working relationships depended greatly on whether they trusted each other or not. This, in turn, was largely based on the types of relationships that had existed before 1994. In both Mvuzane and Ximba, the relationships between the chiefs and the elected councilors were established well before the first local government elections in 1996, and this seemed to make cooperation more likely. In fact, in both Mvuzane and Ximba, the person who was placed on the party list as the candidate was also a close advisor to the chieftaincy structure prior to 1996.

For example, in the IFP-dominated tribal authority of Mvuzane, the elected councilor and chief had known each other since the late 1980s. Vusi was attending high school in Mvuzane in the late 1980s when he got involved with small-scale development projects and began to question the public statements made by Inkatha leaders that funding was coming to tribal authority areas. As a member of the Inkatha Youth Brigade, Vusi led a congregation of youth to an Inkatha meeting in Mvuzane and directly confronted the Inkatha leaders about the whereabouts of these funds. After this meeting, the relationship between Vusi and the chief was strained as the chief feared that Vusi was a member of the ANC and that he wanted to abolish the chieftaincy. Only after many months did Vusi convince the chief that he respected the authority of the chieftaincy and that he only wanted to help the community. Vusi later attended school in Durban, became fluent in English, and by the early 1990s was considered to be the chief's closest advisor. Thus, Vusi and the chief and *izinduna* had established a close relationship before Vusi became the elected councilor.

Similarly, in Ximba tribal authority, which the ANC has dominated, the elected councilor, Simon Ngubane, and the chief had known each other since the 1980s. They were both members of the UDF and actively participated in the anti-apartheid struggle. There were many rumors in this area, however, that the community actually wanted another person to be their elected councilor but that at the last moment, the chief "changed the rules" and was able to secure the election of Ngubane. According to some *izinduna* and others close to the chief, there was a fear that the person the community preferred was not afraid to challenge the chief on issues and that he would carefully "watch the money," whereas Ngubane would know "his place." In addition, whereas Ngubane did not speak English and had little formal education, his competition had a law degree and had more formal education than the chief (who also holds a university degree). Thus, many people speculated that the chief arranged for Ngubane's election because he did not want someone more educated than himself as the elected councilor.

The Struggle over Representation

The ability to cooperate at the local level is a difficult issue because the quest to maintain unity means that elected councilors must alter their behavior in ways that limit their own autonomy and demonstrate respect for the chieftaincy. The result is that local populations see their elected representatives working with, or under, their chiefs. While both chiefs and *izinduna* are able to broaden the scope of their authority to meet the rising expectations for change, elected councilors must carefully situate themselves within the preexisting rules, procedures, norms, and symbols that provide the framework for local politics. They cannot simply claim that their authority was the result of democratic elections and begin working directly with rural communities. Instead, the ideas of "democracy" and "representation" become meaningful only when combined with the proper show of respect to the chieftaincy.

For example, one elected councilor suggested that when he attended a community meeting with an idea, he would always remove his hat and praise the chief and *izinduna* before presenting his ideas. If there was only one chair available, he would let the chief or *izinduna* have it to show the community that he recognized the authority of the chieftaincy. Once this respect was expressed, it was much easier to receive the approval of the chief or *izinduna* for a proposed project.[41] At the same time, it was much easier for the elected councilor to mobilize the community, whether in terms of financial donations, time, or labor, when the elected councilor was able to tell the community that his idea had been approved by the chieftaincy. In this manner, access to the community was dependent upon the acquiescence of the chief or *induna*. With this in mind, it is not surprising that Beall also found that one of the most repeated complaints that traditional leaders have about elected councilors is that they do not follow proper protocols and appear disrespectful (2006: 465). Thus, in many chieftaincy areas, the goal of the leaders was not to separate or divide power, but instead, to combine it in mutually beneficial ways.

In many cases, the boundaries between elected councilor and the chief or *izinduna* became so blurred that it was difficult for people to see any difference. For example, in every chieftaincy, there are a group of community members who made up the *isigungu*. In Mvuzane, Ximba, and Khowleni, the elected councilor was also named a member of the *isigungu* or was represented on the *isigungu*. Sometimes this position was acquired before the elections and sometimes the elected councilor was made a member only after the election. In many instances, people in the community may not have known whether the elected councilor was on the *isigungu*, but they nevertheless recognized that the elected councilor was the closest advisor to the chief. It was not uncommon for elected councilors to also serve as *izinduna* or traditional councilors as well, thereby occupying important positions within the chieftaincy. In fact, there was one instance where an elected councilor had told us during an interview that he was not a traditional councilor, but when the chief was asked the same question, he claimed that the elected councilor was a traditional councilor. Such a scenario only highlights the degree to which these lines can be blurred and the confusion that sometimes accompanied these multiple roles.[42] Thus, for many people living in tribal authority areas there was no difference between the elected councilors and those within the chieftaincy, because they saw the authority of these different actors merge.

There are many other examples of the blurring of authority between elected local government officials and traditional leaders. For instance, Oomen notes that at the swearing in of Billy Sekwati as king of the Pedi in 1998, the mayor and other elected officials were in attendance. Before he was elected mayor in 2000, Abraham Mafiri was the driver of the local chief (Oomen 2005: 144). Later in her analysis, Oomen quotes the mayor as stating that he gets along with 80 percent of the traditional leaders in the area because "he was a 'local boy' and knew the correct procedures to follow" (147). Goodenough reports that two chiefs from the Mtubatuba Municipality in northern KwaZulu-Natal both decided to run for office in 2000 to help "harmonize the *ubukhosi* system and modern democracy" (2002: 145). They both won their elections. Overall, Goodenough's findings in KwaZulu-Natal mirror those from my three case studies.

> There seems to be a good relationship between the traditional leader and elected councilors. This is attributed to a number of things. Firstly, the elected representatives are originally from the area and they have grown up respecting traditional structures and they have an understanding of the historical role of traditional leaders. The leader is the custodian of the land where they can locate development projects,

so without his consent no development can take off. According to inkosi Caiphas Mkwanazi, elected representatives should function as a community-based organizations not as leaders. In this way there would be no tensions regarding the chieftaincy. This has served Khula village well during the transition period. (Goodenough 2002: 150)

The structure of the electoral process from 1996 to 2000 and how this helped to give meaning to the idea of representation is another example of how new norms merged with preexisting ones. Because the elected councilors were elected from a party list through proportional representation, not every chieftaincy—of which there are 280 in KZN—had an elected councilor. Theoretically, however, each elected councilor represented every person who happened to live under the jurisdiction of one of the seven regional councils (see map 5). Thus, even though not every chieftaincy may have had its "own" elected councilor, every area should have been represented by one of the elected councilors, who perhaps lived in a nearby area. In most cases, however, elected councilors chose not to visit areas they were not from because they believed they lacked the authority to do so without the permission of the chief. The fact that many elected councilors were unwilling to cross the existing chieftaincy boundaries, even though they were the elected representatives of people from numerous chieftaincies, highlights the importance of the preexisting tribal authority boundaries.

For example, one of the URC elected councilors who lived in Mvuzane believed it was inappropriate and dangerous for him to do work in other areas. Technically, Vusi Chamane represented the entire URC, which consisted of 1.5 million people and 21,000 square kilometers.[43] Obviously, representing such a large area was impossible, and he was forced to make decisions as to which communities he would expend his resources for. Even though he was born and raised in a tribal authority area adjacent to Mvuzane and had personal connections with the chief and *izinduna* in this area (his father is an *induna* there), he refused to work outside Mvuzane. While initially he tried to coordinate projects for both areas, he admitted that the traditional leaders and the community in Mvuzane could not understand why he was helping other communities when there was so much to be done in Mvuzane. More importantly, the people of Mvuzane and the chief and *izinduna* considered Vusi to be their councilor, and Vusi likewise would often characterize himself as "Mvuzane's representative." Even the chief occasionally referred to Vusi as "his" councilor, such as when he told the community

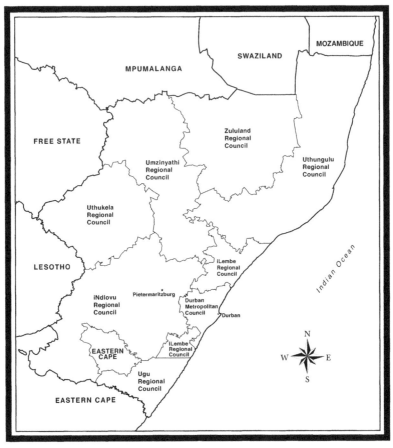

MAP 5. *KwaZulu-Natal Regional Councils (1996–2000). Map designed by Em Hansen Trent and courtesy of the KwaZulu-Natal Department of Local Government and Traditional Affairs.*

at a meeting that he sent "his councilor to Richard's Bay to ask about money."[44] Likewise, the elected councilor who lived in the neighboring chieftaincy of Kholweni concentrated her time on projects for this one area and rarely visited other tribal authorities.

Thus, the chiefs, *izinduna,* communities, and even the regional councils expected elected councilors to work in their home areas. For many, this was a difficult decision as they realized that they technically "represented" an entire region. But because regional council projects were allocated to individual tribal authorities, and only a small minority of the total number of tribal authorities received projects in a given year, elected councilors were forced by circumstance to lobby for specific projects for their own tribal authority.[45] In addition, as I mentioned above, many elected councilors had serious reservations about entering communities where they were not known by the chiefs, the *izinduna*, or the community at large. Elected councilors were hesitant to enter other communities, as the chief and *izinduna* in these areas would be suspicious and consider the elected councilor a stranger to the community (Khandlhela 1998: 8). Thus, there was a high degree of pressure to work only with one's own chief and his communities, even though this practice did not fit with official understandings of "representation." Indeed, the personal relationships between the chiefs and the elected councilors described above only served to reinforce this highly exclusive notion of representation.

The Struggle for Equality

While elected councilors and traditional leaders have been able to forge mutually beneficial ties at the local level, how have the interactions between the chieftaincy and elected councilors developed in other arenas? Specifically, to what extent did the authority of the chieftaincy travel to the institutional level of the local government? What meanings were attached to traditional authority at this level? Similarly, to what extent was their position as ex-officio members of the local state translated into more authority at the local level, and what meanings did communities attach to these newly acquired titles?

From the outset of negotiations in 1993, chiefs demanded to be recognized by the constitution and to be a formal tier of local government. Many government and nongovernment officials suggested that chiefs could not, and should not, be members of formal government at any level, as this would expose them to vigorous debates and "political decision making"—activities that were not becoming of a traditional leader. Some even suggested that chiefs would *lose* authority in the local areas if they were members of local governments.[46] Indeed, some traditional leaders have made this argument as well. Billy Sekwati, king of the Pedi, has stated that "if you as a chief get into politics, you'll lose your respect. People can just chase you there and throw stones at your door if they don't want something. Because you'll be just like any other councilor" (Oomen 2005: 147). As demonstrated above, however, this has not been the case, and chiefs and *izinduna* have maintained their authority at the local level despite their close relationship with local government.

Given the inability of local government to exercise social control in the rural areas, and the negative perceptions people have of local government at the local level, we might expect chiefs to be willing to abandon their place in this institution. This has not been the case, however. According to many chiefs, their authority would be threatened if they were not part of local government (Oomen 2005; Goodenough 2002).

Unlike at the local level, however, most chiefs had very little decision-making power in the formal local government structures. For example, in the KwaZulu-Natal Regional Councils from 1996–2000, they were not allowed to vote, and most decisions were made through the executive committee and the sub-standing regional committee rather than through the regional council as a whole. Each of the seven existing regional councils in KZN had an average of 250–300 members and met once every three months. Because of the large number of people on the regional councils, most of the significant decisions were made at the committee level, where even the vast majority of elected councilors had little influence.

Most elected members who were not part of these committees complained that the regional councils did not encourage participation and that decisions were ultimately made by the few councilors who were committee members. In fact, many elected councilors believed that meetings held in the tribal authority or at the regional authority level were in fact more democratic than the regional council meetings. There was little debate of issues, and the council rarely challenged the decisions of the executive committee. In addition, very few individual council members asked questions during the meeting, and when they did, it was often characterized as a point of clarification that subsequently resulted in a brief answer given by the executive committee, and the meeting continued.

The most important decisions concerning the allocation of resources occurred on the committee level. The thirty executive committee seats were allocated on a proportional basis to the different parties and interest groups (these included chiefs, levy payers, and women's representatives). In the URC, where Mvuzane and Kholweni were located, this meant that the IFP occupied a majority of the positions on the committees. There were chiefs who were appointed to the different committees. Obviously, chiefs who occupied such positions were able to influence the decision-making process to a much greater extent than those who were not. In most cases, however, the chiefs who were members of the executive or sub-standing committees were ones who held powerful positions within the preexisting Bantustan system. For example, from 1996 to

2000, there were a total of six chiefs on the URC executive committee. Of the six, two were the chairmen of their respective regional authorities, four were former members of the KwaZulu Legislative Assembly, two were current members of the KwaZulu Natal House of Traditional Leaders, and all had ranking membership on the Inkatha Freedom Party. Thus, it seems that the authority rooted in the former Bantustan system definitely transferred to the new local government institutions.

At the same time, this authority was limited and challenged within the regional councils. While ordinary elected councilors showed the chiefs the same types of respect as they would at the local level,[47] many of the committee members believed that at the regional council meetings, chiefs were their equals. Some even suggested that within local government, chiefs were inferior to the elected councilors. One chairman of a regional council explained it in this way: "[I]n the Uthungulu meetings and with development they are ordinary people and the chairman is the boss but when the meeting is over, he is their subject again. It is not easy for some of them to get this and there is tension."[48] This was indeed the case as chiefs did not conceptualize any boundaries to their authority and were not as willing to make these types of distinctions. The issue for many within the regional councils was the extent to which "traditional authority" meant the same thing at the official meetings and on committees as it did at the local level.

This tension between chiefs and elected councilors manifested itself in different ways at the meetings. First, the configuration of space at the meeting itself de-emphasized the special status of chiefs. The executive committee sat at the head table on a raised platform. Below them, there were long tables, with folding chairs on each side where the other members sat. Members were divided into different groups (political party, traditional leaders, levy payers, and the women's interest group) and sat in certain sections designated by different colored ribbons on the table. The center space, directly in front of the executive committee, was reserved for chiefs. Unlike meetings held at the regional authority or within tribal authorities, chiefs did not sit at the head table, nor were they given the most comfortable chairs. Instead, the executive committee members were the ones who sat in the padded chairs.

Second, during the meeting itself, chiefs largely remained silent, many of them not even looking toward the raised platform, but instead staring across at each other. The chiefs who were not seated on the executive committee never once spoke or participated in other ways. Again, this was different from how chiefs behaved at regional authority or tribal authority meetings, where they set the agenda, led the discussions, and often talked amongst themselves, laughing and poking fun at each other.

Unlike at the local level, where chiefs were active participants in all aspects of community life, at this level, they were content with simply watching and listening. Some chiefs suggested that they attended these meetings just to make sure that decisions taken concerning their areas were acceptable.[49] In fact, when nongovernmental organizations came to the regional council meetings to propose a particular development project, the chiefs usually refused to ask questions or otherwise participate. One representative from an NGO stated that chiefs purposely did not pay attention at the regional council meetings so that they could then insist, after the meeting, that any proposal be discussed again at the next regional authority meeting. It was only in this forum that they provided the necessary approval for any projects. In this vein, the NGO representative commented that the chiefs "do not use the Regional Council for what it is intended" and only wanted to supervise the actions of elected councilors—"for them, the main decision-making bodies are still the tribal authorities and regional authorities."[50]

It was clear that the authority of chiefs was more contested within the regional councils than at the local level. Within this formal local government arena, there were serious egalitarian pressures. Elected councilors were more likely to treat traditional leaders as equals and to exert their democratic authority. Except for those chiefs who occupied elite positions in other traditional institutions, most chiefs were relegated to the position of quiet observer. There was no doubt that the local government elites, those who occupied positions on the committees, attempted to limit the influence of traditional authority at meetings. As this was a sensitive issue, these boundaries were not discussed explicitly with chiefs but were invoked in other ways. For their part, chiefs treated the meetings as a necessary inconvenience and redirected important policy decisions to a forum where they feel more secure.[51]

At the same time, there was no indication, from chiefs or from local communities, that it was inappropriate for chiefs to sit on these councils. When this issue was raised during the debate over local government, some analysts argued that it would be "undignified" for chiefs to be exposed to the rough and tumble world of local political decision making (Butler 1997; CASE/AFRA 1998). In the midst of the debate over this issue, others suggested that chiefs would "destroy themselves" if they continued to serve on local government.[52] Sometimes these warnings were rooted in misunderstandings as to how decision making worked in the rural areas, not to mention how the process worked at the local government level. More importantly, such an argument ignores the fact that the boundaries of what is considered dignified and proper for the chieftaincy are not static but dynamic. For example, one woman who worked for a nongovernmental organization active in the chieftaincy areas stated that if they served on local government they could "no longer seek the advice from elders or others [for decisions] as in the regional council [decisions] were expected to be made quicker [than in the tribal authority areas]."[53] Instead, decision making within the chieftaincy was increasingly done in conjunction with previous excluded groups such as youth and women. While regional council meetings rivaled "traditional" meetings in their sheer length, they did not offer as much opportunity for debate and discussion as local-level meetings.

Also, there were not many people in the rural areas who argued that the dignity of the chiefs was negatively affected through their participation on local government. First, a majority of the people in the rural areas did not even know that their chief was a member of the local government institution. Except for those advisors who were close to the chief and those people who regularly attended the meetings, many people were surprised to learn that their chief was a member. While most people thought that it would be a good thing if he were a member, mainly because they believed this would make it easier for the community to acquire development projects, others suggested that he did not need to have a say on URC as "Vusi is there as *his* representative"[54]— highlighting yet again the contested notion of representation at the local level. Very few people suggested that it was undignified for the chief to take part in local government decision making, and interestingly, a large proportion of the informants stated it would be good if the chief were to run for political office so as to be closer to government, and thus acquire more development projects.

For their part, at community meetings, traditional leaders very rarely mentioned that they were part of local government. While it was not treated as a secret, it was also something that never appeared to be important enough for the chief to tell the people about. This may explain why so few of the informants in Mvuzane and Kholweni knew that their chiefs were members of the URC. As was pointed out above, the ineffectiveness of local government was often used as a way for both chiefs and *izinduna* to deflect criticism and blame at the local level. Thus, for this reason, it was not surprising they did not mention their presence in the institution. But the position of the chief in local government also worked to his benefit. In those areas where local government was working much more efficiently (usually in areas close to urban centers), people identified much more readily with the institution of local government, and the chief stressed that his role on the government helped to bring resources.

With respect to whether chiefs *should* have a say in local government decision making, an overwhelming number of people insisted that they must have this power. This sentiment was based on a number of factors, such as the need for unity and harmony, the fact that chiefs "own" the land, the fact that chiefs were the leaders of the community, the ability for the chiefs to have access to new government channels, and the persistent fear that "chaos" would result if chiefs were not allowed to participate. There was an obvious connection that was made between the day-to-day interactions between traditional leaders and elected councilors and the maintenance of unity and harmony. As for the fear that chiefs would lose dignity if they participated in local government institutions, it appeared that the loss of dignity was more often correlated with inaction and perceived laziness rather than partaking in local government decisions.

The Weak-State Thesis and Ximba Tribal Authority

The blurring of authority between traditional leaders and elected councils might be expected in places like Mvuzane and Kholweni, where the local government is relatively weak. But how did people understand authority in a place like Ximba, where the local government had many more resources at its disposal and could more effectively implement development projects? While the weak-state thesis assumes that citizens might become less attached to the chieftaincy where there is a greater government presence, the findings from Ximba challenge this hypothesis.

For appreciation of the local dynamics in Ximba, some important differences between URC and the Durban Metro must be highlighted. In 1996, when the URC was established, it encompassed an extremely large area, with over one million people and close to seventy tribal authority areas. There were no major cities within its jurisdiction, and most of its residents lived in rural areas that before 1994 were part of the KwaZulu Bantustan. In 1998–99, the entire URC budget consisted of R110,832,958 (approximately $18.5 million).[55] The most desired development projects were the water projects, but these were difficult to fund in large quantities because they were expensive. Thus, in many cases, tribal authorities received funding for less expensive, and less desired, projects such as community centers and sports fields. For example, in 1998–99, URC allocated R53,816,305 (approximately $8.9 million) for development projects. Of this amount, only R15,500,000 (approximately $2,500,000) was appropriated for twenty-four water projects (*Ezimoti*, February 1999: 8). In the 1999–2000 financial year, the URC sponsored a total of thirty-seven projects totaling approximately R16,000,000 ($2.6 million) for the seventy tribal authority areas falling under its jurisdiction (Uthungulu Regional Council 1999–2000).

The comparison with the Durban Metro Municipality (Durban Metro), where Ximba Tribal Authority was located during this period, is striking. Rather than encompassing seventy tribal authority areas, the Durban Metro had only three in its jurisdiction from 1996 to 2000.[56] It was approximately 2,300 square kilometers in size and had a total population of over three million (Republic of South Africa 2001a). For the most part, those living within the Durban Metro were in urban or peri-urban environments, and only a small percentage lived in the types of rural areas that characterized Mvuzane or Kholweni. For example, in 1996, while just over 7 percent of those in the Durban Metro lived in "traditional dwellings," over 60 percent of those in the URC did so (Republic of South Africa 2001a). In 1996, it was estimated that it had an annual budget of R4.5 billion (approximately $750 million). In addition, not only did more people have access to basic services such as clean water, electricity, and telephones in 1996, the Durban Metro was able to support many more development projects between 1996 and 2000 than the URC. More recently, in 2003, the eThekweni Metro (its name changed in 2000) established a Programme for Amakhosi Support and Rural Development, and the goal was to provide R200 million (approximately $28.5 million) for development in the chieftaincy areas (Beall 2005: 768).

Interestingly, in all three areas a vast majority believed that the most important job for local government was the implementation of development. Thus, the ANC's official policy that has stressed the connection between local government and development appears to have resonated with rural populations. Yet with more resources to distribute and the implementation of a variety of development projects from 1996 to 2000, it was not surprising to find that attitudes about local government were much more positive in Ximba than in Mvuzane or Kholweni. Whereas in Mvuzane and Kholweni, less than 30 percent of the people believed local government helped them improve their lives, nearly 70 percent of the people in Ximba believed this was the case.[57] In addition, many more people in Ximba could correctly identify their elected councilor than those living in Mvuzane and Kholweni. Finally, while over 50 percent believed that their lives had improved since 1994 in Ximba, fewer than 20 percent shared this view in Mvuzane and Kholweni.[58]

These positive attitudes about local government, however, did not result in less affinity toward the chieftaincy. Indeed, the belief that the chieftaincy should continue in the future was just as intense in Ximba as it was in Mvuzane, and the notion that disharmony and division would result if the chieftaincy were to disappear was just as prevalent as well. Not only did those living in Ximba believe that the chieftaincy should have a say on local government issues and on development issues, very few identified the elected councilor as the leader in the community. In fact, of the three case studies, the percentage of respondents who named the elected councilor as the leader in Ximba was only 3.8 percent[59]—compared to 4.5 percent in Mvuzane[60] and 9.2 percent in Kholweni.[61]

These attitudes suggest that the chieftaincy has remained important in Ximba despite the fact that local government has demonstrated greater capacity. At the same time, people in Ximba attached an additional significance to the chieftaincy that was not apparent in Mvuzane and Kholweni. Specifically, there were many more people who talked openly about the responsibilities the traditional leaders had for the "protection of culture" and connection with the ancestors. When I started my research in the rural areas I was keenly interested in the ways the chieftaincy might utilize culture to maintain legitimacy. Instead, I found traditional leaders and local populations much more interested in elections, local government, and development. Yet the conversations I had with people about culture, land distribution, the ancestors, or even the importance of the king revealed that these issues were not as important as others. The exception to this was Ximba, where people were much more inclined to discuss the supernatural powers of chiefs, the importance of King Zwelethini for Zulu unity, and the important responsibilities that the chieftaincy has to promote Zulu culture. This was all the more striking given the fact that Ximba was the least rural area of the three case studies.

To understand these attitudes, it is important to situate Ximba into the broader sociopolitical context that emerged in the early 1990s. In an attempt to mobilize Zulu support before the 1994 elections, the

ANC decide to celebrate Shaka Day in Ximba in 1993 (Mathieson and Atwell 1998: 113). Shaka Day, which was celebrated in the KwaZulu Bantustan each September 24 during apartheid, was a day dedicated to the memory of Shaka and to the promotion of the Zulu identity. Until 1993, Inkatha would lead this celebration in Umlazi, a Durban township, and at Shaka's grave in Stanger (114). Given that the Mlaba chiefs had resisted colonialism and apartheid from the beginning and belonged to the ANC since 1912, the decision to have this celebration in Ximba made historical and political sense. To make the event more multicultural, and thus more consistent with the ANC's principle of non-racialism, it was renamed "Heroes Day" and recognized not only Shaka but also the Xhosa and Basotho monarchies (117).

Rather than promoting cultural diversity, however, the event focused exclusively on the Mlaba clan, chief Mlaba, and thus, the local Ximba identity. For the ten thousand people who were in attendance, chief Mlaba's speech was the most anticipated part of the ceremony. In his speech, while he offered a version of Zulu history and culture that was distinct from Inkatha's, he also reinforced the notion that Zulu identity was rooted in the notion that "a chief is a chief through the people" (Mathieson and Atwell 1998: 120). Even though the ANC did not celebrate Shaka Day in 1994, many of the respondents I met in Ximba told me that the community sponsored unofficial Shaka Day events each September 24.[62] There were also those who told us that King Zwelethini would often visit their area on this day.

These findings suggest a certain amount of "retraditionalization" occurring in Ximba that is consistent with Oomen's (2005) analysis of chiefs in the Northern Province. The fact that this process has unfolded in Ximba, as opposed to Mvuzane and Kholweni, is definitely correlated with the ANC's attempt in the early 1990s to connect with rural KwaZulu-Natal. It also raises the possibility, however, that cultural practices might become more important for local populations, as well as for the legitimacy of the chieftaincy, in areas where there has been more successful implementation of development. At the very least, the degree to which the people in Ximba associate their chieftaincy with the protection of culture, as well as with the delivery of development, highlights the blending together of different sources of legitimacy.

With respect to the weak-state thesis, when compared to Mvuzane and Kholweni, the Ximba case study provides an important example of how the chieftaincy adapts to the presence of more effective state institutions. There is no doubt that those living in Ximba relied upon the local government for their development needs and that the chieftaincy was less involved in this process than in Mvuzane and Kholweni. Despite the local government's performance, the chieftaincy remained central to the residents of Ximba because of its ability to provide unity and harmony in the midst of political, economic, and social changes. The ways in which its authority overlapped with local government was different than in Mvuzane and Kholweni, but nonetheless, Ximba has managed to adapt to the new political environment.

THE ONGOING STRUGGLE FOR HEGEMONY

In official documents, many policymakers assume that the legitimacy of local government will be rooted in its ability to represent the people through elections, its ability to implement development projects, and the fact that it will be the institution closest to the people. An examination of the meanings people attach to local government and the linkages that have been made between chiefs and elected councilors since 1996 reveals that politics at the local level has developed in ways that contradict many of these assumptions.

The establishment of new local government boundaries fails to lessen the meaningfulness of those preexisting tribal authority boundaries. Rather than transform people's understanding of the political landscape, the new boundaries are simply superimposed over the old ones, which leads to confusion at the local level. In the midst of this confusion, many people look to traditional leaders to provide order, harmony, and unity, which only enhances the moral legitimacy of the chieftaincy. Added to this confusion is the fact that most people in KwaZulu-Natal have had very few positive experiences with local government institutions. Even in Ximba, most people associate "local government" with the "elected councilor." The relationships that traditional leaders form with the elected councilors only complicates understandings of authority, and most people still believe their chiefs are the leaders of the community and that elected councilors should respect the wishes of the chiefs. One of the results of this process is that it fundamentally alters the nature of democratic representation and what it means to be "represented." More importantly, for many people in the rural areas their first experience with local-level representation was not one that inspired confidence or trust in the newly established democratic institutions.

Finally, while the chieftaincy provides leadership and is the site for governance, people conceptualize local government as simply a site where development funds are available for the community and elected councilors as those responsible to get those funds. In this way, the legitimacy of local government is linked to the ability to deliver development and not to the fact that it is a democratic institution. How to get these funds, however, remains a mystery to most of the population, which leads to confusion and frustration. The chieftaincy, on the other hand, is the central site of decision making even though most people recognize it does not have the resources to implement major development projects. For much of the local population, local government is too distant to enable any meaningful participation. It seems plausible that this could change in the future as people learn more about local government and as local government has access to more resources, but the case of Ximba cautions against the correlation between the strength of local government and the legitimacy of the chieftaincy.

The struggles that have ensued since the early 1990s have transformed both the chieftaincy and state institutions. Neither has yet to achieve complete hegemony in the rural areas, and it is likely that these struggles will continue, perhaps in different ways, with the establishment of the permanent local government institutions in 2000. These struggles are not new to rural South Africa, however, and the question of whether the chieftaincy is under local government or vice versa will not be answered for some time (Crais 2003b: 1047). Still, the chieftaincy has seemingly withstood the first wave of institutional change at the local level, and the networks the chieftaincy has formed over the last five years, and the lessons learned, will add another dimension to any future attempts of reform. The ultimate irony may be that while many government and nongovernment officials spent the first five years of democratic rule debating the appropriate role for chiefs and *izinduna,* these leaders have been expanding their authority and making crucial linkages with the local state that may prove difficult to completely undo in the future.

THE CHIEFTAINCY AND DEVELOPMENT

SIX

Expanding the Parameters of Tradition

Inkosi is trying. The government is doing nothing. Yes [inkosi should be involved in development], though nothing is happening. We depend on the inkosi in all our needs.

Inkosi is not used to doing this [development]. Some trying now. Educated people need to do things [with development]. No [inkosi should not have a say on development]. [They] need education. Inkosi likes changes but does not know how.

In former times, people did not know anything about development until a few years back. They had no problem with the life they had until this idea of development came.

One of the most critical issues for those living in the former Bantustan areas is the implementation of rural development projects. Given the devastating development policies during apartheid, this is not surprising. What I did not expect, however, was the extent to which those living in these areas expected that the chieftaincy should be actively involved in the rural development process. How traditional leaders have responded to these expectations and how local populations evaluate the performance of traditional leaders concerning development is the central focus of this chapter. It is important to point out that the local dynamics I explore here took place in 1998–99, which was well before the passage of the TLGF Act (2003) and the Communal Land Act (2004); thus, the development function of the chieftaincy was not formally defined or proscribed. In different ways, each of these acts has formally entrenched the chieftaincy into the development process even further than was the case in 1998–99. This is important because before the passage of these acts it was assumed that the issue of rural development was beyond the official jurisdiction of the chieftaincy and that its role with respect to development would be minimal (Republic of South Africa 1998b). For a variety of reasons, this has not been the case. Instead, traditional leaders have sought to expand their authority over development even though it is an issue that appears unrelated to their traditional responsibilities.

DEVELOPMENT IN RURAL SOUTH AFRICA: RISING EXPECTATIONS AND MIXED RESULTS

The promise of development and the establishment of a better life for all have been staples of the ANC's political rhetoric since the transition period.[1] Such promises, however, have never been simply about providing much-needed services to those who were disadvantaged during apartheid. Instead, the delivery of development has been one of the crucial components of the ANC's understanding of democracy in South Africa. Nelson Mandela's remarks during his first State of the Nation speech in 1994 made it clear that democracy in South Africa encompassed much more than the so-called first generation rights:

> Our definition of the freedom of the individual must be instructed by the fundamental objective to restore the human dignity of each and every South African. This requires that we speak not only of political freedoms. My government's commitment to create a people-centered society of liberty binds us to the pursuit of the goals of freedom from want, freedom from hunger, freedom from deprivation, freedom from ignorance, freedom from suppression and freedom from fear. These freedoms are fundamental to the guarantee of human dignity. They will therefore constitute part of the centrepiece of what this government will seek to achieve, the focal point on which our attention will be continuously focused. The things we have said constitute the true meaning, the justification and the purpose of the Reconstruction and Development Programme, without which it would lose all legitimacy. When we elaborated this Programme we were inspired by the hope that all South Africans of goodwill could join together to provide a better life for all. (1994b)

But to what extent is this rhetoric meaningful to ordinary South African citizens? For many, especially those living in the rural areas, the issues of elections, local government, and development are interrelated. As we have seen, one of the hallmarks of the post-apartheid era has been the general expectation that the political reforms in the early 1990s would bring socioeconomic changes as well. In this way, people in South Africa appear to have adopted an understanding of democracy that encompasses both substantive and procedural dimensions (Africa and Mattes 1996: 6; Mattes 2002: 31). In other words, even though South Africans clearly respect the importance of elections and the protection of rights, they also believe that a successful democracy depends on socioeconomic improvements.

Within government circles, there is a keen understanding that the transformation of state-societal relations is directly related to the effective and rapid delivery of resources.[2] This is especially the case in rural areas, where over half of the population resides in extreme poverty and where development projects were either nonexistent or repressive during the apartheid era (Hendricks 1990; Beinart and Bundy 1987; Yawitch 1981; Bundy 1988). Thus, for state officials, the issue of development is not only about helping people improve their dismal living standards, but also about establishing political authority in large segments of the country where people lack positive experiences with state institutions and officials (Koelble 2005).[3] Indeed, the lack of services such as roads, clean water, electricity, and sanitation directly relates to the state's inability to establish its authority and to provide strategies of survival in the former Bantustan areas (Herbst 2000; Migdal 1988).

The major principles for rural development policy were articulated in the Reconstruction and Development Programme (RDP) outlined by the ANC in 1994. While the RDP was replaced as official government policy in 1996 with the pro-market Growth, Employment, and Redistribution (GEAR) policy, the principles set forth in the RDP continue to shape the national political rhetoric as well as local understandings of development. According to this document, central to the transformation process are the following themes: establishing a people-driven development program where civil society can emerge, the democratization of both the local state and society, the decentralization of power to local communities through development committees, and the inclusion of previously excluded groups, most notably women and youth. Nelson Mandela constantly mentioned these goals during his presidency, and President Mbeki rarely missed an opportunity to touch on these imperatives as well.[4]

The ANC has responded to the development challenges in the rural areas with two national policies—the Integrated Sustainable Rural Development Programme (ISRDP) and Project Consolidate. The ISRDP targets thirteen rural development nodes, and Project Consolidate has been expanded to include a large number of municipalities. Both of these policies focus on the lack of capacity of local municipalities to deliver development projects (Makgetla 2007: 160). Despite this focus on capacity building at the local level, many municipalities remain unable to address development effectively. According to the DPLG statistics in 2005, of the 284 existing municipalities, only 81 were able to provide sanitation to 60 percent of their residents, and only 129 were able to provide water to 60 percent of their residents (South African Institute of Race Relations 2006: 551; Atkinson 2007: 60).

At the same time, the ANC's embrace of neo-liberal economic policy with the adoption of GEAR in 1996 meant that the government focused on reducing government spending to reduce deficits. The result was that beginning in the late 1990s, the National Treasury began to cut national spending around 1 percent per year. This had a dramatic impact on the percentage of the national budget that went to local governments for development projects. While local governments received 3.7 percent of the national budget in 1997, they received less than 3 percent in subsequent years until 2002. As Makgetla notes, the result of these cuts was that "the national subsidy to municipalities fell almost 50 per cent in real terms" (2007: 160).

Given the lack of capacity of local government and the budget cuts, it is not surprising that the results have been uneven in the rural areas, where approximately 70 percent of South Africa's poor live (Integrated Sustainable Rural Development Strategy, November 17, 2000). A comparative analysis of development statistics as they relate to the entire country, the urban areas, and select rural areas demonstrates these discrepancies (see table 6.1). For example, Statistics South Africa 2001 Census data reported that 72 percent of all South Africans have access to water in their dwelling, in their yard, or at a tap within 200 meters of their home. More importantly, it also reported that only 7.5 percent were forced to get water from rivers or stagnant water supplies. Similarly, it also shows that 70 percent of all South Africans used electricity for their lighting, while only 23 percent used candles. Finally, according to the countrywide statistics, a majority of South Africans have access to municipal refuse removal (57 percent) and flush toilets (52 percent). These statistics show significant gains from comparable data in 1996 and definitely support the ANC's claims that it has provided services to many citizens since 1994.

Yet, these national statistics look much different in the rural areas. What is most striking is to compare the development indicators between the Durban Metropolitan Municipality, where Ximba Tribal Authority is located, and the Uthungulu District Municipality and the Umlalazi Local Municipality, where the Mvuzane and Kholweni Tribal Authorities are located. Whereas only 7.5 percent of all South Africans use stagnant

TABLE 6.1. Development Comparisons

	South Africa	KwaZulu-Natal	Durban Metropolitan Municipality (Ximba TA)	Uthungulu District Municipality	Umlalazi Local Municipality (Mvuzane TA and Kholweni TA)
RDP/Water	72%	60%	94%	44%	24%
Stagnant/River Water	7.5%	15%	1.5%	31%	46%
Lighting/Electricity	70%	61%	80%	52%	39%
Lighting/Candles	23%	35%	17%	44%	57%
Refuse/Munic	57%	50%	86%	24%	12%
Refuse/Dump	43%	50%	14%	76%	88%
Sanitation/Flush Toliet	52%	41%	64%	25%	15%
Sanitation/Latrine or Dump	40.5%	44%	24%	57%	72%

SOURCE: 2001 Census.

or river water, a total of 31 percent of those in Uthungulu and 46 percent of those in Umlalazi must do so. Similarly, 44 percent of those in Uthungulu and 57 percent of those in Umlalazi still use candles for lighting. And while 76 percent of those in Uthungulu are responsible for disposing of their trash, a staggering 88 percent in Umlalazi are without refuse service. Makgatela's comparison of development data from 2003 between former Bantustan areas and non–former Bantustan areas is consistent with these findings. In his study, he shows that whereas well over 80 percent of the households in the non–former Bantustan areas have electricity for lighting, just over 20 percent of those in the Bantustan areas have access to this service. Similarly, only 20 percent in the Bantustan areas have access to water on site compared to over 80 percent in the non-Bantustan areas (Makgetla 2007: 149). These statistics highlight the extent to which there are still a great number of people who are living without basic services, and thus, without a basic state presence.

These development challenges in the former Bantustan areas affect the authority of the chieftaincy in unanticipated ways. While the 1993 and 1996 constitutions recognize the existence of traditional leaders in a new South Africa, their role concerning the implementation of development is not specifically addressed in these documents. As discussed earlier, the TLGF Act establishes formal linkages between traditional leaders and local government with respect to development. Yet the idea that traditional leaders should be involved with the implementation of development was not always official government policy. For example, during the 1990s, in many of the official government documents it was assumed that traditional leaders would only exercise ceremonial authority and would play a minimal role with respect to development.[5] In addition, the LG White Paper suggested that their role would be one of a gate-keeper and nothing more. At the same time, the LG White Paper noted there were "natural capacities" for both traditional leaders and democratic institutions that needed to be recognized for this interaction to be constructive (Republic of South Africa 1998b: 78). The implication was that while the areas of conflict resolution and maintenance of law and order were traditional functions, other areas—such as bringing water, roads, and electricity—were beyond the traditional responsibilities of the chieftaincy and should fall within the realm of state institutions.

In a similar vein, a KwaZulu-Natal policy document for 1998 stated that while "traditional leaders need to be drawn into development so that they can play a pro-active role, . . . they should not be directly responsible for development" as this may force them to "assume a party political profile, and therefore undermine their capacity to express the common view, or articulate a traditional perspective" (KwaZulu-Natal Legislative Assembly 1998, *An Integrated Rural Development White Paper for KwaZulu-Natal*: v and 21 [hereafter IRD-WP]). In addition, it was feared that "non-delivery . . . [would] likely . . . undermine the legitimacy of customary systems." To avoid this outcome, government officials were admonished to be "sensitised to indigenous value system and knowledge, to enable them to interact meaningfully and positively with traditional communities." The document also noted that the most important institution of development in these areas would be the development committees that "provide a link between local government and traditional authorities" (IRD-WP: 21–22). Thus, on the one hand, there was the argument that traditional leaders lacked the natural capacities to deliver development, and on the other, there was the suggestion that traditional leaders might *lose* legitimacy if they were involved in development due to the fact that they would be forced to take sides or would not have the resources to deliver.

Despite these different concerns, during the late 1990s there seemed to be an overall consensus that while traditional leaders were to be a part of the development process, their role was secondary to that of local government and development committees. Even though the TLGF Act seems to alter this policy at the margins, government officials have sought to keep the boundaries between the two distinct. For example, in the 2005–2006 Department of Local Government and Local Affairs Budget Speech, Minister Mabuyakhulu stated that "we continue to build the capacity of Amakhosi to deal with issues of *conflict and community complaints* . . . [and to establish] synergistic relationships between the institution of Traditional Leaders and Local Government to ensure smooth service delivery on the ground *without any territorial contestation*" (2005: 12; emphasis mine). Thus, there is a clear sense among the national and provincial officials that the chieftaincy is not responsible for delivering development and that this should be the function of local government.

One of the problems for South African government officials, however, is that local communities strongly disagree with these assumptions, and they want their traditional leaders to be active in the development process. A few examples from Mvuzane, Kholweni, and Ximba highlight this point. With respect to the role of traditional leaders addressing the community's needs, about 80 percent were of the opinion that traditional leaders should have a say on whether development projects were brought to the community.[6] When asked why he should have a say on development, 45 percent stated because he was their leader, and another 25 percent stated that it was his land. It is also notable that 30 percent of those interviewed in the three case studies were of the opinion that development was the most important job for traditional leaders, second only to resolving disputes (35 percent).[7] In addition, approximately 50 percent believed that their chief had been actively trying to get development to their areas since 1994. Reflecting the lack of development initiatives during apartheid, an overwhelming 76 percent stated that before 1994, their chief was not trying to get development.

In some cases, people remarked that the chief's role consisted of more than simply providing approval as to whether development projects could be initiated in the community (i.e., a gatekeeper role). Rather, it was often suggested that he should be *actively* trying to get more resources by any means necessary. In many cases, people suggested that this was one of the most important duties of traditional leaders. Moreover, it was common to find that people who lived in areas with less development became jealous of those who lived in areas with more development. Put simply, people desperately want development to occur, and there has been a general rise in their expectations since 1994. Because of this, many believed that traditional leaders should be doing more with respect to development rather than less. To meet these rising expectations, people in Mvuzane, Kholweni, and Ximba stated that the chief should do whatever he can to get into contact with government institutions. In contradiction to the view that chiefs should not be involved in politics, an overwhelming number of people (60 percent) argued that their chief should run for office so that he would be closer to government departments, and thus, have better access to resources.[8] There was generally no feeling that the chief was too dignified, or that it would somehow be disrespectful for him, to run for office. Instead, if becoming an elected leader would enable a traditional leader to have access to more development resources, then he should do so for the good of the community.

Research in other rural areas suggests that these findings are not unique. For example, in Nzimakwe Tribal Authority, which is located in southern KwaZulu-Natal in the Ugu District Municipality, the community chose to allow a woman to serve as acting chief after her husband died, because she was the most qualified to access development projects. One traditional councilor remarked, "[W]e are lucky to have her as our leader because she is not only clever, but she is fearless and works hard to help everyone in the Nzimakwe community. She has brought development" (Goodenough 2002: 154). Other residents commented that "much of *inkosi* Nzimakwe's popularity is the result of her involvement in development in her traditional area" and that "the only structure that has spearheaded development and service delivery is the traditional structure" (Goodenough 2002: 155–56). Oomen finds similar dynamics in the Northern Province in three tribal authority areas that were previously part of the Lebowa Homeland. In particular, she demonstrates that the performance of traditional leaders with respect to development is important for their legitimacy (2005: 195–96).

These attitudes need to be situated in a historical context as well. As was discussed in the previous chapter, most respondents suggested that their traditional leaders had not been involved with development issues before 1994. Given the lack of resources made available for development during apartheid, this is not surprising. These attitudes, of both local populations and traditional leaders, have definitely shifted over the last fifteen years. More importantly, the attitudes concerning traditional leaders and development that are currently held in rural areas are at odds with the assumption that they should be nothing more than ceremonial leaders or gatekeepers. Even though the implementation of development projects has changed since the introduction of GEAR, the RDP's vision of a people-centered, decentralized, inclusive development process has affected the dynamics of local level politics to a significant degree. In fact, these ideas are continually reshaped to coexist with local political norms.

OLD BOUNDARIES AND NEW INSTITUTIONS: MAKING DEVELOPMENT COMMITTEES FIT AT THE LOCAL LEVEL

Recognizing the importance of development committees is crucial to understanding the development process in rural South Africa. These committees are ubiquitous in the rural areas, and many were established even prior to formal local government institutions. By most accounts, they became much more prevalent in the rural areas after the 1994 elections, with most being formed between 1994 and 1997 (Oomen 2005). At this time, the ANC encouraged communities to establish such communities in order to reinvigorate civil society so that development would be "people-driven" (African National Congress 1994). In terms of the development process, they were designed to be the crucial link between rural communities and the government.

For example, consider the case of Mvuzane, where the first development committees were formed in 1994. In the initial stages of this process, chief Biyela took a very proactive stance. Not only did he approve the creation of such committees, but he also helped to arrange meetings where the members of the committee were elected. While most people in the community attributed the creation of the development committees to chief Biyela, this was clearly not the case. In fact, it was actually Vusi Chamane, the person who would be elected local councilor in 1996, who first suggested the idea. Of course, he approached the chief and sought his permission to establish the committees, and the chief agreed. For most people in Mvuzane, this was the proper way to handle this issue. Because the chief was considered to be "the leader of this land," it was only appropriate for him to have the final say on the introduction of any new organizations in the area.[9] This was the case in Kholweni and Ximba as well, where the chiefs were involved with the establishment of development committees.

Indeed, this has been the case in many other areas as well. In the Nzimakwe Tribal Authority, there was a similar dynamic in which the Nzimakwe Development Committee, of which the chief was the leader, was responsible for making all development decisions in the community. Elected councilors were expected to report directly to this body before making decisions concerning development (Goodenough 2002: 156). Similarly, Oomen notes occasions where the authority of the chieftaincy merged with development committees. For example, in Hoepapkranz, the chief's son chaired the African National Congress committee and the development committee. Likewise, the head of the local civics organization was also the chair of the tribal council. Thus, it was common to find different leaders wearing many different hats at the local level, which resulted in forum shopping as people sought out the institution that was most likely to provide them with the services they desire (Oomen 2005: 174).

While the manner in which traditional leaders have successfully become the unofficial, yet de facto, leaders of the development committees has been discussed in the literature,[10] what has been given less attention is how the committees themselves are constructed so as to fit within the existing local political boundaries—in both a normative and an institutional sense.

To understand the way in which development committees were situated into the existing political space, it is important to recall the structure of tribal authorities in KwaZulu-Natal, where power is decentralized. Every tribal authority area, such as Mvuzane, was subdivided into smaller units that were referred to as wards and that were under the jurisdiction of a particular *induna*.[11] In each ward, there was one development committee, which was responsible for securing development projects for its particular area. For example, in Mvuzane Tribal Authority, there were fifteen different wards, and each ward had an officially established development committee that was supposed to meet on a regular basis. Although precise population data on these tribal authority wards are not known, it was most likely that each ward consisted of approximately one thousand people. I have not located an official map where the names of these wards were recorded, and yet the boundaries of the wards were well known to everyone in the community, and they were considered very important. In fact, most people would interact with their *induna* on a more frequent basis than with their chief, and the *induna* was the first person they would contact for land and for dispute resolution. These wards formed a part of a political landscape that was virtually invisible to outsiders but that was extremely important to the daily lives of most people.

Each ward committee consisted of approximately six to fifteen people who were elected for a one-year term. Members of the committees did not receive any compensation for their service, but it was considered an important position of authority within the community. While committees were supposed to meet once a week, in reality they met much less frequently. Each committee chose a chairman, vice-chairman, secretary, and treasurer. In addition, each member of the committee was appointed to a particular portfolio and was responsible for locating funding for specific projects. The different types of portfolios would include water, roads, schools, or electricity. In some cases, development committees even drafted their own constitutions that established the responsibilities of the committee and each of its officers.

Without fail, each ward *induna* was appointed to the ward development committees as an ex-officio member. While technically the *induna* attended meetings only as an observer, in actuality, the *induna* was often involved in the decision-making processes of the committee as well, especially if the committee happened to secure funding for a development project (which was extremely rare). The most common refrain in Mvuzane was that the *izinduna* were required to consult the committee before they made any decisions with respect to development. Of course, the dynamics in each ward varied depending on the personality of the *induna*.

Each ward development committee elected one to two of its members to serve on the tribal authority–wide development committee that was referred to in Mvuzane as the working committee. On this committee, the chief served as an ex-officio member, as did each of the *izinduna* from the different wards. The meetings of the working committee always took place at the tribal court, and the chief was usually the one who was in charge of the meetings. As with the ward committees, the working committee also elected a chairman, vice-chairman, secretary, and treasurer, and different people were assigned particular portfolios of which they served as the "ministers." Whereas the ward committees were supposed to provide the necessary link between the community and development decisions, the working committee was supposed to provide a link between the community and government or nonprofit organizations that could provide resources as well as provide an arena where the concerns of each of the wards could be addressed.[12] In Mvuzane, Kholweni, and Ximba, the chief, or the representative of the chief, had a great deal of influence on the working committee. Theoretically, each of the development committees were supposed to be working toward acquiring funding for their ward, but in reality, even if a ward was able to find funding, it could not implement the project without the permission of the working committee, and more specifically, the chief.[13] People's attitudes on the effectiveness of the development committees varied depending on whether their specific committee had been able to secure funds. As one person stated quite directly, "Development committees are not helping. They were just elected. They do not even know what to do or what they were elected for."[14] In those cases where people did have positive experiences with the development committees, it was a common refrain that "they cannot do anything without *inkosi*."[15]

What was most revealing was that the development committees were simply superimposed over the existing tribal authority structure, and therefore, they were not really autonomous from the chieftaincy structures at all. The result was that development committees were fully integrated within the preexisting sociopolitical space, and traditional leaders were able to maintain authority over development decisions (MacDonald 1998). This description also highlights the extent to which decision making in Mvuzane, as well as other tribal authorities, was extremely decentralized. Despite many assumptions to the contrary, there was very little evidence that traditional leaders were able to rule their areas in a centralized, absolutist manner. For most local issues, whether they were land issues, conflicts, or permission to conduct a particular ceremony, ordinary people interacted with their *induna* and their traditional councilors far more often than with their chief. One of the consequences of such decentralization was that in the rural areas there was little social space that was not controlled by at least some traditional leaders, whether they were the chief, the *induna,* or the traditional councilor. And rather than operating as autonomous civil society associations at the grassroots level, these committees simply shared this space with *izinduna* and traditional councilors. This made any autonomous activity difficult to initiate or sustain. Thus, rather than feeling threatened by the existence of a new, somewhat alien, structure in the community, most traditional leaders have been able to incorporate them into their preexisting decentralized form of rule.

Nonetheless, the existence of the committees has ignited some changes with respect to the authority of the chieftaincy. These changes, however, have not been what many predicted in the early 1990s. The first point is that development committees actually helped to enhance the authority of the traditional leaders because they provided a means for traditional leaders to take control of the most important issue for most people, even though it might appear that this issue lies outside of the realm of their traditional responsibilities. In Mvuzane and Ximba, the legitimacy of the development committees was interlinked with that of the traditional leaders, and specifically chief Biyela and chief Mlaba. The result was a blurring of authority. For example, when describing the structure and responsibilities of the development committees, most people would bring up the role of the chieftaincy spontaneously: "The Mvuzane Working Committee is looking after the needs of the people. There are two people per ward [who serve on this committee]. [These people] report to the chief's committee and then to the community. The working committee deals with everything which involves the community. It meets once a month. The *inkosi* encourages the committees."[16] A comment from a male pensioner in Ximba highlights this point:

Development is a new thing. This started after 1994 with the new government. Before we were just given things not knowing where they come from. Traditional leaders used to keep law and order only. We knew nothing about development. There is peace in this area. Some of the people in this area come from Mkhizwane area when there was violence. Maybe they like that we are united here.[17]

Specifically in Mvuzane, chief Biyela's pro-development stance sent a message to the community that the traditional leaders wanted to be active players in this new area of concern. In short, he attempted to co-opt a social space that was meant, in theory, to be separate from traditional structures. This process was much easier for the chief to accomplish given the preexisting decentralization of power in the community and the relationship he had with Vusi Chamane. Thus, the chief allowed a new structure to exist while simultaneously incorporating this structure into the preexisting forms of rule. This decision made a great deal of sense given the changing expectations in the rural areas. In fact, it enabled the chief both to legitimate the committees, and thus appear as a friend of development, and also to maintain control over the activities of the committees. The extent to which the chief was able to do this also demonstrates how the gatekeeper theory of chieftaincy authority cannot explain what happens once the traditional leader "opens the gates" to his community. Indeed, it is rare to find a situation where traditional leaders just let things happen in their areas without providing at least minimal oversight.

One of the other important changes that the process of development has initiated is the role of women in community affairs. The establishment of development committees provided a forum where women could demonstrate their decision-making skills and their knowledge about development issues. As mentioned above, women were the majority on most of the ward development committees and on the working committee. At the outset, women played an important role on these committees, and in many cases, occupied positions of leadership. In Mvuzane, as well as in Ximba and Kholweni, the chiefs encouraged the active participation of women on these committees, recognizing they had more experience with development issues than the men did. In fact, during apartheid, women were the catalyst for much of the development that occurred in the rural areas as they sought funding for schools, community gardens, and other income-generating projects. In some cases, the experience women gained while serving on the development committees in the mid-1990s allowed for the possibility of other political opportunities. For example, one of the more active women on the Mvuzane Working Committee was Theodore Xulu. After serving for a number of years on this committee, she was eventually able to make the IFP party list, and she won a seat on the Umlazi local council. While this case was the exception, the women who served on the development committees told us that their experience was invaluable because it enabled them to show the men that there were knowledgeable about development issues and that they should be more involved in local matters.

The development committees also introduced a new form of representation. As was discussed earlier, since 1994 the *izinduna* and traditional councilors in Mvuzane had been elected by the community rather than appointed by the chief. While many members of the community did not identify this change with the establishment of development committees, those who were involved with the development process from the beginning suggested that this was the case. More specifically, many people saw the establishment of development committees as an integral part of the democratic transition and the ability for them to have more of a say in community matters. This new ability to have a say has provided the catalyst to demand the election of the *izinduna* and traditional councilors. In addition, as chief Biyela of Mvuzane remarked, it was no coincidence that all of the newly elected *izinduna* are much younger, more educated, and more willing to advance development than their predecessors.[18] Thus, it appears that there was also pressure for the qualifications for being a traditional leader to change because of the desire to acquire development projects.

The final point is that the chief was able to increase his own authority and legitimacy as he quickly became an important source of information for the community about the development committee, its functions, and its goals. In a social context where new knowledge is equated with power (Gluckman 1940a), the chief immediately enhanced his own authority by being the source of this knowledge rather than at the mercy of others who might have more formal education and governmental connections.[19] While some members of the community have blamed the subsequent failure of the development committees on the perceived lack of education and/or "laziness" of the chief, most people nonetheless acknowledged that the chief has an important role to play in development.

For example, in Mvuzane, just over 90 percent of the respondents stated that the chief should have a say on development projects. This is compared with about 74 percent in Ximba and 77 percent in Kholweni who stated the same. Overall, out of 153 people in all three areas, 125 (82 percent) said the chief should have a say, while only 25 (16 percent) said he should not. In addition, most people said that the reason why the chief should have a say was because he was the leader (46 percent), with the next closest reason being that he controls the land (25 percent). In Mvuzane, the responses were similar, with about 49 percent of the people saying that he should have a say because he was the leader and 30 percent saying he should because he controls the land. This general attitude, which was crucial for the ability of the chief to be authoritative and legitimate with respect to development, was positively influenced by the chief's proactive stance and actions in setting up development committees. In addition, because the development committees were officially separate institutions, distinct from the traditional structures, the traditional leaders can likewise blame the lack of development projects on the "laziness" of the people.

THE IMPLEMENTATION OF DEVELOPMENT PROJECTS: DEVELOPMENT BEFORE POLITICS?

The establishment of development committees has been important for rural areas, but they have largely failed to access development resources. When development committees actually received funding, which was rare, the chieftaincy was always involved with its distribution. During this transitional period (1996–2000), before the establishment of permanent local municipalities in 2000, development projects were usually awarded to tribal authority areas, and the decisions concerning exactly where the project would be implemented was left to the working committee. Thus, after it was announced that a tribal authority would get a particular development project, such as a water project, each *induna* lobbied the chief and the working committee for the project to be implemented in his particular ward. This was always a contentious decision because most water projects at this time would provide water for only around three hundred individuals.

The other issue that arose with the implementation of development projects such as water projects was that the development committee chose certain members of the community to help work on the project, thereby enabling them to earn a salary. In most cases, the *izinduna* had the final say on who was able to work on the project and therefore be paid a salary. Not surprisingly, it was often the case that the committee would decide to offer the *induna* the opportunity to work on the project.

Thus, development projects were often used as important resources to help traditional leaders maintain linkages with the community. Not only could the traditional leaders help maintain certain patron-client relationships by using these new resources, but they could also become sources of wealth in and of themselves. In most cases, traditional leaders utilized the development committees as the medium through which they could exercise control over the allocation of these resources.

An example from Mvuzane helps to highlight this process. After the URC allocated funds for a water project in Mvuzane, it was up to the working committee to decide which ward would receive the project. As table 6.1 indicates, most people in Mvuzane did not have access to either taps or boreholes, and they received their water from the river. In fact, this particular water project was the first one allocated by the URC in Mvuzane, and it was only the second water project that Mvuzane had received since the early 1990s.

Because most people in Mvuzane did not have access to clean water, the decision as to which ward would receive this project was controversial. The working committee decided that the Nyimbitwa ward would receive the water project. This ward was located next to the ward where the chief lived, which fueled suspicions that the chief was trying to improve the homesteads closer to his particular ward at the expense of others. Despite the fact that the *induna* from Nyimbitwa should have been the person most involved in this process, as it turned out, the *induna* from the Mbileni ward, which was where chief Biyela lived, was the *induna* who made decisions concerning who would work and be paid for the labor for the project. The *induna* from Mbileni ward had served as *induna* longer than any other *induna* in Mvuzane, and chief Biyela had appointed him to the position of *induna enkhulu,* which meant he served as acting chief whenever the chief was absent. He was, next to Vusi and the chief himself, one of the most powerful people in the community. The fact that this project was placed next to his ward and that he was able to choose who would work on the project left the impression that the working committee's decision was biased and not fair to the rest of the tribal authority. In fact, many in the community openly asked why Nyimbitwa was receiving the project, because there were many other areas with more serious needs.

Previous research on the influence of traditional leaders on development projects has found that these leaders are important because they provide the project with legitimacy and because they are able to mobilize labor to work on the project (Keulder 1998). While the traditional leaders in Mvuzane did take on these responsibilities, they also were accused—along with members of the ward committee—of manipulating the process for their own gain, or for the gain of their friends.

For example, on the Nyimbitwa water project, most of the people who were chosen to work on the project were members of the ward development committee. In effect, the committee members, with the acquiescence of the *induna,* were able to use the development project as way to secure a part-time job. In the past, the coordinators of the projects would encourage people to donate their time so that the allocated funds could be used to extend the water project to as many people as possible. But because local government sponsored this project, there were funds specifically designated for salaries, and the community was told that they had to find people who would work on the project for pay.

After the project had been operating for about two months, Vusi discovered that the workers were being paid unusually high salaries. He also discovered that the committee had created a few "ghost workers," which enabled them to pay themselves even more money. He discovered this only after the tribal secretary received a check from the local government for her work as "storage keeper" for the project. She had never been appointed to this position, nor was she involved in the project in any way. She told Vusi about this, and he decided to inquire into the matter more with members of the Nyimbitwa ward.

Vusi also learned that rather than holding an election to choose the members of the development committee, the *induna* chose the committee on his own. Because of the way the project was being run, both Vusi and the community more generally were becoming angry and frustrated with the way the committee was implementing the project. In public discussions about this issue, while the behavior of the committee was often raised as an issue, never did members of the community complain, specifically about *induna enkhulu,* despite the fact that everyone realized he was effectively in charge.

In fact, even though Vusi had gathered specific information that implicated the *induna* and the committee for misallocating project funds, he was reluctant to tell the *inkosi* what he had discovered or to confront the *induna enkhulu* and the committee about the issue, as such a confrontation might have damaged his relationship with chief Biyela. Vusi did call a community meeting in Nyimbitwa to discuss the project and to listen to the concerns of those in the area. Before the meeting, he stated that he was in a difficult situation because he did not want to accuse anyone of bad behavior but he was very upset about what was going on. At the meeting, which was attended by about forty community members, the ward development committee, and those working on the project (the *induna enkhulu* was not there), Vusi talked in the abstract about the importance of keeping track of funds, making records that detail expenses, and using as much as the money as possible to extend the project to more homesteads. He stated that in his capacity as local government representative for the area he was responsible for monitoring the project and that he wanted the chairman of the committee to report to him more often about the use of funds. He also told the meeting how he had encouraged people in his area to work for free on the Mvula Trust project. After he spoke, many people at the meeting voiced their own criticisms about the project, and the chairman promised that they would do a better job at keeping the community, and Vusi, informed about how the project was progressing and how the funds were being allocated.

This example is not isolated to Mvuzane; similar dynamics occur in numerous other tribal authority areas.[20] Not only have development committees become integrated into the local power structures of the communities, but they have also become part of the local patronage networks. And because so many people in the community are in need of basic services such as water, electricity, and roads, the decisions made concerning development projects have a heightened political value. This happened even though the chief repeatedly told the committee that development was not a "political" issue (by which he meant that decisions should not be made on the basis of party identification). Or as another chief emphasized: "politics comes after development" (Goodenough 2002: 148). The reality, of course, was that the allocation of resources actually invited politics, and it was not surprising that decisions concerning the distribution of such scarce resources were contentious. In this way, the issues concerning development were inherently political in that they involved local, preexisting power relations that constrained and directed choices.

RESOLVING DEVELOPMENT CONFLICTS: DECIDING WHEN TO DECIDE

With the implementation of development projects, new types of conflicts emerged. These conflicts presented an interesting and novel challenge to traditional leaders, as they were forced to decide whether a particular conflict was within the reach of their jurisdiction or whether the development committees should resolve the conflicts on their own.

Prior to 1994, the functions of traditional leaders were usually limited to issues concerning land allocation, the resolution of community problems, and a host of cultural and/or religious duties. More generally, however, traditional leaders have always been expected to solve community problems (*izinkinga umpakathi*) (Zulu 1984). With the introduction of development projects, however, the definition of "community problems" has expanded to include development issues.

It is undoubtedly the case that local populations have increasingly attached more importance to whether the chief could deliver resources. Obviously, this reality created difficulties for the chieftaincy because development resources were scarce and the chances of acquiring these resources were limited. To address this conundrum, traditional leaders have tried to insulate themselves from any criticism for not delivering resources by simultaneously telling the community that they are in favor of development and that it is up to the development committees and the local government to provide the necessary funds. In this way, traditional leaders have been able to deflect blame and earn praise no matter what actually transpires. This is a difficult stance to take, however, and not all traditional leaders are successful with deflecting blame.[21] Still, as the community leader, and as the person who most people believed should resolve significant conflicts in the community, the traditional leader is the person assumed to be responsible for resolving conflicts involving development projects. But even here, traditional leaders have demonstrated the extraordinary ability to make strategic decisions that will not threaten their status as the community leader and as the symbol of unity.

A comparison of two conflicts that arose in Mvuzane and of the manner in which each was resolved by the chief reveals how chiefs tried to establish their authority over new issues. The first conflict involved a water project sponsored in 1996 by the Department of Water Affairs (DWAF). The ultimate aim of this project was to set up a scheme that would pump water from the Tugela River to the city of Richard's Bay. To do this, the water from the Tugela would have to travel through tributary rivers until it reached its final destination. One of these tributary rivers was the Mvuzane River, which passed directly through Mvuzane Tribal Authority. Before this project was started in 1996, a representative from the DWAF visited each of the tribal authorities affected by this project and asked for the chief's permission to enter his area and do the necessary work. In the case of Mvuzane, as probably was the case in other tribal authorities, the project was allowed to proceed only under the condition that the community would receive direct development benefits from it. For example, DWAF promised that the community would receive additional water supplies—through boreholes and taps—and that certain roads would be tarred and bridges would be built. In addition, DWAF said that the project would also create jobs for people in the community. The project was approved by the chief under these conditions, and it commenced in 1996.

As it turned out, the project did not go according to plan. Rather than provide benefits to the community, it actually did considerable harm. Even where DWAF seemed to have delivered on some of its promises, these were incomplete. For example, portions of the main road were tarred, but just in those sections that needed to be finished in order for the engineers to transport their supplies through Mvuzane. In addition, some bridges were built, but they were built too low so that they were not effective when the water level rose. While electricity poles and lines were installed in certain sections of Mvuzane, these main lines were not connected to any households.[22] Finally, according to chief Biyela and Vusi, no jobs were created as a result of the project.

According to those in the community, the most serious problem with this project, however, was the way in which the water was released from the Tugela River and traveled via the Mvuzane River to Richard's Bay. When the water was released, the Mvuzane River transformed from a small stream into a flowing river. The river reached such depths that it flowed over the bridges onto the roads and fields. People lost their clothes, cows were killed, and children were injured when the water was released. To make matters even worse, the people in the community were never warned as to when this would occur, which led to more anger and frustration.

In addition to the loss of property and some injuries, the project had caused the river water to be much dirtier than in the past. Because most people in Mvuzane did not have access to boreholes or taps, they collected their water from the river. The water was so dirty that it was difficult to use it for washing, and it was dangerous to drink. The community complained to the chief about the water situation, and the chief called a meeting with the representatives of the water project to sort out the problems.[23]

The meeting occurred in February 1999 on an overcast and rainy day. Because the inside of the tribal court was being used for a memorial service, the meeting took place outside, against the wall of the tribal court. Chairs and benches were arranged along the sides of the tribal court so that people would be protected from the rain. The chief, *izinduna,* traditional councilors, Vusi, and the representatives from Mhlatuze Water Board sat at one of the corners of the tribal court so that people could sit next to the two adjoining walls and still be able to see the main participants.[24] There were about sixty to seventy people at the meeting, with approximately half of the people being women. Most of the people were middle-aged adults, between forty-five and sixty. Because the representative from Mhlatuze could not speak Zulu, and only a few people from the community could speak English, a translator was used during the meeting. The translator was someone who worked for the Mhlatuze, and he was not from Mvuzane.

The meeting lasted for about one hour, and chief Biyela was the first person to speak. The chief argued that the promises that were made to the community had been broken and that this was unacceptable. Speaking calmly and not raising his voice, chief Biyela nonetheless made it perfectly clear that he was not pleased with this project: "You did not fulfill your promises. You lied to us . . . we will allow you to continue with the project if you fulfill [your] promises." The chief also told the representative that the community was getting the impression that he and his advisors were not taking care of the people's interest. Thus, not only was the project failing to deliver on its promises, but the community was beginning to blame the chief, as the community leader, for this failure. The chief told the representative that the situation had to be reconciled immediately. He insisted that people should be compensated for their lost property and injuries and that DWAF needed to bring the community water services that were promised to them. The river water, the chief said, was now undrinkable, but the people had no choice but to drink it, and they were getting sick. To emphasize this point, chief Biyela had someone go to the river and bring back a glass full of the water. While the representative was responding to the chief's remarks, the glass of muddy water was placed at the representative's feet. Chief Biyela interrupted the representative and asked him if he wanted to drink this water—to which the representative just shook his head no.

The representative's first point was that the chief and his representatives were doing a "very good job" at representing the community's interests and that the problems associated with the water project were not the fault of the traditional leaders. The problem, he said, was that the funds had not yet been allocated to complete the project. When these funds arrived, he promised that all of the services that had been promised would be provided. This, he stressed for a second time, was not the fault of the chief. He explained that his organization was not involved in the early stages of the project and had only recently been subcontracted by DWAF. Thus, he could not comment on the previous promises that had been made, but he promised that he would look into them. He repeatedly said that it was "sad that in this day and age, that these things happen." He also promised that he would send a letter to DWAF outlining the concerns of the community.

At this point, members of the community were given the opportunity to voice their specific concerns to the representative. Numerous people, both men and women, took the opportunity to offer their complaints—often in impassioned and angry tones. The chief would occasionally interject in a diplomatic fashion to keep the proceedings from becoming too critical, but for the most part, those at the meeting were able to speak their minds. After about forty-five minutes of discussion, Vusi asked to be heard. He was one of the last people to speak. He said that he would like to have a copy of the letter that the Mhlatuze was going to send to DWAF because he wanted to see exactly how the community's concerns were articulated on paper. Also, he wanted the representative to arrange for someone to come out and speak with each of the people who had been injured or who had lost property so that they could be properly reimbursed. Vusi later confessed that while he knew these people would not be compensated, he nonetheless wanted to see how the representative would respond to the request. The representative said he would arrange for someone to come out, and then he left the meeting.

The meeting continued, and other business was discussed. A few minutes later, however, the representative's translator came over to chief Biyela and whispered something in his ear and then left. The chief then said something to Vusi, and Vusi left the meeting to go talk with the representative. Apparently, the translator told the chief that the representative would not be able to send someone out to speak with the injured people, but instead, that he needed to arrange for each of the injured persons to write their complaints down and then send them to Pietermaritzburg, which was over 200 kilometers away. Obviously, this was going to be very difficult to coordinate, and chief Biyela did not feel it was his responsibility to arrange this. As the representative and the translator drove off, the chief made his final remarks on the matter. He said that they had already been lied to again by these people and it happened even before they had left the meeting. Six months after the meeting, the problem was unresolved; the community waited for over a year to have this matter resolved.

This conflict and resolution can be compared to another water project that was started around 1993. About this time, Vusi started applying to various organizations for funds to help start a water project. Eventually, he received funds from Mvula Trust for a water project in his ward. The funds were awarded to him, and with contributions of 130 rand plus labor from over fifty households, the water project was completed in 1998. Each household continued to pay 5 rand per month for the water.[25] Each of the communal taps was protected with a lock, and if the 5 rand was not paid then the key to the lock was removed. While there were some problems with collecting the money, for the most part people paid the required amount. The money was put into a savings account at a bank in Eshowe, and it was supposed to be used if any of the pipes needed repairs.

While Vusi was the central figure in this project, in theory, the water project was controlled by the ward water committee, which was formed by Vusi prior to getting the funds from Mvula Trust. The water committee consisted of nine people, of which seven were women. Like other committees, it had a chairperson, vice-chairperson, treasurer, and secretary. This water committee, however, like the others in Mvuzane, were entirely dependent on the leadership of Vusi. For example, even though Vusi had officially resigned from his ward's water committee and served as the minister of education on the working committee, both the ward committee and working committee consulted with Vusi before making any decisions. In fact, many of the ward water committees stopped meeting because they were "waiting for Vusi" to help them acquire funds.

After the project was completed, the water was pumped from a nearby spring to a tank that was located on Vusi's property.[26] The water was distributed through a gravity pump allocation scheme to fifty households. People accessed the water through community taps, or if they could afford to spend an extra 50 rand, they could put a tap directly in their homestead. Only Vusi's family and the Thandi family were able to pay for private taps. Mandla Thandi (this is not his real name) lived about 300 meters from Vusi's homestead and was one of the two *izinduna* for the ward—the other one being Vusi's brother. To guard against waste, some procedures were agreed upon by the community concerning the use of the water. For instance, they agreed that the main water supply could be turned on or off from the tank at Vusi's. It was decided that the water would be turned off at night to prevent people coming from other wards and using the water.

As mentioned above, this particular ward in Mvuzane had two *izinduna*. This was not uncommon in Mvuzane or in other tribal authorities.

The rationale for having two *izinduna* was usually that the ward was uncommonly large and that it was better to have two *izinduna* at different sections of the ward so people did not have to travel too far to have problems resolved. In this case, the two *izinduna* lived right next to each other, which suggested there was another reason for this arrangement. The reasons why this decision was made remain unclear. While it was well known that *induna* Thandi was appointed in 1993 and Vusi's brother was appointed in 1996, it remained a mystery as to whether *induna* Thandi needed help because he was often in Durban searching for work or whether the appointment of Vusi's brother was some sort of gesture to the family for all the work Vusi had done for the community.[27]

The conflict over the water transpired in the following way.[28] *Induna* Thandi was going to be in Durban for about one week searching for work, and he told his neighbors to let Vusi know. After Thandi left for Durban, Vusi began receiving complaints from people that they were not getting any water from the communal taps. When Vusi investigated the situation, he discovered that *induna* Thandi's tap had been left open and that the water was spilling out into his homestead. Because all the water was coming to Thandi's, the water was not continuing to flow down to the taps that were below Thandi's. Vusi not only turned off Thandi's tap, but decided to disconnect his pipe from the main pipe and thereby not allow him to use his private tap. *Induna* Thandi returned from Durban to find that his tap had been disconnected. Rather than go to Vusi to resolve this problem, he went directly to the chief and demanded that a case be heard to resolve the matter. That Saturday there was a meeting called for those living in this ward. It was held at Vusi's homestead. The chief did not attend the hearing but instructed the *induna enkhulu* and his advisors on how the matter should be decided. Everyone present at the meeting, except *induna* Thandi and his father, supported Vusi's right to shut off the water versus *induna* Thandi's claims that this had been done without notice and without proof that he was at fault. *Induna* Thandi also argued that he had not left the tap on and that someone must have done it after he left. The community, as well as Vusi, the *induna enkhulu,* and chief Biyela's advisors, were also of the opinion that *induna* Thandi should not have come directly to the chief with this matter, but instead, that he should have gone to the ward water committee first. *Induna* Thandi argued that because he was an *induna* he was entitled to have the chief resolve the conflict and that as the *induna* he should not have to go to an ordinary person and make an apology.

As these events transpired, Vusi told the community that this was first and foremost a question for the ward development committee. According to Vusi, when it came to development questions or conflicts every person in the community was equal, and the *induna* should have recognized the proper protocol in this situation. But once the *induna* did take the matter to the chief, it then became a matter for the traditional structures to deal with, and he felt the ward development committee no longer had a role to play.

At the end of the day, the decision, as passed from chief Biyela to the *induna enkhulu,* was that this was a matter for the water committee to decide. If *induna* Thandi wanted to have his water turned back on, he would have to address the water committee, which meant that he would have to deal directly with Vusi. It was up to this organization to decide if and when the pipes would be reconnected. In other words, the meeting resolved nothing except the jurisdictional issue of who should decide. In this case, it was decided that the matter was better left to the water committee.

This conflict continued for over three months without resolution. *Induna* Thandi refused to apologize to the water committee or Vusi, and he said that he was looking for permanent work in Durban, and thus, an apology did not matter. In fact, one of the communal taps was only 30 meters from his homestead, so his family still had easy access to water. The issue, so it seemed, was one of pride more than convenience. Vusi later said that he was surprised he had not heard from the *induna* about the matter and that he would like the *induna* to send him a *written statement* outlining his position. There was no indication that this ever occurred.

TRADITION, DEVELOPMENT, AND POLITICAL LEGITIMACY

One of the more frequent statements concerning development in the rural areas was that "[t]hings are starting to change now though nothing has changed."[29] Or to put it more succinctly, as did a woman in Mvuzane, "nothing has happened."[30] Admittedly, there are more visible signs of development in 2009 than there were in 1998, especially in terms of more paved roads, more access to clean water, and more pit toilets. As noted in the previous chapter, however, for a vast majority of rural South Africans, development is happening much too slowly, and their lives have not improved in the ways that they anticipated with the democratic transition in 1994. While the structures of local government have changed, rural communities still have development committees, and traditional leaders are still involved in the development process.

The involvement of traditional leaders with development is an example of how they have remained a potent political force in the rural areas. The extent to which they have been able to expand their authority over development issues, however, was not something that many in South Africa anticipated. While they do not have the capacity to actually access resources, they have nonetheless sought to direct and redirect the introduction of new rules, structures, and conflicts in a way that has enhanced their authority. This appropriation of the development process highlights how the chieftaincy has sought to give meaning to, and gain control over, one of the central features of the government's transformation process. In many ways, the interaction between the chieftaincy and the state over development harkens back to the colonial era, when those in the rural areas utilized the "language of modernity and improvement" as a means to gain control over state institutions and processes and make them "their own" (MacKinnon 2003: 67; Galvan 2004). This not only allows traditional leaders to keep a watchful eye on the activities of development committees, distribute scarce resources, and resolve conflicts over development issues, but because development structures were situated into preexisting boundaries, it also enables members of the community to make sense of this new experience through familiar frames of reference. In fact, the chieftaincy has shown itself to be particularly adept at selectively altering development institutions and processes to enhance their own authority and not simply acting as a gatekeeper.

What is notable is the way in which traditional leaders and local populations have justified their responsibilities over development issues. While most informants suggested that traditional leaders had not focused on development in the past, there was a strong consensus that they must be involved in the process because they were the leaders of the community and because the distribution of development resources without their guidance might result in conflict and disorder. These sentiments were found in all three case studies, even though local populations viewed the chieftaincy and development committees differently in each. Thus, whether there were positive or negative attitudes about the chieftaincy, local government, or development committees, a vast majority of informants believed that the chieftaincy must help direct the development process.

At the same time, traditional leaders have been forced to make decisions in a new political and social environment—one that is in many ways beyond their control. In this vein, the implementation of development resources and institutions has reshaped some aspects of local politics. Not only have communities demanded that chiefs either appoint or allow for the election of more pro-development *izinduna* and traditional councilors, there is also some evidence that women have gained more formal responsibilities with respect to development issues. Unlike the case in the tribal authority structures, the women were able to voice their concerns and maintain some control over the development agenda through the development committees. In addition, some women have effectively used the development committees as a starting point to other positions in the community. The role women play with respect to development cannot be overemphasized, and it is clear that through their work on development projects they have been able to secure the trust of the community and the traditional leaders. At the same time, progress remains slow, and despite the new avenues that are open to women, there is no question that gender equality is still elusive at the local level.

The fact that the legitimacy of traditional leaders is linked to development, while perhaps surprising, is something that many researchers are finding throughout South Africa (Oomen 2005; Goodenough 2002; Beall 2006). The notion that traditional leaders will be held accountable based on what they do, rather than who they are, directly contradicts the assumption that they can ignore the demands of their local populations without risking their legitimacy. Even though there are historical examples that demonstrate how traditional leaders have always had to respond to local populations, the idea that they are able to exercise complete authority with a "clenched fist" remains pervasive (Mamdani 1996). This view of the chieftaincy's legitimacy, however, oversimplifies what has always been a complex process.

LEGITIMACY LOST?

The Fall of a Chief and the Survival of a Chieftaincy

The chief does not care about people. Maybe it is because he has got everything. No one is doing anything for us except the councilors are doing things in their area only.

Once these people are in power they do nothing for the community, only their friends. [Inkosi is] doing nothing. [Induna is] at the moment helping the people.

Yes [the chieftaincy should continue]. There is dignity in the area. There are amakhosi in all areas, though ours are not working. Inkosi is doing nothing. Induna is doing more and he always report to inkosi.

The preceding chapters have explored how the chieftaincy has responded to the sociopolitical changes since the early 1990s. While the rural political landscape has been altered with the introduction of elections, local government institutions, and development projects, many people continue to remain loyal to traditional leaders and rely upon them to help navigate the new political realities. At the same time, even as traditional leaders have maintained their authority, they have also faced a variety of new expectations that have in turn affected the nature of their rule. In particular, people in the rural areas want the chieftaincy to simultaneously adapt to the new realities as well as to remain a symbol of unity. Indeed, finding the appropriate balance between these competing pressures, and selectively adapting to and blending with the newly introduced authority structures, is the defining characteristic of the politics of multiple legitimacies in rural South Africa.

The next issue is what happens to the legitimacy of the chieftaincy when it is unable to achieve this balance. What are the limits of authority for the chieftaincy and how do people in the rural areas hold their traditional leaders accountable when they fail to promote unity? The justifications that underwrite the authority of the chieftaincy, its claim to be a symbol of unity, and its ability to cooperate with new forms of authority are the same reasons given to strip individual traditional leaders of their authority. Thus, the basis of the chieftaincy's moral and performance legitimacy is simultaneously a mechanism to empower disgruntled citizens to challenge its authority. But there is an important distinction between the authority of individual traditional leaders and the authority of the chieftaincy as a whole. In the example discussed below, when faced with the opportunity to abolish the chieftaincy, the people in Kholweni Tribal Authority refused to do so and decided to simply replace the chief and *izinduna* with leaders they believed would be more effective.

LEGITIMACY UNDER THREAT: CHIEF MTEMBU'S FALL FROM POWER

This particular story unfolded in Kholweni Tribal Authority in 1998–99, and it centered on the reign of chief Mtembu. He had ruled in Kholweni since 1973, when he was "elected" by select members of a church committee. Unlike the chieftaincy in Mvuzane or Ximba, the chieftaincy in Kholweni is not one based on hereditary rule. Instead, an "elective" chieftaincy was established when King Mpande ceded the area, which is now called Kholweni, to the Norwegian missionary Hans Paludin Schreuder in 1852. From that period, the people in Kholweni elected their chief, and this continued during apartheid. In 1973, chief Mtembu was "elected." As it turns out, the election process consisted of a church council choosing the chief and appointing him for life. While many people in the community believed the chief was supposed to be chosen every five years, no election was held after 1973.

One of the more interesting rumors surrounding the chieftaincy in Kholweni was that the chieftaincy itself was cursed. As the story is told, before chief Mtembu was chosen in 1973, the church committee had appointed two other people to the position, but both had died within months of their inauguration. The rumor was that the previous chief had used witchcraft to secure his reign and that those who followed him refused to consult the appropriate *inyanga* (witchdoctor) and acquire the necessary *muthi* (medicine) for protection. Many believed that the reason chief Mtembu was able to reign for so long was that he was able to obtain *muthi* that was extremely powerful and that protected him from the curse.

In Kholweni, the frustration concerning the lack of development and the ineffectiveness of local government had reached the breaking point in 1999. The fact that there were complaints in this community about the allocation of resources, the performance of the leaders, and local government ineffectiveness, however, was not exceptional. As we have seen, similar criticisms were common in both Mvuzane and Ximba. The main difference in Kholweni, however, was the intensity, as well as the openness, of the debates and the particular anger that those in the community directed at chief Mtembu.

Many overlapping factors contributed to the state of affairs in this area. Some of these were directly attributable to chief Mtembu and his *izinduna,* such as the perception that they were no longer providing security, resolving disputes, or looking after the community welfare. Other concerns, strictly speaking, were beyond the direct control of the chieftaincy, such as the fact that there had been no development projects completed in Kholweni since the establishment of local government in 1996. One of the reasons for the lack of development projects in Kholweni was the perception of many local government officials and nongovernmental organizations that Kholweni actually had better access to roads, water, and electricity than did most other chieftaincies in the area. Thus, there was a belief that Kholweni did not need resources as badly as other areas.

Indeed, the 2001 census data appeared to confirm this point. With respect to access to electricity, sanitation, and clean water, there were much greater needs in Mvuzane than in Kholweni. For example, while 92 percent of those living in Mvuzane used candles for electricity, only 40 percent in Kholweni did so. Similarly, only 45 percent of those living in Kholweni had no access to any sanitation system, compared to Mvuzane, where 74 percent of the population had no access. Finally, with respect to water, while 49 percent of those living in Mvuzane collected their water from a river or stream, only 32 percent in Kholweni were in this position.[1]

Obviously, despite such statistics, those living in Kholweni nonetheless believed that they had many unmet needs, which they did, and they blamed chief Mtembu and his *izinduna* for the lack of development. Many feared increasing division and disunity and the deterioration of the community. Unable to provide a persuasive counter to these complaints, the community spoke openly about the need to replace him, and there were rumors that a delegation was going to visit the provincial Department of Traditional Affairs in Ulundi, one of KwaZulu-Natal's two provincial capitals, to make these demands. Rather than wait for this to happen, chief Mtembu voluntarily resigned his position in early 1999. His resignation initiated a series of events that culminated in the election of a new chief later that year. It also provided the opportunity for some in the community to question whether the chieftaincy structure should be abandoned for something resembling city government.

Unlike the situation in Mvuzane and Ximba, where the chieftaincy had responded with some success to the new expectations associated with political change, the chieftaincy in Kholweni did not react in a similar fashion. With respect to development, local government, democratic elections, and resolving community disputes, the chieftaincy was not able to convince the people that it was up to the task of governing in the new dispensation. As was the case in most tribal authority areas, in Kholweni chief Mtembu was considered the most important part of the institution and represented the unity of the area. As the division in the community increased, community members ultimately blamed chief Mtembu and his *izinduna*. In fact, before chief Mtembu resigned in early 1999, two of his *izinduna* also chose to resign as well. What was most interesting, however, was how the community used the failings of their individual leaders to reexamine the desirability of the chieftaincy institution more generally. In the end, the chieftaincy remained in Kholweni, but the process of choosing new leaders highlighted the increasing pressures on this institution to respond to community needs and be held accountable for their decision making.

While some suggested that chief Mtembu had been a good chief early in his reign, the overwhelming impression was that he was now incapable of performing as the community demanded. These sentiments fueled a general resentment against the chief and some *izinduna,* which reached a crescendo in 1999. Unlike in most areas, where people were generally complimentary of their leaders, even when they believed they were not performing as well as they should, in Kholweni the negative comments concerning chief Mtembu were made consistently, and in some cases were unsolicited.[2] The specific list of complaints against chief Mtembu and some of his *izinduna* included the lack of development, the lack of cooperation with local government, the inability to control crime in the area, and the lack of consultation with the community. In most cases, people used these specific complaints to highlight a more general belief that the community as a whole was suffering under the current leadership. In this vein, people complained that the community was divided, that it lacked harmony, and that it was no longer unified.[3]

One measure of the discontent regarding chief Mtembu is to compare the attitudes of people living in Kholweni with those in Mvuzane and Ximba. For example, when asked whether they thought it was a good idea for the chieftaincy to continue in their area, over 90 percent of the informants responded "yes" in Mvuzane and Ximba. This compared with *only* 80 percent in Kholweni. Of course, this percentage is still quite high, but it should be situated into the broader context of frequent negative comments made about chief Mtembu individually. For example, with respect to maintaining law and order, over 90 percent believed that chief Biyela and chief Mlaba were doing a good job.[4] In Kholweni, however, only 70 percent were pleased with chief Mtembu on this issue.[5] What is clear is that the negative perceptions people had about chief Mtembu were also affecting attitudes about the chieftaincy as a whole, if only at the margins. Similarly, even though chief Biyela from Mvuzane and chief Mtembu from Kholweni were the same age and had the same educational background, a majority of the informants in Mvuzane suggested that it would be good for chief Biyela to run for an elected office, while a majority in Kholweni thought this would be a bad idea. In short, there was the perception that chief Mtembu did not have the skills to work with local government, and it was common for people to refer to chief Mtembu as a "drunk" and to insist that he was a "lazy chief."

Development and the Chief: "He is too slow"

As was the case in most tribal authorities in KwaZulu-Natal, the people in Kholweni were most frustrated with the lack of development and the lack of jobs since the democratic changes in the 1990s. What was different in Kholweni, however, was that people were more likely to blame the chieftaincy for their condition rather than other entities, such as the local government, the ANC, or the national government, as was the case in Mvuzane and Ximba.

The reasons for this were varied. In the first instance, very few projects had been implemented since 1994. With respect to local government funding, since its inception in 1996, the URC had not provided any resources to Kholweni for development projects. While the resources were scarce and competition between chieftaincies for projects was intense, some members in the community were under the (mistaken) impression that the URC had done more in Mvuzane than Kholweni. While there were a few boreholes in the community that were provided during apartheid, most people collected their water from the rivers.

After five years of the new government, many people found this situation intolerable.

While chief Mtembu was not directly to blame for what happened at the URC, many in the community believed that his inaction demonstrated that he simply did not care about the welfare of the community. To substantiate this point, many people were often anxious to suggest that chief Mtembu had never done anything to help bring development to the community even when there were opportunities to do so. One person, who had been in Kholweni his entire life, explained how chief Mtembu often failed to help those in the community who were willing to help bring development projects. One particular example concerned a group of women who wanted to build a crèche in the 1980s. Apparently, they had collected the necessary funds but needed the chief to sign a letter and send it to the authorities in Ulundi, one of the two capitals of the province. He refused to do so, and the ladies were not able to open the crèche.[6] On another occasion in the early 1980s, someone in the community located orange trees that could be bought for only R2 (approximately $1.50).[7] When he went to the chief and asked for his help to sell these orange trees to the community, the chief refused; as a result, this project was never established in the community.[8]

Finally, many in the community could also recount a more recent example of such inaction that involved the implementation of a water project that was partially funded by the Zululand Joint Services Board (ZJSB).[9] The project was designed so that water was pumped from a river to a tank located on a hill. The water was then distributed using gravity to those living down hill from the tank. The river used for this project was actually the boundary between Mvuzane and Kholweni. Both chiefs were notified and asked to attend meetings and provide assistance with this project. While chief Biyela was active in this project, chief Mtembu was not. This was the case even though the tank was located on the Kholweni side of the river and the people who initiated the project were from Kholweni. Those involved in the project were dismayed that their chief had not been more cooperative, and some suggested chief Mtembu's attitude was embarrassing for the entire community.[10] Not surprisingly, those who benefited from the project credited the women who contacted the ZJSB and chief Biyela. Thus, even when there was a successful development project in his area, chief Mtembu was not given credit. These stories, as well as others, were discussed frequently in the area and helped to reinforce the growing negative feelings about the chief.[11]

In addition, many in the community described chief Mtembu as a "selfish" person[12] who did not understand how to implement development,[13] and who was more concerned with his individual gain than with the community welfare.[14] Perhaps there was no greater evidence of this than the fact that while most of the community did not have easy access to water, electricity, or telephone service, these were all available at chief Mtembu's large block home located on ten acres of land. As discussed earlier, there was a growing sentiment in the rural areas that every person had an equal right to development and that it was inappropriate for traditional leaders to receive development before people in the community. The unbalanced allocation of these resources in Kholweni resulted in even more frustration with the chief. As a retired minister in the area noted, the "only problem is that people are given money for development and use it for their personal use."[15] Another person added that "the problem here is that people are concerned with their own living."[16] These sentiments reinforce the more general notion that there is an expectation that traditional leaders put the interests of the community before their own individual interests.

While some people in the community believed the chief had received water and electricity in the 1980s, chief Mtembu suggested that he got electricity in 1992 and water in 1994. In each case, there was no dispute that he had paid for these projects personally without community support.[17] Members of the community alleged that electricity could have been extended to many other homes in the area except that, as was the case with the crèche, chief Mtembu refused to sign the necessary papers and give the required consent to the electricity company, Eskom.[18] The chief rejected these allegations and argued that he had tried to bring electricity to the rest of the community, but when Eskom told the community they had to collect a deposit for the service, most people could not afford it. The chief also noted that his electricity bill was at least R500 per month ($83) and that most people would not be able to afford this given the poverty in the area.[19] Still, the fact that chief Mtembu had access to these resources, while a majority of the community did not, served to heighten suspicions that he was not working for the community interest.

The issue of development affected chief Mtembu's *izinduna* as well. While the *izinduna* were part of the ward development committees, as was the case in Mvuzane and Ximba, these committees were no longer meeting on a regular basis, and most of the *izinduna* were not doing much with respect to development. In one case, the *induna* resigned when the community accused him of misallocating money that had been collected for a specific development project. The community elected another *induna*, Xolani Dube, who was the husband of Victoria Dube, the elected councilor in the area. Xolani Dube promised to make connections with URC, vis-à-vis his wife, and to bring development resources to the community. Without question, *induna* Dube was one of the more popular people in Kholweni, and many people trusted he was trying to bring development to the community. There was obvious tension between chief Mtembu and *induna* Dube, and at one point, chief Mtembu threatened not to register Dube as an *induna* with the Department of Traditional and Environmental Affairs in Ulundi. After he became aware of this threat, *induna* Dube held a meeting and told the community that he would avoid a conflict with chief Mtembu and submit his resignation if that would bring harmony to the community. Those at the meeting pleaded with *induna* Dube not to resign, and he decided not to. It was probably not a coincidence that chief Mtembu sent his own letter of resignation to Ulundi soon after this community meeting was held. As one person suggested, *induna* Dube used "development to get community support." Some in the community even suggested that *induna* Dube's offer to resign was simply a way to make himself more popular with the community.[20]

There exists a great deal of data that the legitimacy of the chieftaincy is now related, either directly or indirectly, to the issue of development (Oomen 2005; Goodenough 2002). While resources have been scarce in the rural areas, in Mvuzane chief Biyela focused much of his time on development, and he utilized the decentralized nature of the institution to establish ward-based development committees to facilitate local-level decision making. He also stressed to his *izinduna* that they needed to assist their communities with development matters. He routinely held meetings on development, encouraged the formation of development committees, made and enforced rules concerning the allocation of development resources, and resolved disputes when they arose. In other words, he utilized his authority as chief to at least give the impression that he was working to bring development. Indeed, perhaps even more important than whether the leaders were actually providing development resources was whether those in the community believed their leaders were attempting to do so. Chief Mlaba in Ximba demonstrated similar skills, and most informants believed he was trying to acquire development for the community. In Kholweni, however, this was definitely not the case, as chief Mtembu rarely took an active stance with respect to this issue. In the end, it appears that politics in the rural areas, like politics elsewhere, was as much about perception as anything else.

Despite chief Mtembu's bad reputation with respect to development, a majority of the community nonetheless believed that the chief's most important responsibility was to provide development. In fact, of the three case studies, Kholweni was the only one where development was considered the chief's most important job. In addition, when asked if the chief should have a say on development issues, most people responded that he should. Similar to the findings in Mvuzane and Ximba, people in Kholweni were adamant that he must have a say on these matters because he was the leader of the community and it was "his land." Thus, even though chief Mtembu had failed to bring development to the community, there was evidence that the community believed development issues remained within the authority of the chieftaincy.

Local Government and the Chieftaincy: The Lack of Unity

Chief Mtembu's unpopularity in Kholweni was not only the result of his poor performance with respect to development. A contributing factor was the perception that he was not cooperating with local government or the local government representative, Victoria Dube. Not only was she a member of the URC, but she was also a member of the all-important executive council, which acted as the main decision-making body. Like the elected councilor in Mvuzane, Vusi Chamane, she was a well-educated and articulate person who spoke fluent English and was accustomed to negotiating with people outside the rural areas. While chief Biyela in Mvuzane considered Vusi his closest advisor, this was not the case with chief Mtembu and councilor Dube in Kholweni. Whether this was a result of chief Mtembu's bias against women in positions of power or whether it was the result of the growing animus between chief Mtembu and *induna* Dube was difficult to know. Whatever the reason, chief Mtembu and councilor Dube did not have a close working relationship, which most likely contributed to the chief's negative public perception.

Perhaps even more importantly, the lack of public interaction between councilor Dube and chief Mtembu meant that many members of the community did not even know chief Mtembu was an ex-officio member of the URC. While this was also the case in Mvuzane, in Kholweni the lack of knowledge about the role chief Mtembu had on the URC was striking. For example, only 36 percent of those interviewed knew that he was a member of local government, and only 34 percent could recall a time when chief Mtembu reported to the community about the URC. This compares to Mvuzane, where 48 percent knew chief Biyela was on the URC and 55 percent claimed that he had reported back to the community about the URC.[21] Moreover, in Mvuzane chief Biyela was able to garner the trust of the community through his cooperative working relationship with the URC, but chief Mtembu could not, or chose not to, use the URC to help enhance his own authority. Those who were aware that chief Mtembu was involved with the URC complained that he did not report back to them what this body was doing.

To assess how people perceived the relative authority of local government institutions and the chieftaincy, I asked informants whether they believed the chief should be allowed to overrule a local government decision. The majority of those asked this question in Kholweni responded that the chief could not and should not overrule the decision of local government. The reasons why he should abide by local government decisions reveal much about people's perceptions of his qualifications, judgment, and authority. Many noted that the chief could not overrule local government because he was "under" them, or alternatively, that the government was "above" him.[22] Others challenged the underlying assumption of the question and stated that he could not do anything without the agreement of the community—implying that his authority to override a decision of the local government was based on whether he consulted with the community first.[23] The most revealing statements, however, were the ones that questioned whether the chief had the appropriate judgment to make decisions for the community at all. One woman, who was the wife of a traditional councilor, stated that chief Mtembu's decisions in the past had been bad for the community but "good for other people."[24] A former *induna* added that if the chief were to overrule local government decisions then "they will tell him you do not want to develop your place."[25] Finally, the elected councilor answered that he should not be able to overrule "if [the decision was] for the benefit of the community."[26]

These sentiments reflect the precarious balance between the authority of the chief and local government institutions and how they influence the legitimation process at the local level. While it is important for chiefs and *izinduna* to forge close working relationships with local government institutions, they must do so in a manner that does not threaten their own autonomous authority in the community. In the case of Kholweni, even though most people believed the URC was not doing a good job, they nonetheless accepted that its authority was greater than that of the chief. This was not the case in Mvuzane and Ximba, where both chief Biyela and chief Mlaba were able to forge close alliances with the elected local councilors while also maintaining an autonomous source of authority. Most importantly, in both Mvuzane and Ximba there was the belief that the chief was seeking to promote the community welfare and was using local government to help him do this. As we have seen, for various reasons, this was not the case in Kholweni.

The final point is similar to the one made above with respect to development. While there were negative perceptions concerning chief Mtembu's ability to work with local government institutions, this did not translate into the belief that there was no role for the chieftaincy with respect to local government. Despite the fact that many informants suggested the chief was "under" local government, there was also widespread agreement that the chief must be allowed to participate in the decision-making process within local government. For example, even though chief Mtembu did not have the trust of his community, when asked whether "a chief should" have a say on the URC, an astounding 86 percent claimed that he should. One traditional councilor stated that "the Uthungulu Regional Council is working for the community and because the government cannot do anything here without the chief's permission," he must be involved in the decision making."[27] Thus, even in a situation where the community had lost trust in the judgment of their individual leader, they still believe that he *was* the leader of the area and that nothing could happen there without his consent. These seemingly contradictory perceptions about the chieftaincy's authority highlight the importance of making a distinction between evaluations of the individual leaders and the more general attitudes concerning the role of the institution in society.

Order and Security: A Chief Who Does Not Solve Problems

The inability of the chief, *izinduna,* and traditional councilors in Kholweni to promote the community welfare through the implementation of development and to cooperate with local government institutions was not the only reason why the community had lost faith in their ability to govern. In addition to these concerns, there were complaints that the these leaders were no longer maintaining law and order, resolving community disputes, or consulting with the community. In short, the overall behavior of Kholweni's leaders threatened those basic principles underlying the idea of unity.

With respect to questions of law and order, the resolution of disputes, and consultation, it was difficult to quantify or verify the complaints and fears shared by many informants. While such complaints were common in both Mvuzane and Ximba, in Kholweni they were more frequently a topic of conversation. Perhaps most importantly, unlike in the other areas, the negative comments were often made in a manner that directly related to the moral authority of the traditional leaders—their ability to promote unity and harmony in the community.

The maintenance of law and order was one of the main concerns in Kholweni. Many informants believed that crime had increased since the early 1990s and complained that the traditional leaders were not doing a good job at keeping order. The issue of crime was raised in most conversations, as people feared burglary, assault, and murder.[28] In addition, there was little faith that the chief, *izinduna*, traditional councilors, or police could do anything to help provide security. These statements concerning the chief and the maintenance of law and order highlight this sense of helplessness: "[The chief] is not doing a good job. Maybe it is because he has got everything. He does not care about his community";[29] "No one [is providing security]. The traditional leaders have failed. They know some people who are stealing livestock but they do nothing to report them to Eshowe";[30] "People are out on bail for serious things. Community is not well. Discipline is not good. Present government is not keeping discipline."[31]

In Kholweni, as in other communities across South Africa, people decided to form "policing forums," which provide protection for the area (Oomen 2005). The policing forum in Kholweni was established in 1997 and consisted of ordinary members of the community.[32] In some instances, the members of this forum cooperated with the chieftaincy, but they did not do so routinely. Instead, it was an autonomous organization where members of the community could report crimes and arrange for security at festivals or parties. This service was not free, however. Each household who wanted protection paid R10 per year to the forum. What was most notable about these policing forums was that the community had decided to create them in the first place. In Mvuzane and Ximba, for example, I was told that members of the chieftaincy, usually the *izinduna* or *amaphoyisa*, were responsible for providing security at public events, and the idea that policing forums were necessary was never even mentioned. Even in Ximba where there was a police station located within the tribal authority area, the *izinduna* and *amaphoyisa* were still responsible for local events, and most people suggested the police were called only for "major" issues. The fact that these duties were delegated to another body was another indicator of the extent to which the chieftaincy had lost its ability to exercise social control in Kholweni.

In addition, people in Kholweni consistently complained that the chief or *izinduna* were no longer hearing cases and that no one was helping with the resolution of disputes.[33] Again, it was sometimes difficult to assess whether such perceptions were real or whether they simply were the product of the negative feelings toward the chief more generally. For example, during the three months I spent in Kholweni, I never observed a meeting at the court where disputes were resolved. In addition, on numerous occasions I would visit the court at the time when cases were supposed to be heard, but nobody was there. When I examined the court record books in July 1999, I found that no cases had been recorded since December 1998, and the tribal secretary confirmed that no cases had been heard during this period. Still, the tribal secretary did suggest that the chief still resolved disputes at his home and that these were not recorded. Indeed, on two different occasions I had interviews scheduled with chief Mtembu that had to be canceled because he was at someone's home "resolving disputes." Yet there were even questions raised about this process, as there were also suspicions that given his poor health and his propensity to drink too much alcohol, his wife had taken over many of his functions. Some even suggested that she convinced him to resign and actually drafted and delivered his resignation letter to Ulundi.[34] Whether these suspicions were valid or not was difficult to ascertain. Nonetheless, when I finally did have a chance to interview chief Mtembu at his home, I was told his wife was in the kitchen "discussing" an issue with a family that the chief would "resolve" later. While I do not have the evidence to refute the existence of a distinction between the discussion and the resolution of a problem, based on informal discussions with people in the community, I have little doubt that she had assumed many of the chief's responsibilities, including dispute resolution.

Whether he was still hearing cases or not, some informants suggested that they chose not to take cases to him because he was unable to resolve the problems or because they did not trust his ability to make neutral decisions. For example, one male informant noted that "people no longer take issues to these people [the chief, *izinduna*, and traditional councilors] because even if you go to them no steps are taken. I complained in 1994 about boundaries but nobody has come to solve the problem."[35] Another informant said that "we report to the chief but he does not take any steps. For example, two people were shot but nothing was done."[36] Finally, a member of a ward development committee was concerned that the traditional leaders would not resolve issues fairly. She stated that problems were solved, but "it depends on who you are. Leaders do favors to their friends."[37]

In addition, many people complained that the chief did not consult with the community before making decisions. While during apartheid the magistrate "did not allow" consultation,[38] many believed the chief now had an obligation to communicate more frequently with them.

Thus, when asked whether they believed the chieftaincy was "acting like a democracy," 48 percent in Mvuzane[39] and 77 percent in Ximba[40] asserted that this was the case, while in Kholweni, only 10 percent had this opinion.[41] Given that those living in these areas associate democracy with the promotion of unity and harmony, these attitudes only reinforce the notion that the chieftaincy's legitimacy in Kholweni was threatened.

As these various comments from Kholweni reveal, there were a variety of complaints against chief Mtembu and his *izinduna*. On the surface, these complaints were essentially about what these leaders did, or failed to do, for the community. In other words, the concerns about development, local government, security, resolving disputes, and consultation highlighted the importance of the performance dimension of the legitimation process. Yet while these negative evaluations concerning performance are an important aspect of the legitimation process, it should not be forgotten that similar complaints were often mentioned in Mvuzane and Ximba as well. The crucial difference in Kholweni was not that there were complaints about performance, but rather, that the poor performance of the leaders was interpreted as threatening the unity of the community and the dignity of the chieftaincy. That is, rather than attempting to justify decisions and rules as necessary for maintenance of unity, chief Mtembu and some of his *izinduna* acted in ways that were ultimately interpreted as promoting disunity and division. In effect, what proved detrimental to the chieftaincy in Kholweni was that people linked the poor performance to the moral dimension of legitimacy, which was based on the importance of promoting unity.

The only notable exception to these negative perceptions about the chief and his *izinduna* was the opinion regarding *induna* Dube. Where chief Mtembu did not care about development, Dube was trying. Where chief Mtembu did not understand local government, Dube did. Where chief Mtembu was not resolving disputes or consulting with the community, Dube was. Indeed, in the election for a new chief, which has since been nullified, Dube was the choice of the community. How this election proceeded and the discussions it prompted about the chieftaincy more generally is the focus below.

THE ELECTION OF THE CHIEF AND THE RECONSTITUTION
OF THE POLITY

The poor performance of the chief, *izinduna,* and traditional councilors threatened not only the general welfare of the area but the actual composition of the polity itself. For some in Kholweni, the election process enabled them not only to choose a new chief, but to reexamine authority relations more broadly. The election for a new chief took place on June 6, 1999. Unlike in the past, when a church committee elected the chief, this election was open to the community as a whole. A total of 600 people registered to vote in the election, and 316 cast their ballots. The unofficial vote count showed that *induna* Dube had received the majority of the votes. Before announcing the results, however, the officials from the KwaZulu-Natal Department of Traditional and Environmental Affairs, who were monitoring the election, nullified the contest. They had received complaints, from both the candidates and members of the community, that the registration process was truncated in some areas and that many people were not told when the election was taking place. It was decided a new election would take place on July 23, 1999.

Indeed, the feeling throughout the community was that the registration process had been designed in a way to favor some wards over others and that there was little information about this process. One reason for the confusion was that this election took place only a few days after the national elections. As I have explained, the registration process for the national elections was a challenging event, but one that people actively took part in. For example, while there was no information concerning the specific registration rates in Kholweni for the 1999 election, the voting results for the three polling stations within Kholweni show that approximately 2,880 people voted.[42] In the 2000 local government elections, approximately 3,350 people voted at the same three polling stations. With a voting-age population of around 4,200 people in Kholweni according to 2000 statistics, the voter turnout in the 2000 was about 80 percent.[43] Thus, the notion that only 600 people registered for the election of the chief and only 300 people, or 7 percent of the voting population, voted raised serious concerns—not surprisingly—about this particular election in Kholweni.

For most people, the confusion began with the registration of eligible voters, which took place in the few months preceding the election. What caused this confusion remains unclear, except that there was poor communication between those in charge of the registration process and the members of the community. This was the first time the entire community was involved in the election of the chief, and thus there were few precedents available to help guide the process. Even more important, there were no formal rules in place for the election. Chief Mtembu had resigned his position in late 1998, and the election was not until June 1999. During this period, even though Mtembu was officially the chief until another one was chosen, the community essentially lacked a local leader with *de facto* authority.

For the election, the *izinduna* of each of the three wards were responsible for registering the people in their area. While I never saw a copy of the registration form, I was told that the names of the people were given to the provincial Department of Traditional and Environmental Affairs, which was in charge of the election. Many people complained that the residents of some wards were told the deadline for registration was in May while in other wards the registration process continued until the election. Specifically, those living outside of *induna* Dube's ward complained that he had allowed the registration to continue in his area to help him in the election.[44] Messages concerning the registration were given at schools to children, who were then supposed to tell their family. The lack of community meetings held by chief Mtembu during this period only caused more communication problems.

In addition to registration, each ward was also responsible to select up to two candidates who would run in the election. These candidates were supposed to be chosen at a ward meeting, but most people admitted that they were not aware of any such meetings actually taking place. Instead, certain people were chosen, and their names were sent to the Department of Traditional and Local Government Affairs. In addition, there were also complaints that some wards were overrepresented and others were underrepresented.[45] Some informants even suggested that some *izinduna* made their own decisions concerning whose names would be sent to Ulundi, whether or not these were the people the community had chosen. Of the six people who were on the ballot, three were either *izinduna* or former *izinduna,* one was an IFP member of the National Council of Provinces and a former member of the KwaZulu Legislative Assembly and lived most of the year in Cape Town, and the final two were former businessmen. In addition, all of the candidates were male.

Given the frustration with the performance of the chieftaincy under chief Mtembu, it was not surprising that many people believed they should elect a chief who understood how to get development, how to make connections with local government, and how to solve community problems. For example, one woman stated that one of the candidates, Senator Bhengu, "was not elected because he made a road to his house only. He did not do anything for us while in Ulundi. With respect to water, Bhengu said that all these people have rivers."[46] *Induna* Dube, on the other hand, was described as "trying a lot"; "maybe he will do a good job as he is still young."[47] Of the six candidates, many considered *induna* Dube to be the most active with respect to development projects.

In addition, there was some discussion concerning whether the chief should be a Christian. Unlike the issue of performance, where there was a consensus in the community, the question of religion was much more divisive. There were those who did not think it was appropriate for a non-Christian to be chief and even suggested that the church council and not the community should choose the chief.[48] Others did not believe the chief's religion was important as long as he worked hard for the community. If the chief was a non-Christian, however, he should nonetheless recognize certain community traditions involving Christianity, such as not holding meetings on Sundays. Perhaps more importantly, even if the chief was not a Christian, he should "have Christian qualities."[49] Because it was well known in the community that *induna* Dube was rumored to have many mistresses, some suggested that this behavior should eliminate him as a candidate.[50]

Many of the comments made about the registration and election highlighted the confusion and the skepticism concerning the fairness of the process: "The *inkosi* was chosen while other members of the community did not know";[51] "In this area, no one is elected to be a chief if he is not a Christian";[52] "It [the election] has not been done democratically. Not done fairly. Everything should be done democratically because of the 1994 elections";[53] "I didn't hear about the elections until it was over. Bhengu not nominated but forced on as one of the candidates";[54] "The elections were during the week. People not here [to vote]. [It was] not fair."[55]

Claims that the registration and election were "unfair" or "undemocratic" were common, which highlights the extent to which the expectations of "free and fair" elections for national and local government positions had been adopted as the standard for tribal authority elections as well. One of the consequences of this entire process, however, was to prompt some members of the community to suggest more fundamental political reforms in addition to the elections. In fact, some cautioned that without a written constitution limiting the chief to a five-year term, it was possible that the next chief could rule just as long as chief Mtembu.

This inclination for communities within chieftaincies to draft written constitutions as a way to hold leaders accountable appears to be increasing throughout South Africa (Oomen 2000: 27–28).[56] In Kholweni, in the wake of the election debacle, an informal committee had formed to propose a written constitution as well as to research the history of the area. As one committee member stated, he was doing research to find out "why the Kholweni tribe was invented and help to decide how to do elections."[57] This informant also insisted that the seven people working on these issues were self-appointed and did not constitute a "recognized committee." Instead, they simply wanted to gather as much information as possible about Kholweni's past, as well as how ruler-ruled relations have developed in other areas, and present this information to the community. After the information was gathered, the community would then appoint a formal committee to offer more specific recommendations.

As part of this investigation, some members of the community were contemplating whether Kholweni should abolish the chieftaincy and simply adopt what was referred to as the township model, where there was an elected mayor rather than a chief.[58] Other members of the community argued that if they were going to have a written constitution forcing the chief to run for office every five years, there was no reason to abandon the chieftaincy, because the chief would ultimately end up functioning more like a mayor in the future.[59] More importantly, however, many suggested that the chieftaincy could not be abolished, as this would threaten the dignity, respect, and unity of the community.[60] While the chief's functions and tenure could be limited in a written constitution, for many, the idea of abolishing the chieftaincy entirely did not register as within the realm of the possible.

These perceptions were highlighted when informants discussed the advantages and disadvantages of electing the chief. Given the general excitement about the election of the chief, and the momentum toward a written constitution, it was surprising that many informants, while still a minority, preferred the hereditary chieftainship to the one in Kholweni. The most appealing aspect of the elected chief was that the community had the freedom to dismiss chiefs who were not working hard or producing results. The focus was on choosing someone who had strong leadership qualities and who could do things for the community: "You can elect the person you think can do a good job";[61] "You can change him at any time for a new one";[62] "Hereditary system not good because someone may not have education and will not be able to communicate in other languages";[63] "Changing the leadership now and then helps to make things happen";[64] "[Election is good] because get rid of useless *inkosi*—the drunkards."[65]

On the other hand, those who favored a hereditary chieftainship focused on the importance of training and the fact that the election of the chief ultimately divides the community: "With hereditary he grows up being groomed to be the chief";[66] "Child grows up under supervision and taught how to be a leader of the people";[67] "No elections. Here [in Kholweni] today you are a chief and tomorrow not. More discipline and dignity with hereditary chief. Must respect chief's and *induna*'s sons";[68] "With hereditary, they know all the rules and culture of the Zulu kingdom. With election, they work for their families";[69] "Elections divide the community";[70] "Hereditary is better. These are my father's people and I must treat them this way."[71] Some even noted that hereditary must be better as there was more development in chief Biyela's area: "Elected *inkosi* just misuse our money rather than seeing to our needs. Look at Biyela's place. They have roads and water."[72]

Given the claims that the election in June 1999 was not free and fair, another election was held a few months later, and former *induna* Xolani Dube was declared the winner. As I mentioned above, many in the community believed he was the best choice for chief because of past efforts to access development projects in the community as well as his personal relationship with Victoria Dube. Xolani Dube was the chief for only four years because he died unexpectedly in 2003.

Upon his death, the community was once again asked to choose a chief, and this time they decided to elect Victoria Dube. Upon being chosen in 2003, chief Dube was an elected councilor for the URC, and she served as both the chief and an elected councilor for a brief time before she decided to resign from her position as elected councilor. When asked why she decided to resign her post, chief Dube mentioned that she believed that she could help her community more as a full-time chief than she could if she remained a member of the URC.[73]

LEGITIMACY AND THE CHIEFTAINCY IN KHOLWENI

Given the arguments raised in this analysis, two lingering questions deserve attention: Why did the legitimation process proceed in a more precarious manner in Kholweni than in Mvuzane or Ximba? Why was chief Mtembu forced to resign in 1998–99? These questions focus attention on the comparative aspect of this study as well the extent to which democratization has affected the relationship between the chieftaincy and society at the local level.

Some might argue that what happened in Kholweni was the result of its peculiar institutional design—that is, the fact that the chieftaincy was not hereditary. I do not believe, however, Kholweni should be categorized as an exceptional case given its non-hereditary institutional design. In practice, while not officially, the chieftaincy in Kholweni functioned as a hereditary institution. In this way, before 1999, members of the community, as a whole, were never allowed to select their chief. There is also evidence that even within hereditary chieftainships, disputes arise and those who aspire to become the chief can manipulate the rules to their advantage (Comaroff 1978). Thus, while I do not have evidence concerning the succession process in Kholweni as it unfolded within the church committee, I doubt that this process was free of conflict, intrigue, or negotiation.

Moreover, the manner in which the legitimation process unfolded in Kholweni was similar to Mvuzane and Ximba except that in Kholweni the leaders' poor performance, along with rising expectations, prompted the community to search for methods to hold them accountable. There were similar dynamics in Mvuzane and Ximba concerning the election of *izinduna,* traditional councilors, and various development committees. Most importantly, however, unlike the situation in Mvuzane and Ximba, where chiefs, *izinduna,* and traditional councilors utilized the idea of unity to maintain legitimacy, in Kholweni, we begin to observe the boundaries and limits of this concept, and with it, the boundaries and limits of the chieftaincy's legitimacy.

The timing of these events raises other interesting issues concerning the mutually transformative interactions between the ideas and practices of democratization and the ideas and practices of the chieftaincy. According to most people in Khowleni, the leadership style of chief

Mtembu was unchanged over the last ten years. That is, the concerns and frustrations with chief Mtembu were not new to the community, and many of the complaints people had against him concerned events that had occurred in the 1980s. While his performance remained unchanged, however, it appears that community expectations increased with the democratic transition in the 1990s. Unlike the situation in Mvuzane and Ximba, where the chieftaincy sought to create innovative ways to maintain authority in the midst of these pressures, the leadership in Kholweni failed to do so. Chief Mtembu was unable to justify his decisions, or lack thereof, as consistent with the goal of unity, as the most important aspects of the ruler-ruled relationship—security, consultation, neutral decision making, and community welfare—were absent from community life.

The way this dilemma was resolved in Kholweni should caution against predictions that democracy and the chieftaincy are incompatible. In the final analysis, for many people in Kholweni, it seemed appropriate to use the same electoral rules and processes as were utilized in the government-sponsored contests in 1994, 1996, and 1999 to elect the new chief—a chief who would provide security, consult the community, resolve disputes fairly, and promote the community welfare, especially with respect to the implementation of development. Thus, the safeguards of a "free and fair" election were invoked to help select a chief who would unify the community. At the same time, the community seemed hesitant about abolishing the chieftaincy in favor of a different institutional design. For many informants, even if the chief and mayor were elected in the same manner, and even if they were given similar responsibilities, there was nonetheless an important difference between the two. To understand the reasons for this distinction requires that we examine not only the functional attributes of the chieftaincy but its symbolic and normative features as well.

In the end, Kholweni demonstrates the important distinction between the legitimacy of individual leaders and the legitimacy of the chieftaincy more generally. There is no question that people in Kholweni lost faith in the ability of most of its leaders to solve community problems and provide development resources. For most of the community, however, the bad performance of these leaders did not necessarily impugn the chieftaincy form of governance or the idea of the chieftaincy more generally. While some members of the community sought reforms to abolish the institution of the chieftaincy, most viewed these proposals as beyond the realm of the politically possible.

Nonetheless, Kholweni also illustrates that the chieftaincy is not completely immune from criticism and attack and that bad leadership can ultimately enable people to think of forms of governance other than the chieftaincy. In other words, what is considered politically appropriate and what values are given priority are not fixed. In Kholweni, as was the case in Mvuzane and Ximba, there was a growing tension between the central importance of unity, as well as the chieftaincy's representation of this unity, and the desire to choose leaders who have the necessary qualities to make and enforce rules, and make decisions, that will promote the community welfare. There is no question that these tensions, and contradictions, will continue to shape chieftaincy-society relations in the future.

CONCLUSION

EIGHT

The Chieftaincy and the Post-Apartheid State:
Legitimacy and Democracy in a Mixed Polity

In my own region my forebears fought wars and battles
against colonial and later apartheid regimes in order to
maintain our traditional democracy. We cannot afford to
dispose of our traditional government institutions in favor of
Western kind of democracy. That would mean we fought in
vain against domination by foreign powers. Let us merge the
two types of democracies for the general good of the people.

Ubukhosi is like a two-edged sword. Depending on the
person wielding it, it can damage; it can easily be used to
injure and cause harm; equally it can be used to defend and
therefore build. It is common knowledge that service delivery
in rural areas has gone smoothly in areas where government
structures had good relations with traditional leaders, while
the opposite has been true of those areas where relations
have been bad. . . . [I]t is immoral for people to be made to
choose between traditional leaders and service delivery—they
deserve and are entitled to have both. . . . The present strug-
gle is not about the retention of power for its own sake, it is
for the retention of power so that it can be used to safeguard
the African value systems which are the bedrock of society.

When South Africans went to the polls in 1994, it not
only marked the culmination of an arduous tran-
sition process but also initiated the establishment of a mixed polity.
Through its incorporation of the chieftaincy, South Africa joined a
growing number of African states that have decided to blend together
the principles of liberal democracy with the principles of hereditary rule.
While there were many reasons to officially incorporate the chieftaincy

into the constitutional dispensation, few could have predicted how this decision would affect the legitimacy of the democratic post-apartheid state as well as the legitimacy of the chieftaincy. Indeed, after fifteen years of democratic rule, we are only just beginning to understand how people at the local level manage to make sense of and give meaning to these different sources of authority. What does seem clear at this point, however, is that the legitimation process is one that has been both contradictory and mutually transforming, and the developments in South Africa since 1994 challenge many of our assumptions concerning the nature of state authority and the consolidation of democratic rule.

To understand the struggle for legitimacy, I have focused on relations between the chieftaincy and society as well as between the chieftaincy and the state at the local level. My argument is that we cannot understand the chieftaincy's continued authority in the rural areas unless we take seriously what it does for people and what it means to people. Whether the chieftaincy establishes and maintains political legitimacy will depend upon the extent to which it performs in a manner that promotes the norms and values of the society over which they rule. More importantly, as these norms and values transform, so must the actions of traditional leaders. In other words, the authority of the chieftaincy, similar to the authority of the state, must be rooted in society if it is to be followed voluntarily. In a mixed polity, where there exists more than one moral order, the legitimation process will be particularly complex and contradictory, especially as the chieftaincy and those living in the rural areas incorporate the democratic norms and values of the post-apartheid state. As such, the legitimation process is one that is ongoing and is likely to promote constant negotiation and contestation. As an approach to understand authority in South Africa, the multiple legitimacies framework resists categorizations that are oftentimes utilized in the debate over the chieftaincy, such as suggesting that all chiefs, or the chieftaincy itself, are illegitimate or undemocratic. Instead, it invites analyses that focus on the interactions between the chieftaincy, the state, and the people.

THE NATURE OF POLITICAL LEGITIMACY IN A MIXED POLITY

Obviously, these dynamics have taken place in a broader sociopolitical and economic context, and I have situated the struggles for legitimacy into this context. In many cases, the various external factors have created both new opportunities and new challenges for the chieftaincy. It is clear that during the first fifteen years of democratic rule, there has been a mixture of continuity and change in rural South Africa. Through a number of policies, the ANC has tried to transform the rural areas and to make the chieftaincy more democratic. Its ability to dictate what happens on the ground, however, has been limited. Due to a lack of development resources, and dysfunctional local governments, most people in the rural areas have seen only marginal changes in their daily lives since 1994. In addition, for the first ten years of democratic rule, traditional leaders were able to govern much as they had during apartheid, utilizing the same Bantustan structures and boundaries. Given this continuity with the past, it was not surprising that when I asked whether elections had changed the chieftaincy, most people simply laughed and shook their heads no. Thus, for many, there is the desperate feeling that life has not improved at all since 1994, and in some cases, they suggested that their lives had actually gotten worse.

Despite the perception to many that nothing has changed, the reality is that in a variety of ways rural South Africa today is much different than what it was in the early 1990s. Unlike during the apartheid period, the rural areas are now plural institutional environments with a range of governmental and nongovernmental institutions. These institutions, such as development committees, local government, and political parties, compete with the chieftaincy for political and social space. At the same time, while institutional alternatives now exist, for many people the chieftaincy continues to be the central pillar in this post-apartheid political landscape. It has not only continued to resolve conflicts and provide resources to local populations, but it has remained the moral centerpiece in a changing and unpredictable political environment. For many living in the rural areas, it is the idea of the chieftaincy itself, even more so than its individual leaders, that provides a sense of unity and harmony. Indeed, chief Holomisa's quotation at the beginning of this chapter that "it is immoral for people to be made to choose between" the chieftaincy and development makes sense only if there is a recognition of the moral foundations of its authority.

In this way, the ability of the chieftaincy to function as a lens through which those in the rural areas can imagine and comprehend the new political reality has provided it with an even greater relevance at the local level than many had anticipated. Even in a community such as Kholweni, where chief Mtembu had lost the respect of the people, there was a general consensus that the chieftaincy should continue, but only after it was infused with new leadership. Undoubtedly, when the negotiators agreed to accommodate the chieftaincy, and to establish a mixed polity, they could not have anticipated that it would remain such a meaningful institution fifteen years later.

While there have been a range of responses to these changes, for the most part, traditional leaders have proven to be nimble, flexible, and adaptable, showing once again that they are not simply "card-board props"[1] or puppets of the state.[2] Indeed, one of the consistent themes in this book is that the chieftaincy has been transformed in many ways since 1994. What is interesting, however, is that this transformation process was often initiated from the bottom up rather than from the top down. There are numerous examples of people living in Mvuzane, Ximba, and Kholweni, who pressured their traditional leaders to become more inclusive, participatory, and accountable. In some cases, formally excluded groups, such as women, have been able to have a much greater influence on the chieftaincy, and attitudes concerning the role of women in the community appear to be changing. Even though the ability of local populations to effectuate these reforms is limited, it is a mistake to assume that those living in the rural areas are simply dupes who are content to accept their fate or wait passively for change to occur. Instead, ordinary citizens in the rural areas have utilized the chieftaincy to gain access to state institutions and resources and to help them provide meaning to the changing political environment. Unfortunately, much of the research on the chieftaincy has not examined the relations between local populations and traditional leaders and the dialogues that take place between the two over the nature of authority. Understanding these dialogues, and taking them seriously, is crucial if we want to understand the implications that the establishment of a mixed polity and the politics of multiple legitimacies have for the nature of authority and the development and quality of democracy in rural South Africa.

I began this book with the suggestion that there existed multiple sources of political legitimacy in South Africa, each with a distinct worldview concerning the appropriate relationship between rulers and ruled. For analytical purposes, it is possible to distinguish between the two and to specify the specific norms, rules, and institutions that encompass each worldview. In the rural areas, however, these differences become blurred as the democratic values of the post-apartheid state and the preexisting values of the chieftaincy overlap and blend together in ways that are contradictory and mutually transforming. The result is that for many people living in the rural areas it is difficult to disentangle the two, creating a complex sociopolitical space that complicates authority relations.

Within this space, I have argued that the chieftaincy is evaluated based on what it does for the people as well as what it represents to the people. The challenge for traditional leaders is that to maintain their legitimacy they must perform in ways that are consistent with preexisting values, especially the maintenance of unity, as well as allowing for the introduction of new norms and institutions that facilitate more development, participation, and accountability. As such, the legitimation process necessitates that they balance these contradictory demands for both continuity and change. Obviously, to accomplish this feat requires astute political skills, and whether traditional leaders succeed or fail depends, in large measure, upon the decisions they make at the local level. Thus, rather than attribute the resurgence and legitimacy of traditional leaders solely to external factors such as the existence of a weak state, the central argument in this book is that we must consider internal factors as well, such as what they do and the values they seek to uphold and reproduce.

Significant social and political changes are occurring in the rural areas, and those living in these areas are both intimidated by the changes and invigorated by the opportunity to improve their lives. As it negotiates these changes, the chieftaincy faces a challenging situation because it must simultaneously rely upon the state for the delivery of development resources and try to remain autonomous from the state for the purposes of local governance. This is a difficult process, and the chieftaincy's ability to successfully walk this tightrope is linked to whether it is able to carve out a space, distinct from the state and society, where it functions as a semi-autonomous polity. Indeed, many of the most heated debates in South Africa over the chieftaincy involve the drawing and redrawing of boundaries, both physical and moral, which affect the contours of this space.

It is crucial that there is an appreciation for the ways in which the chieftaincy seeks to achieve as much rule making and rule enforcement as possible with the aim to govern at the local level. In doing so, it has also sought to expand its authority over a range of issues that were presumed to be under the direct control of the state. The examples from Mvuzane, Ximba, and Kholweni demonstrate that traditional leaders have managed to make decisions and resolve disputes that concern elections, development, and local government. Even during the 1999 election, when the state was clearly present in the rural areas, traditional leaders were seen as a critical part of the process. In Mvuzane, chief Biyela worked with Vusi Chamane to provide information to the people about the voting process, and on Election Day, chief Biyela and his *izinduna* were at the polling sites to provide guidance and assistance. Indeed, throughout the rural areas, the chieftaincy's involvement in the election process actually helped to legitimize the elections and mobilize voters. Similar to the role the marabouts played in past elections in Senegal, traditional leaders have been able to gain some influence over voting, one of the most cherished and sacrosanct aspects of the liberal democratic process (Schaffer 1998; Comaroff and Comaroff 1997). With respect to development issues, the expansion of authority was even more thorough and complete because of the incredible lack of state presence. Because it is the most important issue in many rural communities, traditional leaders have attempted to make themselves indispensable to the development process. Not only are traditional leaders expected to access development resources, but once development projects are implemented, they are able to direct who benefits, and they are expected to resolve any disputes over its use or misuse. The influence they seek to have over development extends well beyond the role of a mere gatekeeper. Instead, as a semi-autonomous polity, they are determined to gain as much control and autonomy as possible at the local level.

The larger point is that those at the local level expect their traditional leaders, as the leaders of the area, to govern them, and they evaluate these leaders based on how well they perform their responsibilities (Oomen 2005: 164–99). The importance of development, and how it relates to authority, should not be underestimated. One of the results of political change in South Africa is that people expect their traditional leaders to do their best to bring development to their areas. For the most part, traditional leaders have not been immune from those rising expectations that accompanied the transition to democracy, and while in most cases they lack the capacity to access development on their own, they must at least be *perceived* as working for the community's benefit, and thereby promoting unity and harmony. Indeed, chief Mtembu's problems in Kholweni had less to do with the fact that there were no development projects and more to do with the perception that he was not trying and that he was no longer working for the benefit of the community.

The ability of the chieftaincy to make and enforce rules not only enables it to control the daily lives of those living in the individual chiefs' areas, but is also a way for it to reproduce its moral order. The moral dimension of legitimacy directs attention to how political actions must align with the norms, values, and symbols in which the authority of the chieftaincy is embedded. I have argued that the moral legitimacy of the chieftaincy is intertwined with the notion of unity and that the chiefs' decisions as the leaders of the community are evaluated in this context. In other words, the authority of traditional leaders is rooted in society, and it is simply not the case that they can do whatever they want without consequence. To remain effective, they must address the material needs of the community as well as the broader moral framework in which their authority is situated. Moral legitimacy, however, is inherently ambiguous and open to contestation, and it is bound to change over time (Schatzberg 2001). Thus, depending on the particular circumstances, traditional leaders can use it to expand authority, as was the case in Mvuzane and Ximba, or local populations can utilize it to limit authority, as in Kholweni. In this way, identifying the moral dimension of legitimacy is a way to understand the contours of the subsequent struggles over authority but it in no way predetermines the ultimate winners or losers (ibid.). Such struggles will be particularly complex and contradictory as multiple moral legitimacies intersect, overlap, and mutually transform.

My argument that the legitimation process has both a moral and a performance dimension parallels Comaroff's observations concerning the succession process in a Tswana chieftaincy. Briefly stated, his argument is that the succession rules are open to multiple interpretations and that there is room for political competition in a hereditary chieftaincy. He finds that the right to rule is determined by more than just birthright and that the quality of the potential chief mattered as well. Accordingly, Comaroff argues that "achievement and ascription may be seen as two levels of one reality, rather than as opposed principles" (1978: 17). He also notes that

> the very concept of an *ascriptive political system* would appear to be self-contradictory. For, if the devolution and incumbency of authority, or access to power, were entirely a function of non-negotiable ascription, the system would not admit *political* action as this term is generally understood today. Similarly, in order to have any enduring currency or social meaning, political action and achievement must be organized by means of established cultural categories. In other words, the logic of a political system necessarily resides in the dialectical process whereby the ongoing negotiation of power relations is mediated in terms of the cultural order. (Ibid.)

The point here is similar in that we cannot understand the decisions that traditional leaders make or the evaluations of their performance without taking seriously the cultural context in which they are situated and the way in which their authority is rooted in society (Crais 2006; Koelble 2005; Schatzberg 2001; Schaffer 1998; Comaroff 1997). Once we recognize the significant linkages that exist between traditional leaders and society, it is much easier to understand and appreciate the difficulties the post-apartheid state has had establishing their own connections with the people, independent from the chieftaincy's influence. As one of the "two publics" struggling for hegemony in the rural areas, the chieftaincy competes with the state, and in the process it has influenced the course of state formation and democratic consolidation. Given what we have learned about state-society relations in Africa over the last two decades, this is not particularly surprising, and many analyses have examined in some detail how social forces in society have altered the nature of state authority (Crais 2006; Ashforth 2005; Boone 2003; Forrest 2003; Villalon 1995; Reno 1995; Bayart 1986; Laitin 1986).

Indeed, consistent with these state-in-society analyses, one of the themes of this book has been to examine the limits of the post-apartheid state. After comparing the state's policy goals with what is actually happening on the ground, it is clear that it has been unable to transform the authority of the chieftaincy as it had anticipated. For example, while the 1998 LG White Paper envisioned that the authority of traditional leaders and elected councilors would be distinct, this has not been the case, and the lines between the two have been blurred. In fact, in the case of elections, development, and local government, people in the rural areas have relied upon the chieftaincy as a sort of lens through which they are able to give meaning to these new forms of authority.

The extent to which the chieftaincy has been able to appropriate and transform state authority is especially clear when we examine political dynamics at the local level. As is well documented, from the outset of the transition process, traditional leaders fought against the introduction of "foreign" institutions into "their areas." The fear was that new forms of authority would restrict their autonomy, and thereby weaken their influence. In actuality, the introduction of elections, development committees, and elected councilors has not weakened their authority, and in some cases, depending on the skills of the traditional leaders, their authority has actually expanded despite the fact that it must now compete with other institutions. The chieftaincy's ability to appropriate and transform state authority is linked to the continued meaningfulness of tribal authority boundaries at the local level. Rather than disrupt these preexisting boundaries, state authority was simply superimposed over them. For example, the ANC hoped that the introduction of development committees would create a civil society autonomous from the chieftaincy. Instead, development committees are simply situated within the tribal authority ward boundaries, and chiefs and *izinduna* positioned themselves as the leaders of the committees. Similarly, elected councilors find it difficult to represent communities that are outside their own tribal authority. Not only is it difficult for them to travel to these places, but when they do, they are often seen as outsiders. More importantly, to work in another community is seen as an affront and insult to the elected councilor's own community and to his own traditional leaders. The fact that these new forms of authority are made to fit within the preexisting boundaries enables the chieftaincy not only to gain control over them but to control the meanings people attach to them. As such, development has become part of the traditional leaders' responsibilities, and the elected councilor is seen, first and foremost, as the closest advisor to the chief, and in many cases, as the chief's representative as well as the people's representative.

Yet even though the introduction of elections, local government, and development has not changed authority relations as the ANC had hoped, it is clear that the chieftaincy's authority has definitely transformed since 1994. This is not surprising; throughout South African history the interactions between the modern state and the chieftaincy have often had unanticipated consequences. For example, Crais's observations concerning the colonial state in South Africa highlight how this process of mutual transformation unfolded in the Bantustan areas in the past. He argues that South Africans interacted with unfamiliar, modern structures and sought to incorporate and disseminate aspects of these structures into their daily lives (2003b: 1054). A similar dynamic seems to be occurring in the post-apartheid period, although the discourse of "democracy" and "development" has changed the nature of this process and the scope of the dissemination. In contemporary rural South Africa, we find that there is a steady expectation for more development, participation, and accountability, and the chieftaincy has been forced to respond to these concerns. In the end, through its involvement with elections, local government, and development committees, the chieftaincy has entered into this debate, and by doing so it has undoubtedly changed the nature of its own authority.

Perhaps one of the most obvious examples of this is the fact that in Mvuzane, Ximba, and Kholweni, people now demand the right to elect their *izinduna* and traditional councilors. Before 1994, the chief appointed these leaders, and they usually served for life. The demand for more development, and for leaders who have the skills to access development, has changed, and each ward now has the ability to elect and dismiss their *izinduna* and traditional councilors. In order to promote development in their areas, the chiefs in Mvuzane, Ximba, and Kholweni "allowed" this change to take place, and they have actually warned *izinduna* that they could be removed from office if they do not perform adequately.

Related to the election of traditional leaders and the need to put more development-oriented people into office is the issue of the participation of women. Those living in Mvuzane, Ximba, and Kholweni believed that women should have a role to play within the chieftaincy structures and that traditional leaders should consult women with respect to development. Indeed, there are examples of women serving as acting chiefs in KwaZulu-Natal, including the election of Victoria Dube as chief in Kholweni. While in many cases women still face extreme discrimination in the rural areas, the demand for development has provided an opportunity for them to become more involved. As noted above, these changes have most often occurred from the bottom up, and all of the examples used in this book predated the passage and implementation of the TLGF Act in 2003.

Another example is the attitudes that local populations have concerning whether traditional leaders should receive development resources before the rest of the community. Even though an overwhelming number of people in each case study described traditional leaders as the leaders of the community and believed they should be involved in every aspect of governance at the local level, there was also a strong sense that traditional leaders are not entitled to get development before the rest of the community. It is true that despite this attitude most traditional leaders did receive preferential access to development, and local populations had few institutional mechanisms available to stop this from happening. There is no doubt that significant gaps exist between what people expect and want and their ability to affect the decision-making process. Still, given that such attitudes are developing and that traditional leaders have shown a grudging willingness to adapt to changing expectations, it is worth examining how the distribution of development projects in rural areas unfolds over time.

With a focus on local-level dynamics, it seems obvious enough that the chieftaincy's authority in rural South Africa is complex and defies simple classification. As Koelble and LiPuma note, hereditary leaders are, culturally, time-occupying signs so positioned in social space that they have come to mediate the connectivities between rural and urban, community and state, local and global, in ways that are reproducing the institution of chieftainship in very modern, very transformative, forms. To think of chiefs as either traditional or modern is to ignore the very transcendence of their role that is critical to their resurgence. (2005: 93)

It is true that the chieftaincy's authority is rooted in more than just tradition. In rural South Africa, there are multiple sources of legitimacy, and the chieftaincy has sought to selectively incorporate those norms, rules, and institutions that will enable it to continue to exercise control. This "syncretizing genius" of the chieftaincy, according to Marks, it what has enabled it to remain relevant in the post-colonial era (1986: 11). In this way, while Koelble, LiPuma, and Marks have correctly identified the hybrid nature of the chieftaincy's authority and the external factors that contribute to its resurgence, it seeks to do more than simply mediate—it also seeks to govern with as much autonomy as possible.

DEMOCRACY AND DEMOCRATIC CONSOLIDATION IN A MIXED POLITY

Understanding the manner in which the chieftaincy has exercised authority since 1994 allows us to now examine more critically what this means for democracy in South Africa. For some, the fact that the chieftaincy continues to exercise authority at the local level means that democracy has been compromised and that the process of democratic consolidation is bound to fail because of its presence (Ntsebeza 2005; Munro 1996; Mamdani 1996). While I believe the evidence offered in this book gives us reasons to think more critically about these arguments, the difficulty of engaging in debates about the compatibility of the chieftaincy and democracy is that it presumes we have settled upon what democracy means in South Africa, for South Africans. At this stage in its democratic development, I am not convinced this is clear. What does seem certain, however, is that the democracy that rural South Africans *seem* to be imagining is one that complicates our more conventional understandings of liberal democracy and the consolidation of liberal democracy (Diamond 1999a).

As we have seen, both in national surveys and in the interviews conducted in Mvuzane, Ximba, and Kholweni, people tend to define democracy in substantive terms (Mattes and Thiel 1997). In other words, minimalist definitions of democracy, which focus on free and fair elections and the protection of basic freedoms, do not capture how most South Africans imagine democracy. Instead, the success or failure of democracy is linked to existence of specific public goods, such as employment, development, or, in the case of rural South Africa, the maintenance of unity. Of course, we should not assume that South Africans must choose between procedural democracy and substantive democracy. In their discussion on the discourses of democracy in post-colonial politics, Comaroff and Comaroff (1997) argue that "elections are important to the degree that they open up a space, periodically at least, for *substantive* democracy. On the other hand, voting—*procedural* democracy—is much less salient, save at moments of crisis" (139–40). This is an important reminder that as we analyze the development of democracy in South Africa, we should take the attitudes of South Africans seriously, even if they are inconsistent with our own experiences. Koelble is correct when he argues that in post-colonial spaces democracy is more than just institutions and practices and that we should look for the ways in which understandings of democracy are negotiated through different cultural prisms (2005: 5). This conception of democracy seems even more appropriate in a mixed polity, where citizens may be presented with different conceptions of democratic values and practices.

Of course, the attitudes that people have about democracy may not remain static over time and will be influenced by the experiences they have with democratic institutions (Mattes and Bratton 2007). Whatever type of democracy South Africans create will be the result of ongoing negotiations and dialogues, and it is impossible to know how this process will unfold in the long term. What we do know, however, is that for many people living in the rural areas, their experiences with democratic elections and institutions have not taken place in a political vacuum, and the chieftaincy has both formally and informally become a critical feature of the democratic process. Not surprisingly, the development of democracy has been ambiguous, and in many cases, it appears that the chieftaincy has influenced local-level understandings of elections, consultation, and representation. Again, in a mixed polity, where there are multiple sources of authority for people to choose, this is not surprising. As both King Zwelethini and chief Holomisa's comments at the beginning of this chapter indicate, over the years there has been a great deal of discussion in South Africa concerning the possibility of merging "liberal democracy" and "African democracy." What is ironic is that as these discussions persist within both national and provincial parliaments, at the local level, people have actually started to find ways to bring democratic institutions and the chieftaincy together.

The problem is that the attitudes people have about democratic institutions and the chieftaincy confound our conventional understandings of democratic consolidation, because neither democracy nor the chieftaincy is seen as "the only game in town." Instead, there is ample evidence that people want both democratic institutions and the chieftaincy. More importantly, they want these institutions to work together. For most people in the rural areas, the notion that they should choose one or the other would be considered absurd. What we have in rural South Africa is a type of "double-mindedness" that Whitaker first observed in Northern Nigeria. While there is a tendency to dismiss such double-mindedness as something that is bound to fade away as development occurs, this may not be the case in South Africa, as the Ximba case study illustrates. Indeed, the establishment of mixed polities ensures a type of politics where a variety of political actors will promote different legitimacy logics. In such circumstances, the ways in which people understand and practice democracy are unlikely to conform to the models that some in the West consider to be "conventional" or "appropriate." In South Africa, the incorporation of the chieftaincy into its constitutional framework invites, rather than discourages, double-mindedness. Such a reality requires a more nuanced understanding of democratic consolidation that can explain why and how people might find it appropriate and necessary to accept multiple types of political authority simultaneously, without any recognition that such attitudes are contradictory.

The more normative question is whether this type of double-mindedness is dangerous for South Africa's democracy. There is no denying that the chieftaincy presents many problems for the development of liberal democracy in South Africa and that the chieftaincy may in fact be inconsistent with liberal democracy. At the same time, it is fair to say that one-party rule, increased nepotism, and the continued rise in inequality between the rich and the poor are problematic as well. Indeed, in recent years a growing literature has warned of the gradual decay of democracy in South Africa (Robins 2005). Many of these studies focus on particular institutional and economic developments that challenge the quality of democracy (Southall 1998 and 2007; Gumede 2005; Herbst 2005; Alence 2004; Bond 2003; Sparks 2003; Beall, Gelb, and Hassim 2005). Of more interest here are those analyses that examine how issues of magic, sorcery, and witchcraft intersect with South Africa's democracy (Ashforth 2005; Crais 2002). In a revealing study of witchcraft in Soweto, Ashforth argues that the South African democracy must address the "problem of witches" (Ashforth 2005: 280). The reason is that "the risk of ignoring issues of spiritual insecurity in an African context is that people who see their lives as subject to the ravages of 'evil forces' may suspect, or continue to doubt, that the practice of democratic government, with its doctrines of 'rule of law' and 'human rights,' doctrines that are very recent in the history of political subjection in this part of Africa, represent alien impositions with little connection to their own needs, particularly their desire for security and justice" (284). What this suggests is that as a non-Western democracy South Africa must face a host of issues that other liberal democracies may not have to address. More precisely, issues such as witchcraft, magic, and the chieftaincy highlight Koelbe's point that for democracy to develop in South Africa the people must have the opportunity to imagine it in ways that in the West would simply seem "unthinkable" (Koelble 2005; Schatzberg 2001; Schaffer 1998).

The establishment of a mixed polity has provided the parameters through which South Africans will continue to debate and negotiate questions of authority and democracy, but institutional arrangements alone will not predetermine the outcome of this process. In the long term, the role that the chieftaincy will have in society will undoubtedly transform as it responds to changes that occur at the global, national, and local levels. The transformation of the chieftaincy, however, will ultimately depend upon whether traditional leaders will make decisions that are consistent with the existing moral order. Thus, the legitimation process will vary throughout rural South Africa. As President Mbeki suggested at the annual opening of the National House of Traditional Leaders in February 2007, traditional leaders must attempt to emulate those leaders of the past who "embodied the core values and principles of justice, unity, peace, [and] freedom" and recognize that "[t]hey secured the respect and allegiance of the people because of what they did, in the interest of the people, fully understanding that they only serve as leaders because the people agree that they should serve as leaders." It remains to be seen whether traditional leaders will be able to integrate successfully the different moral orders, rules, and institutions that encompass contemporary South Africa and allow for the creation of a political order that meets the demands and the aspirations of those they govern.

For those living in Mvuzane, Khowleni, and Ximba, there have been significant changes since 1998–99. Victoria Dube was elected as chief in 2005 and is currently serving in this capacity. Although she resigned as an elected local councilor upon becoming the chief, she has sought to utilize her connections with the local municipality to secure development projects for Kholweni. Informal discussions with residents of Kholweni in 2007 suggested that there is a general consensus that she has been a more effective chief than chief Mtembu or her husband.

In Mvuzane, chief Biyela passed away in 2006 after serving as chief for forty years. In 2007, his son, May Biyela, assumed the duties as the new chief in Mvuzane, although as of April 2009 he was not yet "officially" installed into this position. Chief Biyela will face many of the same challenges that his predecessor did from 1994 to 2006, but he will have to confront these without the assistance of Vusi Chamane. In 2006, Vusi decided not to run for reelection as the local councilor, to give someone else a chance to help the community. While Vusi still remains active in the community, he is not as involved in community development projects as he was in the past and has been focused on starting his own business.

Finally, chief Mlaba stepped down as chief in 2007, and his nephew, Simangaye Mlaba, was installed as the chief in Ximba. At his installation celebration, both the KZN local government and traditional affairs MEC Mike Mabuyakhulu and King Zwelethini were in attendance. During his remarks, Mabuyakhulu emphasized that "Amakhosi need to be in constant dialogue with the newly-formed ward committees to ensure the development needs" of their areas and that "we cannot do this along, we need the full co-operation of the Amakhosi" (Maphumulo 2007). Despite these changes within the chieftaincy, Zibuse Mlaba continues to serve as an ANC MP for the KZN Parliament, and Simon Ngubane was reelected as local councilor for the Ximba ward in 2006. These three chiefs have come to power in the midst of more changes in the rural areas that will undoubtedly affect how they rule. Most importantly, with the passage of the TLGF Act in 2003 and the passage of parallel legislation in KZN in 2005, every tribal authority in the province has been changed to traditional councils and every regional authority has been replaced with local houses of traditional leaders. As mandated in the TLGF Act, in 2007 elections were held for traditional councils throughout KZN. How these new bodies will interact with chiefs, *izinduna,* and local government institutions remains to be seen, but I am certain that every chief will seek to use traditional councils to expand his authority.

In addition, the national and provincial elections in 2009 that have propelled Jacob Zuma to the presidency will also change the dynamics in each of these areas. As the first Zulu to serve as president, and as someone who was born and raised in a tribal authority only fifteen miles from Mvuzane and Kholweni, Jacob Zuma is unabashedly in favor of protecting and even expanding the authority of the chieftaincy. While only time will tell whether the chieftaincy will actually benefit from Zuma's rule, there is no question that traditional leaders will expect a lot from him. How traditional leaders lobby a Zuma administration and how this administration responds to this pressure will be one of many dynamics to watch in the next few years.

Given the moral legitimacy of the chieftaincy in rural South Africa, there is no reason to believe that the installation of these three new chiefs will affect how local populations perceive the institution of the chieftaincy. Still, to maintain his legitimacy each of these chiefs will be forced to respond to the needs of the community and to perform in ways that are consistent with the underlying moral legitimacies at the local level. In fact, these changes in Mvuzane, Kholweni, and Ximba are part of a broader pattern in KwaZulu-Natal in which there will be an ever-growing number of chiefs who were installed in the post-apartheid era. In fact, of the chiefs now in power in KwaZulu-Natal, 32 percent of them were installed after January 1, 1993. Another 9 percent of the chieftaincies in this province are officially vacant, which means that there will be even more new chiefs installed in the near future.[3] Such changes, however, do not guarantee that the chieftaincy will become more democratic in the future or that the struggles with the state will become any less contentious. Instead, given the existence of multiple legitimacies in South Africa and the emergence of a new generation of traditional leaders who are even more intimately tied to these overlapping moral orders than their predecessors, the legitimation process is most likely to result in the mutual transformation of both the chieftaincy and the state in the years to come.

NOTES

I. INTRODUCTION

The first epigraph is from Oomen 2005: 164; the second epigraph is from Republic of South Africa 1996.

1. According to the Draft White Paper on Traditional Leadership and Governance, there are 12 kings and queens, 774 chiefs, and 1640 headmen in South Africa (2002: 39). Of the six provinces that have traditional leaders, KwaZulu-Natal has 280 chiefs, Limpopo has 188 chiefs, the Eastern Cape has 173 chiefs, with the remainder found in Mpumalanga, the Free State, and the North West. The accuracy of these numbers is open to some debate as it has proved difficult for the government to keep track of these leaders. While the Department of Local Government and Provincial Affairs has a database that includes all kings, queens, and chiefs, the information in this database is often outdated. For example, there are numerous chiefs who I know are no longer in power but who are listed in this database. In addition, while the Draft White Paper states that there are no headmen in KwaZulu-Natal, this is definitely not the case. In addition, the KwaZulu-Natal Department of Local Government and Traditional Affairs estimates there are 308 chiefs in the province and not 280.

2. There are eleven official languages in South Africa: English, Afrikaans, Zulu, Sotho, Xhosa, Tswana, Swazi, Ndebele, Pedi, Tsonga, and Venda.

3. As will be discussed in chapter 3, in the 2003 TLGF Act the term "tribe" was replaced with the term "traditional community."

4. Nationwide, approximately 42% of the population resides in rural areas. The provinces where there are a majority of people living in the rural areas include KwaZulu-Natal, Eastern Cape, North West, Mpumalanga, and Limpopo (Republic of South Africa 2001a).

5. This conversion is based on an exchange rate of 11.2 rand per dollar on October 21, 2008.

6. Mamdani 1996; Ntsebeza 2005.

7. Rouveroy van Nieuwaal 1996; Alexander 1995.

8. Oomen 2005; Comaroff and Comaroff 2004.

9. Ntsebeza 2005.

10. Rouveroy van Nieuwaal and van Dijk 1999; Rouveroy van Nieuwaal 1999; Rouveroy van Nieuwaal 1996; Ray 1996; Von Trotha 1996; Rouveroy van Nieuwaal 1987.

11. Koelble 2005.

12. While the chieftaincy gained official recognition in many states over the last twenty years, there is little evidence that the efforts to abolish its de facto influence during the 1950s and 1960s were ever completely successful (Rathbone 2000; Rouveroy van Nieuwaal 1996; Moore 1986; Callaghy 1984).

13. The weak-state thesis is addressed in more detail in chapter 5, where I examine the authority of the chieftaincy in an area where the local state has been able to deliver resources.

14. Unlike other studies on the chieftaincy in South Africa, Oomen (2005) does seek to measure and explain political legitimacy, and she dedicates one chapter to this issue. The main difference with my analysis is that I focus more narrowly on political legitimacy, and I examine how it is manifested in ways other than lawmaking.

15. For an analysis of this process in post-colonial Africa, see Bayart (1986).

16. See Whitaker (1970) for an analysis of this dynamic in northern Nigeria.

17. While the delivery of development is technically not a norm, it is nonetheless a critical aspect of the state's moral claim of legitimacy. As Mandela has suggested, the idea of freedom in South Africa is one that has a procedural as well as a substantive component (1994a).

18. Mandela 1994a.

19. At the same time, while it has stressed liberal democratic values, it has also sought to promote more indigenous values, such as the idea of *ubuntu*. For the most part, however, its commitment to *ubuntu* is more often than not overshadowed by an institutional and ideological apparatus that focuses on rights, elections, and the delivery of development to disadvantaged communities (Marx 2002).

20. The studies that I have found particularly helpful are Forrest 2003; Schatzberg 2001; Heywood 1998; Geschiere 1997; Vansina 1990; Laitin 1986; Ashforth 2005; Berry 1993; Crais 2002; Mahoney 1998.

21. I encountered this phrase many times in KwaZulu-Natal. Oomen reports similar findings in Limpopo (2005: 164). Speaking of the Zulus in 1940, Gluckman noted a similar refrain in the rural areas that "the people respect their chief, but the chief ought to respect his people" (1940a: 44).

22. See Karlstrom (1996) for a similar dynamic in Uganda.

23. N = 172.

24. N = 138.

25. Schatzberg makes a similar argument in his analysis of political legitimacy in middle Africa (2001). A historical analysis of the idea of unity as it relates to the chieftaincy is developed in chapter 2. I am interested in understanding how traditional leaders justify their rule in moral terms. Based on the time I

have spent in the rural areas, I have no doubt that the idea of unity provides the frame through which the actions of traditional leaders are evaluated, and I provide many examples of this in subsequent chapters. Whether the chieftaincy actually represented unity during the pre-colonial period does not affect my particular line of inquiry—even though there are plenty of historical references on this point (Gluckman 1940a, 1940b; Cope 1993; Lambert 1995; Hamilton 1998; Laband 1995; Gump 1990; Guy 1979). For example, whether the "founding fathers" in the United States actually believed that "all men are created equal" is irrelevant as to whether American citizens currently evaluate their government based on this moral claim. Whether it is possible that the political principles and practices of the pre-colonial period could survive to the present day, in one form or another, is an important historical question. More recently, scholars from a variety of disciplines have demonstrated how the colonized engaged the colonial state and how they were able to influence and manipulate the nature of rule (Crais 2002; Hamilton 1998; Forrest 2003; Berry 1993; Marks 1986).

26. The idea that the chieftaincy has "traditional legitimacy" is less than helpful for an analysis like this one. Rather, what I am trying to do is to articulate and problematize the actual substance of the chieftaincy's moral claims to rule.

27. Just as politicians in the United States may advocate for diametrically different measures to promote the value of "freedom." Unity, just like freedom, can justify a broad range of political actions and political resistance.

28. In 2000, the Durban Metropolitan Council was renamed eThekweni Municipality.

29. In the 2009 national and provincial elections, a majority of voters in Mvuzane and Kholweni chose the ANC for the first time.

30. Between 1998 and 1999, the exchange rate fluctuated between 6 and 6.5 rand per U.S. dollar. Thus, at the time of this study, 5 rand equaled approximately 80 U.S. cents. Unless otherwise indicated, I use an exchange rate of R6/$1 in this study.

31. The name "Kholweni" is derived from the Zulu word *kholwa* which means "believer."

32. Kholweni is discussed at much greater length in chapter 7.

2. "THE BINDING TOGETHER OF THE PEOPLE"

1. Mamdani concludes that one of the effects of indirect rule was that local populations respected the lawmaker (i.e., the chief) more than the law (1996: 125). My evidence, however, suggests a different dynamic, as people tended to be much more critical of individual rulers than they were of the institution of the chieftaincy itself.

2. Unity was not a concept that figured in the initial research design of this project. It was only after months of fieldwork that I started to encounter frequent, unsolicited references to the idea of unity and the other principles.

This continued to occur as I visited different research sites. The possibilities of broader historical linkages were not considered until I visited, and revisited, the secondary literature and primary sources. In this sense, an inductive, rather than deductive, methodological approach suggested the importance of the idea of unity and its possible explanatory power.

3. In the field, these principles became apparent after speaking with people about the chieftaincy and observing the decision-making and conflict-resolution processes. While I do not claim these are the only principles at work in the political arena, they were the most pronounced in KwaZulu-Natal.

4. In chapters 4–7, I demonstrate how the legitimation process takes different routes in three separate chieftaincies even though the idea of unity and its principles are equally important in each.

5. For readers familiar with the development of American political culture, what I hope to highlight through the use of these principles is what we find in the American experience with the principles that inform the idea of "liberty." One could argue that the principles that give meaning to the idea of liberty include individualism, private property, and the establishment of distinct private/public spheres of activity. Over time, distinctions are blurred to the extent that one might claim individualism is not possible without liberty and vice versa. Analytically, however, it is important to keep these ideas separate. In the context of my argument here, a comparison, albeit rough, would be to equate the idea of "unity" with that of "liberty" as each is a crucial ideological building block for the development of a more coherent political culture.

6. In addition, the idea of unity can be found in other areas of South African politics. For example, unity was an important ideological component of the African National Congress and its policy of an all-inclusive South Africa (Gerhart 1978; Mandela 1965). Future research might focus on comparing how this term was used by urban-based political groupings or whether this term has the same currency throughout South Africa or the region. Obviously, this study is limited to the use of this concept within a narrow scope of inquiry—the institution of the chieftaincy in KwaZulu-Natal.

7. I refer to these rulers as "kings" even though both the colonial and apartheid governments classified them as "paramount chiefs" from 1879 to 1994.

8. In fact, Shaka was not the son of the "great wife," and King Cetshwayo, Shaka's grandson who ruled from 1872 to 1879, utilized the battlefield as well as succession rules to claim power.

9. As Marks has pointed out, what eventually became the policy of indirect rule was more accurately the aggregation of pragmatic decisions, made mostly by Shepstone from 1846 to 1876. When he left his position in Natal, the indirect rule system nearly collapsed because it was so dependent on Shepstone personally (Marks 1970; see also Welsh 1971).

10. It is estimated that approximately 100,000 migrated from Zululand to Natal during the early nineteenth century (Brookes and Webb 1965: 58).

11. The reigns of the Zulu kings are as follows: Shaka (1816–28), Dingane (1828–40), Mpande (1840–72), Cetshwayo (1872–79 and 1883–84), Dinizulu (1884–1913), Solomon (1913–33), Cyprian Bhekuzulu (1948–68), Goodwill Zwelethini (1971–present).

12. This title was subsequently dropped in the mid-1850s at the request of colonial secretary Earl Grey, who believed the term "diplomatic" incorrectly implied that the chieftaincies were separate, sovereign African powers existing in Natal (Welsh 1971: 25).

13. Whether these different early experiences may have affected the legitimation process in Natal and Zululand will be discussed more fully in subsequent chapters. Obviously, this brief summary of Zulu history does not address many of the significant events that occurred during this period. For a more detailed account of this period, I recommend Lambert (1995), Guy (1979), Morris (1965).

14. In 1976, the exchange rate fluctuated around R0.86/$1.00 (Federal Reserve Statistical Release 2000; available from http://www.federalreserve.gov/releases/H10/hist/thru89.htm; accessed September 13, 2001). Thus, R200 equaled approximately $172.00.

15. See Marks (1970) for an exhaustive analysis of the Bambatha rebellion. Also, see Mahoney (1998) for an insightful examination of political culture during this period.

16. This tribal authority was one of my three research sites.

17. All of the following information is located in the Durban Archives Repository in a file entitled "Biyela Succession Dispute." The material is available upon request.

18. In fact, this succession battle is similar to Gluckman's analysis of a bridge-opening ceremony in KwaZulu-Natal in the 1930s. In this essay, Gluckman argues that the colonial experience resulted in the establishment of one society of both blacks and whites rather than a divided one. At the same time, however, he notes how colonial administrators and chiefs differ with respect to the authority they wield and the processes through which legitimacy is established and maintained (1940b).

19. I could not locate any systematic examinations of this appeal process. Thus, it is unclear what percentage of the chiefs' decisions were appealed and what percentage the magistrate actually overturned. Many informants suggested that very few people appealed their decisions due to financial constraints, lack of information about the process, and, most importantly, the threat of public condemnation.

20. There are, however, excellent analyses focusing on the construction and implementation of customary law that shed some light on this (Costa 1998; Chanock 1991). Unfortunately, these studies tend to examine formal and informal rules and structures rather than judicial processes and perceptions of justice, fairness, and impartiality. For examples of an application of the process-oriented

approach in Africa and Asia, see Mann and Roberts 1991; Starr and Collier 1989.

21. I will discuss the issue of defining and redefining "politics" in more detail in chapters 4–7.

3. THE MAKING OF A MIXED POLITY

The first epigraph is from *Ex Parte Chairperson of the Constitutional Assembly: In re Certification of the Constitution of the Republic of South Africa, 1996* 1996 (4) SA 744 (CC) (*First Certification Judgment*), heard on 1–5 and 8–11 July 1996 and decided 6 September 1996: 5; the second epigraph is from Republic of South Africa, 1998, *Local Government White Paper:* 78; the third epigraph is from Republic of South Africa, 2002, *Draft White Paper on Traditional Leadership and Governance,* Notice 2103 of 2002: 1.

1. In their description of "transformative movements," Koelble and LiPuma suggest that it consists of two promises: "to periodise and encapsulate the lack of freedoms of the past by adopting transparently different and more democratic policies, and by implementing institutions that remedy the injustices inherited from the past" (2005: 77).

2. The ANC's dominance at the national, provincial, and local levels of government has enabled it to control much of the debate and policies concerning the chieftaincy. While the Inkatha Freedom Party has remained extremely active at the provincial level, its influence at the national level has waned.

3. In fact, in 2007, Nelson Mandela's grandson, Mandla Mandela, was installed as the chief of the Mvezo Traditional Council in the Eastern Cape. While Nelson Mandela was the legitimate heir, the authorities decided to allow his successor to fill the position ("Mandela's Grandson a Xhosa Chief," BBC News, April 16, 2007).

4. As part of the negotiation process, the parties adopted a number of constitutional principles that were intended to guide the writing of the final constitution. In its certification decisions, the Constitutional Court evaluated the final constitution based on whether its provisions were consistent with the constitutional principles.

5. The interim constitution required that the CC determine the validity of the final constitution before it could become law. The CC judged the final document against the constitutional principles set forth in 1993–94. The CC accepted arguments from all parties who believed the final constitution was invalid. In the end, the CC found some provisions of the final constitution invalid. The assembly was required to amend these provisions and then resubmit the constitution to the CC.

6. In *Bhe v. Magistrate Khayelitsha, Shibi v. Sithole,* and *South African Human Rights Commission v. President of the Republic of South Africa* (2005 (1) B.C.L.R. 1 (CC)), the Constitutional Court ruled that the principle of male primogeniture

concerning succession violated the right to equality under section 9 of the Constitution. See Grant (2006) for a discussion of this case.

7. The pre-interim phase was from 1993 to 1995 and the interim phase was from 1995 to 2000. The final phase of this transition was completed in November 2000, when local democratic elections were held for the second time. The new local government institutions, as well as the electoral boundaries, are different from the ones described in this chapter. This process has renewed the debate in South Africa concerning the chieftaincy, and many chiefs are fearful that the new institutions and boundaries will limit their constitutionally guaranteed authority.

8. Jimmy Seepe, "Mufamadi Assures Chiefs of Their Role," *The Sowetan,* October 27, 1999; "SA Can Meld Hereditary Rule with an Elected Leadership," *Business Day,* January 20, 2000; Jubie Matlou, "Chiefs Face Mbeki over Traditional Land," *Mail and Guardian,* February 3, 2000.

9. *Mail and Guardian,* "Chiefs Want More Power in Local Government," August 18, 1995.

10. *Mail and Guardian,* "The Iron Hand Resists the Ballot Box," February 3, 1995.

11. *Mail and Guardian,* "Buthelezi Mobilizes for Campaign Battle," February 3, 1995.

12. *Mail and Guardian,* "Chiefs Want More Power in Local Government," August 18, 1995.

13. Charles Phahlane, "'Divide and Rule' Move Slammed by Chiefs," *The Mercury,* January 31, 2003; "Traditional Leaders Ask Mbeki to Keep Government Promises," *Business Day,* April 2, 2003.

14. William Mervin Gumede, "Mbeki Not Budging on Chiefs Demands," *Financial Mail,* September 8, 2000.

15. "Chiefs Call for Constitutional Change," *South African Press Association,* April 1, 2003.

16. Interview with local government chief executive officer, November 19, 1998.

17. Interview with local government chief executive officer, November 19, 1998.

18. It is a mistake to assume that this hostility emanated only from KwaZulu-Natal and that it was a product of broader IFP-ANC rivalries (see Lodge 2001: 23). While this rivalry is an important factor to consider when examining traditional leaders in South Africa, it has become less important since the early 1990s. As was discussed above, traditional leaders began to act as one as early as 1995–96 when they were confronted with the interim phase of local government reform. By 2000, traditional leaders had formed an organization, the Coalition of Traditional Leaders, that cut across old IFP-ANC divisions and that promoted the interests of all traditional leaders in the country. Thus, some of the apartheid-era divisions between different "homeland" traditional leaders,

which were based on ethnicity, appear to be transforming into a broader-based chiefraincy organization.

19. There was some discussion in the committee to require the traditional councils to consist of 50% women. It was noted that this might be a difficult target, as political parties, such as the ANC, have had trouble meeting the 30% requirement for candidates.

20. See Oomen 2005.

21. "Traditional Leaders' Issues Must Not Become a Political Football," *Business Day,* February 12, 2003.

22. "Mpumalanga's 'Royal' Transport Scheme Flounders," *African Eye News Service,* February 10, 2003.

23. Justin Arenstein, "Mpumalanga Chiefs Go Cybernetic," *African Eye News Service,* February 24, 2003.

24. This clause was not present in the TLGF Bill but was added during the committee deliberations.

25. Under the 1951 Bantu Authorities Act, traditional authorities were exclusively male dominated, and the government had more power to appoint and dismiss traditional leaders without the consent of local communities.

26. Even those most closely involved in the process recognized the limitations of legislating in this area. Yunus Carrim, ANC MP and chairman of the Portfolio Committee, claims that the transformation envisioned in the legislation is perhaps twenty years away, and that in any case, there may be important unintended consequences that may alter the nature of this transformation (Yunus Carrim, in discussion with the author, June 2005).

4. THE CONTESTED NATURE OF POLITICS, DEMOCRACY, AND RIGHTS IN RURAL SOUTH AFRICA

The first epigraph is from an interview with male member of development committee, Ximba, March 23, 1999; the second epigraph is from an interview with male traditional councilor, Mvuzane, March 3, 1999; the third epigraph is from an interview with male member of development committee, Kholweni, July 13, 1999.

1. Number of people interviewed (hereafter N) = 181.

2. When there is no Zulu word equivalent to an English one, the typical practice is to simply add the prefix "i" to the English word. For example, the English word "video" would be referred to as *ivideo* in Zulu.

3. Mervyn Frost defines politics as "talk and action directed at changing (or maintaining) the general rules of association governing some social entity" (Frost 1996). In addition, he states that "[w]here people operate according to well settled rules and feel no need to challenge or change them, there is no politics" (16). This definition highlights the disruptive capacity of politics that seems particularly relevant for what has happened, and continues to happen, in rural

areas under the chieftaincy. Schaffer finds similar feelings to the idea of *politig* in Senegal as well (1998: 76–79).

4. Interview with male member of development committee, Ximba, March 23, 1999.

5. Interviews with unemployed male, Mvuzane, February 16, 1999; female member of development committee, Mvuzane, February 22, 1999; female member of development committee, Mvuzane, Februrary 24, 1999; female student, Ximba, March 23, 1999; male sugarcane farmer, Kholweni, June 29, 1999; male member of development committee, Kholweni, June 30, 1999; unsalaried female, Kholweni, July 3, 1999; female pensioner, Kholweni, July 9, 1999.

6. Interviews with unsalaried female, Mvuzane, February 11, 1999; male member of development committee, Mvuzane, February 17, 1999; male traditional councilor and member of development committee, Mvuzane, March 2, 1999; male traditional councilor, Mvuzane, March 3, 1999; unemployed male, Kholweni, June 19, 1999; female member of development committee, Kholweni, July 1, 1999; unemployed female, Kholweni, June 30, 1999; female teacher, Kholweni, July 14, 1999.

7. Interviews with female pensioner, Kholweni, June 28, 1999; female pensioner, Kholweni, June 28, 1999; female sugarcane farmer, Kholweni, July 7, 1999; male member of development committee, Kholweni, July 9, 1999; female pensioner, Kholweni, July 9, 1999; unemployed female, Kholweni, July 15, 1999.

8. Interview with male traditional councilor, Kholweni, July 15, 1999.

9. Interview with male *induna*, Mvuzane, February 11, 1999.

10. Interview with unsalaried female, Mvuzane, February 16, 1999.

11. Interview with unsalaried female, Mvuzane, February 23, 1999.

12. Interview with unemployed female, Mvuzane, February 23, 1999.

13. Interview with female member of development committee, Mvuzane, February 24, 1999.

14. Interviews with unemployed female, Kholweni, June 30, 1999; male traditional councilor, Kholweni, June 30, 1999; unemployed female, Kholweni, July 1, 1999; unsalaried female, Kholweni, July 12, 1999; unemployed male, Kholweni, July 14, 1999; female teacher, Kholweni, July 14, 1999; female elected councilor, Kholweni, July 25, 1999; unemployed male, Ximba, March 23, 1999; male teacher, Ximba, April 8, 1999; unsalaried, female, Ximba, April 9, 1999; male traditional councilor, Ximba, April 12, 1999.

15. Interview with chief Biyela, Mvuzane, July 10, 1999.

16. Interview with chief Mlaba, Ximba, April 15, 1999.

17. Interview with male pensioner, Kholweni, July 2, 1999.

18. The notable exception in Ximba is discussed below.

19. A total of 61% of those interviewed in the three case studies did not want their chiefs involved in politics (N = 124). In Mvuzane and Kholweni, approximately 70% had this opinion, while only 45% had such a view in Ximba.

20. A majority of informants in Kholweni believed this would be bad for the community. The Kholweni example will be discussed in more detail in chapter 7.

21. While there is no question that chief Mlaba has been influential in getting resources to Ximba, especially projects related to roads, it is really his brother, Obed Mlaba, who has been the mayor of Durban since 1996, who has been in a better position to get development projects to the area.

22. Interviews with male member of development committee, Mvuzane, February 12, 1999; unsalaried female, Mvuzane, February 16, 1999; unsalaried female, Mvuzane, February 17, 1999.

23. Interview with unemployed male, Mvuzane, February 16, 1999.

24. Interview with unsalaried female, Mvuzane, February 16, 1999.

25. Interviews with unsalaried female, Mvuzane, February 16, 1999; female member of development committee, Mvuzane, February 22, 1999.

26. Interview with unemployed male, Ximba, March 30, 1999.

27. Interview with male, Ximba, March 31, 1999.

28. Interview with male traditional councilor, Ximba, April 12, 1999.

29. Interview with male *iphoyisa,* Ximba, April 15, 1999.

30. Interview with businessman, Ximba, April 12, 1999.

31. Since 1994, the Institute for Democracy in South Africa (IDASA) has conducted a series of public opinion surveys measuring attitudes toward democracy. IDASA has recently joined with the Centre for Democratic Development in Ghana and Michigan State University to conduct additional surveys in South Africa, as well as throughout the African continent. These surveys can be located at http://www.afrobarometer.org.

32. Support for democracy is measured by asking respondents whether they prefer democratic institutions to alternative institutions. The specific questions asked in the survey are whether "democracy is preferable to any other kind of government" and whether "democracy is always the best form of government even if things are not working" (Mattes 2002: 30).

33. Interview with male member of development committee, Mvuzane, February 17, 1999.

34. Interview with male traditional councilor and member of development committee, Mvuzane, March 2, 1999.

35. Interview with male traditional councilor, Mvuzane, March 3, 1999.

36. Interview with unsalaried female, Mvuzane, February 11, 1999.

37. Interview with unemployed female, Mvuzane, January 21, 1999.

38. Interview with chief Biyela, Mvuzane, July 10, 1999.

39. Interview with male *iphoyisa,* Kholweni, June 18, 1999.

40. Interview with unemployed male, Kholweni, June 29, 1999.

41. Interview with male *iphoyisa* and member of development committee, Ximba, March 23, 1999.

42. Interview with male pensioner, Ximba, March 31, 1999.

43. Interview with female member of development committee, Ximba, March 18, 1999.

44. Schaffer found in Senegal a similar tendency for people to associate the concept of democracy with consensus building (1998: 57–59). In middle Africa, Schatzberg found that many believed in the indivisibility of power, which might be considered an example of unity. He has argued that the notion of the indivisibility of power is one that may challenge liberal understandings of democracy (2001: 221).

45. Interviews with unemployed male, Mvuzane, January 19, 1999; female day laborer, Mvuzane, February 5, 1999; unsalaried female, Kholweni, June 28, 1999; female pensioner, Kholweni, June 28, 1999; male student, Kholweni, July 13, 1999; chief Mtembu, Kholweni, July 17, 1999.

46. Interviews with female day laborer, Mvuzane, February 5, 1999; male pensioner, Mvuzane, February 8, 1999; unsalaried female, Mvuzane, February 23, 1999; unsalaried female, Mvuzane, February 23, 1999; male traditional councilor, Mvuzane, March 3, 1999; male pensioner, Ximba, March 31, 1999; male traditional councilor, Ximba, April 12, 1999; male member of development committee, Ximba, April 14, 1999; male *iphoyisa*, Ximba, April 15, 1999; chief Mlaba, Ximba, April 15, 1999.

47. Interview with unemployed female, Mvuzane, January 21, 1999.

48. A total of 82% claimed that a woman could become a chief, *induna*, or traditional councilor, while 64% believed this was a good thing (N = 171).

49. This woman, Theodore Xulu, is currently serving as an elected councilor for the Umlalazi Municipality. This municipality was created in 2000 with the establishment of permanent local government.

50. Interview with female member of development committee, Kholweni, June 18, 1999.

51. Interviews with female sugarcane farmer, Kholweni, July 7, 1999; male teacher, Kholweni, July 14, 1999.

52. I am grateful to Catherine Burns at the University of Natal-Durban, who suggested I ask specific questions about "rights" in the rural areas. Unfortunately, I had completed research in Mvuzane when I adopted these questions, and thus, I was able to gather data only for Ximba and Kholweni. However, upon returning to Mvuzane for a final visit in July 1999, I informally discussed the question of rights with about ten people and found their comments to be consistent with my findings in the other areas.

53. Interview with male *iphoyisa*, June 18, 1999.

54. Interviews with male *iphoyisa* and member of development committee, Ximba, March 23, 1999; male pensioner, Ximba, March 25, 1999; unemployed male, Ximba, March 25, 1999; male *induna*, Ximba, April 1, 1999; male traditional councilor, Ximba, April 12, 1999; unemployed female, Kholweni, June 19, 1999; female teacher, Kholweni, June 19, 1999; unemployed female, Kholweni, June 19, 1999; female member of development committee, Kholweni, July 1,

1999; female sugarcane farmer, Kholweni, July 7, 1999; female pensioner, Kholweni, July 12, 1999; male day laborer, Kholweni, July 15, 1999.

55. Interviews with male *iphoyisa* and member of development committee, Ximba, March 25, 1999; male sugarcane farmer, Kholweni, June 29, 1999; unemployed male, Kholweni, June 29, 1999; male traditional councilor and member of development committee, Kholweni, June 30, 1999; female pensioner, Kholweni, July 2, 1999; unemployed female, Kholweni, July 5, 1999; female day laborer, Kholweni, July 5, 1999; female pensioner, Kholweni, July 9, 1999; male student, Kholweni, July 13, 1999; chief Mtembu, Kholweni, July 17, 1999.

56. Interviews with unemployed female, Kholweni, June 30, 1999; male minister, Kholweni, June 30, 1999; female pensioner, Kholweni, July 6, 1999.

57. Interview with female member of development committee, Kholweni, July 2, 1999.

58. Interview with male day laborer, Ximba, March 30, 1999.

59. Interview with male pensioner, Kholweni, July 2, 1999.

60. Interview with male member of development committee, Kholweni, July 9, 1999.

61. Interview with non-salaried female, Kholweni, July 12, 1999.

62. Interview with male member of development committee, Kholweni, July 13, 1999.

63. Interview with unemployed male, Kholweni, July 14, 1999.

64. Interviews with unemployed male, Ximba, April 8, 1999; unsalaried female, Ximba, April 9, 1999; businessman, Ximba, April 12, 1999; unemployed male, Ximba, April 12, 1999; male traditional councilor, Ximba, April 12, 1999; male pensioner, Ximba, April 13, 1999; businessman, Ximba, April 15, 1999.

65. Interview with female tribal secretary, Ximba, April 8, 1999.

66. This is discussed in greater detail in chapter 7.

67. Interviews in Mvuzane, 1998–99. Mvuzane is located in northern KwaZulu-Natal and has a population of approximately 15,000. It is a typical tribal authority area in that most people do not have access to clean water, electricity, or telephone service and rely upon pension disbursements or employment outside of the area to sustain themselves.

68. It is still unclear why this was the case on registration day, unless perhaps there was miscommunication between the officials and the chiefs. On Election Day, in June, the school near the court, not the court, was used as a voting site.

69. As one of the few people at the registration site with a car, I was the one who volunteered to drive the election officials to retrieve the batteries.

70. Despite recent electoral setbacks in KwaZulu-Natal, the IFP continues to dominate the elections in Mvuzane. It has received a vast majority of the votes in this area in each of the subsequent elections.

71. Interviews in Mvuzane and Kholweni, 1998–99.

72. These years of service are dated from July 1999 and are based on discussions with chief Biyela, the local government representative, and *izinduna*.

The first epigraph is from an interview with unemployed female, Mvuzane, February 24, 1999; the second epigraph is from an interview with female traditional councilor, Mvuzane, February 17, 1999; the third epigraph is from an interview with unemployed female, Mvuzane, January 21, 1999.

1. In addition, a solid minority of people in each area were even more specific and suggested that the sole responsibility of local government was to provide clean water.

2. In KwaZulu-Natal, local government MEC Mike Mabuyakhulu criticized the performance of local governments at a two-day provincial conference in April 2005. He referred to a recent report that 13 of the province's 61 municipalities were on the brink of "total collapse" (*Daily News,* "MEC 'Losing Patience' with KZN Municipalities," April 20, 2005).

3. *SAPA,* "Holomisa Says Local Politics 'Nauseating'," March 21, 2004.

4. *SAPA,* "ANC Mayors Must Deliver or Leave—Mbeki," March 17, 2006.

5. IDASA, "Municipal Protests Indicate Struggle of Communities," February 20, 2006 (available from http://www.idasa.org.za); *The Sowetan,* "Municipal Protests Indicate Struggle for Communities," February 17, 2006.

6. *The Sunday Independent,* January 22, 2006.

7. Afrobarometer, "South Africa's Ratings of Government Performance." Afrobarometer Briefing Paper No. 44, June 2006.

8. In Mvuzane, it was 66% who gave this response and in Kholweni it was 78%. N = 71 in Mvuzane. N = 49 in Kholweni.

9. Interview with male development worker, February 18, 1999.

10. *Mail and Guardian,* "South Africans Now 'Used to Voting'," March 1, 2006.

11. *The Sunday Independent,* January 22, 2006; Mbeki 2006.

12. Many conferences and workshops were sponsored by national, provincial, and local institutions, as well as many nongovernmental organizations, such as the Regional Consultative Forum, IDASA, and the Institute for Multi Party Democracy.

13. Interview with female member of NGO, Durban, July 21, 1999.

14. Interview with Vusi Chamane, Mvuzane, July 10, 1999.

15. Interview with male member of KwaZulu-Natal Government.

16. Interviews with female traditional councilor, Mvuzane, February 17, 1999; female pensioner, Ximba, March 24, 1999; female member of development committee, Kholweni, June 18, 1999. In Mvuzane, Kholweni, and Ximba, 63% stated that the main difference between traditional leaders and elected councilors was that the former were problems solvers and the latter were responsible for development (N = 118).

17. This elected councilor, Victoria Dube, would eventually become the *inkosi* in this area as well. The issues surrounding the leadership struggles in Kholweni will be discussed in greater detail in chapter 7.

18. In the case of Kholweni, however, there were serious consequences when the chief and *izinduna* did not take an active role in development. As I explain in chapter 7, in 1999, the community in Kholweni chose to remove chief Mtembu and eventually replaced him with someone who was more active with local government and development issues.

19. Similar dynamics have been found in other parts of South Africa as well as in other African countries (see Oomen 2000 and 2005 for discussion of Northern Province, South Africa; see Keulder 1998 for discussion of Namibia).

20. Interview with unsalaried female, Mvuzane, January 20, 1999.

21. Interview with male *induna,* Mvuzane, March 3, 1999.

22. Interview with female member of development committee, Mvuzane, February 22, 1999.

23. Interview with chief Biyela, Mvuzane, July 10, 1999.

24. Interviews with Vusi Chamane, Mvuzane, July 10, 1999; Simon Ngubane, Ximba, April 1, 1999; Victoria Dube, Kholweni, July 25, 1999.

25. N = 38.

26. N = 43.

27. N = 53.

28. Even though there was a considerable amount of importance attached to cooperation, few people within the rural areas understood the institutional mechanisms that sought to facilitate this cooperation. For example, in KwaZulu-Natal, even though chiefs were ex-officio members on the regional councils that existed from 1996 to 2000, most local residents were not aware of this.

29. *Daily News,* "MEC 'Losing Patience' with KZN Municipalities," April 20, 2005.

30. *The Natal Witness,* "Councils Vow to Speed up Delivery," April 21, 2005.

31. Interview with unemployed male, Mvuzane, February 16, 1999.

32. Interview with unsalaried female, Mvuzane, February 9, 1999.

33. N = 77 for Mvuzane. N = 49 for Kholweni. N = 55 for Ximba.

34. Interview with unsalaried female, Mvuzane, February 23, 1999.

35. Interview with female member of development committee, Kholweni, June 18, 1999.

36. Each tribal authority area was further divided into wards, and *izinduna* ruled these areas. The ward boundaries were not officially recorded, as were the tribal authority boundaries, but have always been important boundaries for people in the past and are becoming even more important as development projects are ultimately allocated to specific wards within tribal authorities.

37. Interviews with male minister, Mvuzane, February 18, 1999; female tribal secretary, Ximba, April 8, 1999.

38. Interviews with female traditional councilor, Mvuzane, February 17, 1999; male minister, Mvuzane, February 18, 1999; male sugarcane farmer, Mvuzane, February 3, 1999.

39. *Mail and Guardian,* "The Iron Hand Resists the Ballot Box," February 3, 1995.

40. Interview with chief Biyela, Mvuzane, July 10, 1999.

41. Interview with Vusi Chamane, Mvuzane, July 10, 1999.

42. Interviews with Vusi Chamane, Mvuzane, July 10, 1999; chief Biyela, Mvuzane, July 10, 1999.

43. *Ezimoti,* no. 1, May 1997.

44. Field Log, 2/15/98. Available upon request.

45. In the 1999–2000 financial year, Uthungulu Regional Council sponsored a total of thirty-seven projects totaling approximately R16,000,000 ($2.6 million) for the seventy tribal authority areas falling under its jurisdiction (Uthungulu Regional Council 1999–2000).

46. Interview with female member of NGO, Durban, July 21, 1999.

47. This includes taking off any hats, never standing above the chief, and greeting the chief with the appropriate praise name.

48. Interview with male elected councilor, Nkandla, July 8, 1999.

49. Interviews with chief Biyela, Mvuzane, July 10, 1999; chief Mtembu, Kholweni, July 17, 1999; male chief, Port Elizabeth, June 24, 1999. While some would argue they took on the role of "gatekeepers" at the local level, as members of the Uthungulu Regional Council they appeared to be more like watch dogs.

50. Interview with female member of NGO, Durban, November 1, 1998.

51. This finding is interesting in light of the fact that many policymakers wish to keep chiefs out of these meetings, while these meetings might be the one venue where egalitarian pressures can actually work and start to change attitudes about the chieftaincy. Thus, it might facilitate the democratization process to allow traditional leaders the opportunity to participate at these formal levels.

52. "The Iron Hand Resists the Ballot Box," *Mail and Guardian,* February 3, 1995; "Withdraw Explosive Proposals, IFP Tells Moosa," *Business Day,* January 28, 1998. Chief Wellington Hlengwa from the South Coast noted that local government would lead to the destruction of the chieftaincy because "I will have no land; no people and no control. I will become a councilor to the mayor, and then too I will be one of the many councilors. When I die, who on the council will come along to say my son should take over and, if so, to do what?" ("The Iron Hand Resists the Ballot Box").

53. Interview with female member of NGO, Durban, November 1, 1998.

54. Interview with female member of development committee, Mvuzane, February 22, 1999.

55. Exchange rate in 1998–99 = R6 per $1.00.

56. In 2000, new boundaries were drawn for the newly established eThekweni Metropolitan Municipality and there are now sixteen chieftaincies under its jurisdiction. Of the three million people who live in eThekweni, approximately 35% would be characterized as living in urban areas and the rest of the population living in either peri-urban or rural areas (Beall 2005: 766).

57. N = 120 for Mvuzane and Kholweni. N = 49 for Ximba.

58. N = 181.

59. N = 53.

60. N = 67.

61. N = 43.

62. Shaka Day has been officially renamed "Heritage Day," and it is a national holiday, September 24.

6. THE CHIEFTAINCY AND DEVELOPMENT

The first epigraph is from an interview with unemployed female, Mvuzane, January 20, 1999; the second epigraph is from an interview with unemployed male; Mvuzane, February 16, 1999; the third epigraph is from an interview with male chairman of garden committee, Mvuzane, February 9, 1999.

1. For example, in 1994, it stressed its Reconstruction and Development Programme (RDP), which proposed an integrated development program in both the rural and urban areas financed through government borrowing and international investment (African National Congress 1994). During the 1995–96 local government elections, the ANC focused on creating developmental local government institutions that would "ensure that democratic local government deals with the basic needs of all our people" (ANC 1995 Election Manifesto). In 1999, the ANC promised to "accelerate change" throughout the country; in the 2000 local government elections, it stressed the fact that it could "speed up change." In 2004, its manifesto was entitled "A People's Contract to create work and fight poverty," and in 2006, its local government manifesto included a code of conduct for elected local councilors that focused on the delivery of development projects (ANC 1999 Election Manifesto; ANC 2000 Election Manifesto; ANC 2004 Election Manifesto; ANC 2006 Election Manifesto).

2. Interviews with male member of KwaZulu government and KwaZulu-Natal provincial government, Durban, November 21, 1998; female member of KZ government and KZN provincial government, Durban, July 21, 1999.

3. Interview with male member of KZ government and KZN provincial government, Durban, November 21, 1998.

4. Thabo Mbeki, "State of the Nation Address at the Opening of Parliament," February 4, 2000.

5. There was a fundamental shift in policy with the TLGF Act in 2003, which formally established traditional leaders as partners in the development process. The argument here is that this policy switch was the result of events on the ground that are explained in this chapter.

6. This percentage is based on interviews in three separate tribal authorities in KwaZulu-Natal. For this particular question, N = 153.

7. N = 172. In Kholweni, development ranked first, with 49% of the respondents stating that development was the most important responsibility of the

chief (N = 47). In chapter 7, I explore why Kholweni ranked development as the most important responsibility. For other examples of how development has become central to the chieftaincy's legitimacy, see Oomen's (2005) analysis on the dynamics in the Northern Province.

8. N = 85.

9. Interview with Vusi Chamane, Mvuzane, July 10, 1999.

10. Christine MacDonald, "The Construction of State and Development in Rural KwaZulu-Natal: Implications of Dominant Discourses in the KwaZulu-Natal Land Reform Pilot Programme," *Transformation* 37 (1998). In this article, MacDonald argues that traditional leaders have taken over the operation of most land committees in rural areas.

11. These "tribal authorities wards" should not be confused with the "municipal wards" established in 2000.

12. Interviews with Vusi Chamane, Mvuzane, July 10, 1999; male member of development committee, February 3, 1999.

13. In other cases in KZN, some traditional leaders have denied the implementation of projects for their community for political reasons. While I did not observe this in Mvuzane or the other two case studies, there were cases reported where an IFP-aligned chief refused to accept "ANC water" and the funds were used for other tribal authority areas (Interview with female member of NGO, Durban, July 21, 1999.

14. Interview with male day laborer, Mvuzane, February 8, 1999.

15. Interview with male *induna,* Mvuzane, February 11, 1999.

16. Interview with female secretary of development committee and traditional councilor, Mvuzane, February 17, 1999.

17. Interview with male pensioner, Ximba, March 25, 1999.

18. Interview with chief Biyela, Mvuzane, July 10, 1999.

19. Vusi Chamane immediately comes to mind here. There was no question that the community recognized that Vusi had more knowledge and connections concerning development than chief Biyela had. Still, because of the close relationship between the two, and possibly because Vusi was a young man, most community members recognized that he was working for the chief and that anything he did in the community was with the consent of chief Biyela.

20. Interviews with male member of KZN provincial government, Durban, November 21, 1998; female member of NGO, Durban, November 1, 1998. Through discussions with a representative at Data Research Africa—an organization that helps to implement government-sponsored development projects throughout South Africa—I learned of many other examples where traditional leaders and development committees were misallocating resources (interview with female member of NGO, November 1, 1998).

21. See Marks (1986) for a historical perspective on the ambiguity of the chieftaincy authority during the apartheid period.

22. I found that the existence of the electricity poles led to the most confusion,

and frustration, as people could not understand why they could not get access to electricity given the close proximity of the poles. Further, the poles were sometimes placed in the middle of grazing lands or garden areas.

23. This meeting followed earlier attempts by the chief to have the matter resolved. Chief Biyela told the community that he had "sent *my councilor* [Vusi] to Richard's Bay to talk about this" but that the issue had not been resolved (emphasis mine).

24. Since the project had started, DWAF had subcontracted the implementation services to an NGO called Mhlatuze. Thus, the person at the meeting was from this NGO and not from DWAF. He promised that he would be in direct contact with DWAF about the community's complaints.

25. Five rand converted to approximately 80 U.S. cents.

26. Vusi lives with his brother and other relatives in one homestead.

27. At one point, I asked Vusi whether he wanted to be *induna* and why he has not been appointed *induna*—given the respect he has in the community. He laughed at this suggestion and told me that not only was he too young to be an *induna* but that the responsibilities of the *induna* are more conflict resolution than development, and he would rather be active in the latter than the former.

28. What I provide here is the interpretation of these events as they were told to me by *induna* Thandi, Vusi, and their neighbors.

29. Interview with unemployed female, Mvuzane, February 23, 1999.

30. Interview with unemployed female, Mvuzane, February 17, 1999.

7. LEGITIMACY LOST?

The first epigraph is from an interview with male sugarcane farmer, Kholweni, June 29, 1999; the second epigraph is from an interview with unemployed male, Kholweni, June 29, 1999; the third epigraph is from an interview with female sugarcane farmer, Kholweni, July 7, 1999.

1. The 2001 census data provides information based on municipal wards. In the Umlalazi Local Municipality, Mvuzane is coterminous with Ward 1 and Kholweni is coterminous with Ward 8 (Republic of South Africa 2001a).

2. Kholweni was my final research site, although I was familiar with the area because I had conducted four months of research in nearby Mvuzane. While in previous areas informants only rarely offered negative comments about the chieftaincy without some initial prompting, in Kholweni, we were surprised to find so many informants who would offer passionate and detailed comments even before we asked questions specifically about the performance of the chieftaincy.

3. Interviews with male traditional councilor, Kholweni, June 30, 1999; male pensioner, Kholweni, July 2, 1999; female pensioner, Kholweni, July 6, 1999; female sugarcane farmer, Kholweni, July 7, 1999; male pensioner, Kholweni, July 13, 1999.

4. N = 67 for Mvuzane. N = 53 for Ximba.

5. N = 41.

6. Interview with businessman, Kholweni, July 9, 1999.

7. In the 1980s, the exchange fluctuated from R0.81/$1.00 in January 1980 to R1.99/$1.00 in December 1984. For the purposes of this example, I used the average exchange of this five-year period, which is approximately R1.40/$1.00.

8. Interview with businessman, Kholweni, July 9.

9. The Zululand Joint Services Boards were created in the 1980s to help provide development projects to the Bantustan areas. They consisted of both KwaZulu government and Natal government officials working together on development.

10. Interview with female pensioner, Kholweni, June 18, 1999.

11. Interviews with female pensioner, Kholweni, June 28, 1999; male sugarcane farmer, Kholweni, June 29, 1999; unemployed male, Kholweni, July 14, 1999.

12. Interviews with female pensioner, Kholweni, June 18, 1999; male *iphoyisa,* Kholweni, June 18, 1999; male sugarcane farmer, Kholweni, June 29, 1999.

13. Interview with businessman, Kholweni, July 9, 1999.

14. Interview with male student, Kholweni, July 13, 1999.

15. Interview with male minister, Kholweni, June 30, 1999.

16. Interview with businessman, Kholweni, July 9, 1999.

17. Interview with chief Mtembu, Kholweni, July 17, 1999.

18. Interviews with female pensioner, Kholweni, June 18, 1999; businessman, Kholweni, July 9, 1999.

19. Interview with chief Mtembu, Kholweni, July 17, 1999.

20. Interviews with female pensioner, Kholweni, June 18, 1999; businessman, Kholweni, July 9, 1999.

21. In Ximba, 63% (N = 55) knew that chief Mlaba was a member of the provincial government and 52% (N = 44) claimed that he reported back to the community.

22. Interviews with female pensioner, Kholweni, June 18, 1999; male *iphoyisa,* Kholweni, June 18, 1999; unemployed male, Kholweni, June 19, 1999; male pensioner, Kholweni, June 29, 1999; female sugarcane farmer, Kholweni, July 7, 1999; unemployed male, Kholweni, July 9, 1999; female pensioner, Kholweni, July 9, 1999; male day laborer, Kholweni, July 15, 1999. Of the 51 interviews in Kholweni, 60% did not want chief Mtembu to overrule local government.

23. Interviews with unemployed female, Kholweni, June 30, 1999; male pensioner, Kholweni, July 2, 1999; male, Kholweni, July 2, 1999.

24. Interview with female pensioner, Kholweni, July 2, 1999.

25. Interview with male pensioner, Kholweni, July 14, 1999.

26. Interview with Victoria Dube, Kholweni, July 25, 1999.

27. Interview with male traditional councilor and member of development committee, Kholweni, June 30, 1999.

28. Interviews with female pensioner, Kholweni, July 2, 1999; unsalaried

female, Kholweni, July 3, 1999; unemployed female, Kholweni, July 5, 1999; female pensioner, Kholweni, July 9, 1999.

29. Interview with male pensioner, Kholweni, June 29, 1999.

30. Interview with male student, Kholweni, July 13, 1999.

31. Interview with female sugarcane farmer, Kholweni, July 2, 1999.

32. Interviews with female member of development committee, Kholweni, July 1, 1999; female member of development committee, Kholweni, July 2, 1999; businessman, Kholweni, July 9, 1999.

33. Interviews with unemployed female, Kholweni, June 19, 1999; unsalaried female, Kholweni, June 28, 1999; businessman, Kholweni, July 9, 1999; unsalaried female, Kholweni, July 12, 1999; male traditional councilor, Kholweni, July 15, 1999; Victoria Dube, Kholweni, July 25, 1999.

34. Interview with female pensioner, Kholweni, June 18, 1999.

35. Interview with unemployed male, Kholweni, June 19, 1999.

36. Interview with unsalaried female, Kholweni, July 3, 1999.

37. Interview with female pensioner, Kholweni, June 18, 1999.

38. Interview with male sugarcane farmer, Kholweni, July 2, 1999.

39. N = 50.

40. N = 39.

41. N = 30.

42. Republic of South Africa 2001a. These results are available at http://www.elections.org.za. The three polling stations in Kholweni were Ntabantuzuma School, Gcininhliziyo School, and Enhlisa School.

43. The number of votes in Kholweni and the approximate voting age population are available at http://www.demarcation.org.za/demarcprocess/wards/ver3e/warddemogstats.asp.

44. Interviews with female pensioner, Kholweni, June 18, 1999; businessman, Kholweni, July 9, 1999.

45. Interviews with female pensioner, Kholweni, June 18, 1999; businessman, Kholweni, July 9, 1999.

46. Interview with unemployed female, Kholweni, July 1, 1999.

47. Interview with unemployed male, Kholweni, June 29, 1999.

48. Interview with male minister, Kholweni, June 30, 1999.

49. Interview with chief Mtembu, Kholweni, July 17, 1999.

50. Interviews with chief Mtembu, Kholweni, July 17, 1999; businessman, Kholweni, July 9, 1999; female pensioner, Kholweni, June 18, 1999.

51. Interview with female teacher, Kholweni, June 19, 1999.

52. Interview with male pensioner, Kholweni, June 29, 1999.

53. Interview with female teacher, Kholweni, July 13, 1999.

54. Interview with male teacher, Kholweni, July 14, 1999.

55. Interview with male traditional councilor, Kholweni, July 15, 1999.

56. This phenomenon is an interesting development that deserves more detailed and comparative research. The constitution writing process, as well as

the content of the document itself, can provide scholars with important insights concerning the chieftaincy-societal relations and the modern/tradition and state/society dichotomies.

57. Interview with businessman, Kholweni, July 9, 1999.

58. Interview with businessman, Kholweni, July 9, 1999.

59. Interview with female pensioner, Kholweni, June 18, 1999.

60. Interviews with female pensioner, Kholweni, June 28, 1999; male pensioner, Kholweni, June 29, 1999; male traditional councilor and member of development committee, Kholweni, June 30, 1999.

61. Interview with female pensioner, Kholweni, July 1, 1999.

62. Interview with male traditional councilor, Kholweni, June 30, 1999.

63. Interview with unemployed female, July 15, 1999.

64. Interview with male traditional councilor, Kholweni, July 15, 1999.

65. Interview with Victoria Dube, Kholweni, July 25, 1999.

66. Interview with unemployed male, June 19, 1999.

67. Interview with unemployed female, June 30, 1999.

68. Interview with male pensioner, July 2, 1999.

69. Interview with female pensioner, July 2, 1999.

70. Interview with female sugarcane farmer, July 7, 1999.

71. Interview with female teacher, July 14, 1999.

72. Interview with male sugarcane farmer, June 29, 1999.

73. Interview with chief Victoria Dube, Kholweni, July 2007.

8. CONCLUSION

The first epigraph is from King Goodwill Zwelethini, *Sapa*, October 21, 2000; the second epigraph is from chief Holomisa, *Mail and Guardian*, February 16, 2000.

1. McClendon 2003: 56.

2. Koelble and LiPuma 2005: 94.

3. This information was generated from the DPLG's Traditional Communities and Leaders Database in October 2008.

BIBLIOGRAPHY

Adinkrah, K. O. 1991. "'We Shall Take Our Case to the King': Legitimacy and Tradition in the Administration of Law in Swaziland." *CILSA* 24: 226–239.

Africa, Cherrel, and Robert Mattes. 1996. "Building a Democratic Culture in KwaZulu Natal: The Present Terrain." *IDASA: Public Opinion Service* 9: 1–23.

African Eye News Service. 1990–2009.

African National Congress. 1994. *Reconstruction and Development Programme.*

————. 1995. Local Government Manifesto. "A Better Life: Let's Make It Happen Where We Live."

————. 1999. National Election Manifesto. "Change Must Go On at a Faster Pace!"

————. 2000. Local Government Manifesto. "Together Speeding Up Change: Fighting Poverty and Creating a Better Life for All."

————. 2004. National Election Manifesto. "A People's Contract to Create Work and Fight Poverty."

————. 2006. Local Government Manifesto. "A Plan to Make Local Government Work Better for You."

Aitchison, John. 1989. "The Civil War in Natal." In *South Africa: Contemporary Analysis,* ed. G. Moss and I. Obery. London: Hans Zell.

Alagappa, Muthiah. 1995. *Political Legitimacy in Southeast Asia: The Quest for Moral Authority.* Stanford, Calif.: Stanford University Press.

Alence, Rod. 2004. "South Africa after Apartheid: The First Decade." *Journal of Democracy* 15, no. 3: 78–92.

Alexander, Jocelyn. 1995. "Things Fall Apart, the Centre Can Hold: Processes of Post-War Political Change in Zimbabwe's Rural Areas." In *Society in Zimbabwe's Liberation War,* vol. 2, ed. N. Bhebe and T. Ranger. Harare: University of Zimbabwe Publications.

Anderson, Benedict. 1983. *Imagined Communities.* London: Verso.

Appiah, G. W. 1994. "Chiefship in the Transkei under the Tribal Authority System: A Case Study." M.A. thesis, Department of Social Anthropology, University of Natal-Durban, Durban.

Apter, David E. 1967. *The Politics of Modernization.* Chicago: University of

Chicago Press.

Ashforth, Adam. 2005. *Witchcraft, Violence, and Democracy in South Africa*. Chicago: University of Chicago Press.

Askvik, Steinar, and Nelleke Bak, eds. 2005. *Trust in Public Institutions in South Africa*. Burlington, Vt.: Ashgate.

Atkinson, Doreen. 2002. *Local Government, Local Governance and Sustainable Development*. Cape Town: Human Sciences Research Council Press.

———. 2007. "Taking to the Streets: Has Developmental Local Government Failed in South Africa?" In *State of the Nation: South Africa 2007*, ed. Sakhela Buhlungu et al. Cape Town: Human Sciences Research Council Press.

Ayittey, George. 1991. *Indigenous African Institutions*. New York: Transnational Press.

Bank, Leslie, and Roger Southall. 1996. "Traditional Leaders in South Africa's New Democracy." *Journal of Legal Pluralism* 37–38: 407–31.

Barker, Rodney. 1990. *Political Legitimacy and the State*. Oxford: Clarendon Press.

Bates, Robert H. 1981. *Markets and States in Tropical Africa*. Berkeley and Los Angeles: University of California Press.

Bayart, Jean-Francois. 1986. "Civil Society in Africa." In *Political Domination in Africa: Reflections on the Limits of Power*, ed. Patrick Chabal, 109–25. Cambridge: Cambridge University Press.

———. 1993. *The State in Africa: The Politics of the Belly*. London: Longman.

BBC News. 1990–2008.

Beall, Jo. 2006. "Cultural Weapons: Traditions, Inventions and the Transition to Democratic Governance in Metropolitan Durban." *Urban Studies* 43, no. 2: 457–73.

Beall, Jo, Stephen Gelb, and Shireen Hassim. 2005. "Fragile Stability: State and Society in Democratic South Africa." *Journal of Southern African Studies* 31, no. 4: 681–700.

Beall, Jo, Sibongiseni Mkhize, and Shahid Vawda. 2005. "Emergent Democracy and 'Resurgent' Tradition: Institutions, Chieftaincy and Transition in KwaZulu-Natal." *Journal of Southern African Studies* 31, no. 4: 755–71.

Beetham, David. 1991. *The Legitimation of Power*. Atlantic Highlands, N.J.: Humanities Press International.

Beinart, William. 1982. *The Political Economy of Pondoland, 1860–1930*. Cambridge: Cambridge University Press.

Beinart, William, and Colin Bundy. 1987. *Hidden Struggles in Rural South Africa: Politics and Popular Movements in the Transkei and Eastern Cape*. London: James Currey.

Bekker, J. 1993. "The Role of Traditional Leaders in a Future South African Constitutional Dispensation." *African Insight* 23, no. 4.

Bennett, David. 1998. *Multicultural States: Rethinking Difference and Identity*. London: Routledge.

Bennett, T. W. 1995. *Human Rights and African Customary Law.* Cape Town: Juta.

Bentley, Kristina A. 2005. "Are the Powers of Traditional Leaders in South Africa Compatible with Women's Equal Rights? Three Conceptual Arguments." *Human Rights Review* July–September 2005: 48–68.

Berglund, Axel-Ivar. 1989. *Zulu Thought-Patterns and Symbolism.* Bloomington: Indiana University Press.

Berry, Sara S. 1993. *No Condition Is Permanent: The Social Dynamics of Agrarian Change in Sub-Saharan Africa.* Madison: University of Wisconsin Press.

———. 2001. *Chiefs Know Their Boundaries: Essays on Property, Power, and the Past in Asante, 1896–1996.* Portsmouth, N.H.: Heinemann.

Bierschenk, Thomas, and Jean-Pierre Olivier de Sardan. 2003. "Powers in the Village: Rural Benin between Democratisation and Decentralisation." *Africa* 73, no. 2: 145–73.

Bond, Patrick. 2003. *Against Global Apartheid: South Africa Meets the World Bank, IMF and International Finance.* Cape Town: University of Cape Town Press.

Boone, Catherine. 2003. "Decentralization as Political Strategy in West Africa." *Comparative Political Studies* 36, no. 4: 355–80.

Booysen, Frikkie le R. 2003. "Urban-Rural Inequalities in Health Care Delivery in South Africa." *Development Southern Africa* 20, no. 5: 659–74.

Botha, T. 1994. "The Role of Traditional Leaders in Local Government." Seminar Report. Johannesburg: Konrad Adenaur Stifung.

Bourdillon, Michael. 1976. *The Shona Peoples.* Gwelo, Zimbabawe: Mambo Press.

Bratton, Michael. 1989. "Beyond the State: Civil Society and Associational Life in Africa." *World Politics* 41, no. 3: 407–30.

———. 1994. "Civil Society and Political Transitions in Africa." In *Civil Society and the State in Africa,* ed. J. Harbeson, D. Rothchild, and N. Chazan. Boulder, Colo.: Lynne Rienner.

Bratton, Michael, and Eric C. C. Chang. 2006. "State Building and Democratization in Sub Saharan Africa: Forwards, Backwards, or Together?" *Comparative Political Studies* 39, no. 9: 1059–83.

Bratton, Michael, and Robert Mattes. October 1999. "Support for Democracy in Africa: Intrinsic or Instrumental?" Afrobarometer Paper no. 1. Michigan State University, East Lansing.

———. 2001. "Support for Democracy in Africa: Intrinsic or Instrumental?" *British Journal of Political Science* 31, no. 3: 447–73.

Bratton, Michael, Robert Mattes, and E. Gyimah-Boadi. 2005. *Public Opinion, Democracy, and Market Reform in Africa.* Cambridge: Cambridge University Press.

Bratton, Michael, and Mxolisi Sibanyoni. 2006. "Delivery or Responsiveness? A Popular Scorecard of Local Government Performance in South Africa."

Afrobarometer Briefing Paper no. 62. Department of Political and Administrative Studies, Sociology, and Statistics, University of Botswana.

Bratton, Michael, and Nicolas van de Walle. 1997. *Democratic Experiments in Africa: Regime Transitions in Comparative Perspective.* Cambridge: Cambridge University Press.

Brookes, Edgar H., and C. de B. Webb. 1965. *A History of Natal.* Pietermaritzburg: University of Natal Press.

Buhlungu, Sakhela, et al., eds. 2006. *State of the Nation, 2005–06.* Cape Town: Human Sciences Research Council.

Bundy, Colin. 1988. *The Rise and Fall of the South African Peasantry.* Cape Town: David Philip; London: Currey.

Burr, Lars, and Helene Maria Kyed. 2006. "Contested Sources of Authority: Reclaiming State Sovereignty by Formalizing Traditional Authority in Mozambique." *Development and Change* 34, no. 4: 847–69.

Business Day. 1990–2008.

Butler, Jeffrey, Robert I. Rotberg, and John Adams. 1977. *The Black Homelands of South Africa: The Political and Economic Development of Bophuthatswana and KwaZulu.* Berkeley: University of California Press.

Butler, Mark. 1997. "Participative Democracy and Rural Local Government in KwaZulu-Natal." *Indicator South Africa* 15, no. 3: 74–77.

Callagy, Thomas M. 1984. *The State-Society Struggle: Zaire in a Comparative Prospective.* New York: Columbia University Press.

CASE/AFRA. 1998. *Rural Local Government, KwaZulu-Natal.* South Africa.

Chabal, Patrick. 1992. *Power in Africa: An Essay in Political Interpretation.* New York: St. Martin's Press.

Chanock, Martin. 1985. *Law, Custom, and Social Order, the Colonial Experience in Malawi and Zambia.* Cambridge: Cambridge University Press.

———. 1991. "Law, State, and Culture: Thinking About 'Customary Law' after Apartheid." *Acta Juridica* 52: 52–70.

———. 2001. *The Making of South African Legal Culture 1902–1936: Fear, Favour and Prejudice.* Cambridge: Cambridge University Press.

Chazan, Naomi. 1988. "Patterns of State-Society Incorporation and Disengagement in Africa." In *The Precarious Balance: State and Society in Africa,* ed. N. Chazan and D. Rothchild. Boulder, Colo.: Westview Press.

———. 1992. "Africa's Democratic Challenge." *World Policy Journal* 9, no. 2: 279–307.

Chazan, Naomi, and D. Rothchild, eds. 1988. *The Precarious Balance: State and Society in Africa.* Boulder, Colo.: Westview Press.

Cheru, Fantu. 2001. "Overcoming Apartheid's Legacy: The Ascendancy of Neoliberalism in South Africa's Anti-Poverty Strategy." *Third World Quarterly* 22, no. 4: 505–27.

Claessen, Henri J. M. 1988. "Changing Legitimacy." In *State Formation and Political Legitimacy,* ed. Ronald Cohen and Judith D. Toland. New Brunswick,

N.J.: Transaction Books.

Clough, Marshall S. 1990. *Fighting Two Sides: Kenyan Chiefs and Politicians, 1918–1940.* Niwot: University Press of Colorado.

Cohen, Ronald, and Judith D. Toland, eds. 1988. *State Formation and Political Legitimacy.* New Brunswick, N.J.: Transaction Books.

Comaroff, John L. 1978. "Rules and Rulers: Political Processes in a Tswana Chiefdom." *Man* 13: 1–20.

Comaroff, John, and Jean Comaroff. 1991. *Of Revelation and Revolution.* Vol. 1, *Christianity, Colonialism, and Consciousness in South Africa.* Chicago: University of Chicago Press.

———. 1997. "Postcolonial Politics and Discourses of Democracy in Southern Africa: An Anthropological Reflection on African Political Modernities." *Journal of Anthropological Research* 53, no. 2: 123–46.

———. 1999. *Civil Society and the Political Imagination in Africa.* Chicago: University of Chicago Press.

———. 2004. "The Struggle between the Constitution and 'Things African.'" *Interventions* 7, no. 3: 299–303.

Cope, Nicholas. 1990. "The Zulu Petit Bourgeoisie and Zulu Nationalism in the 1920s: Origins of Inkatha." *Journal of Southern African Studies* 16, no. 3: 431–51.

———. 1993. *To Bind the Nation: Solomon kaDinuzulu and Zulu Nationalism, 1913 1933.* Pietermaritzburg: University of Natal Press.

Cope, T. R. 1968. *Izibongo, Zulu Praise-Poems.* Oxford: Oxford University Press.

Costa, A. A. 2000. "Chieftaincy and Civilization: African Structures of Government and Colonial Administration in South Africa." *African Studies* 59, no. 1: 13–43.

Costa, Anthony. 1998. "The Myth of Customary Law." *South African Journal of Human Rights* 14: 525–38.

Crais, Clifton C. 2002. *The Politics of Evil: Magic, State Power, and the Political Imagination in South Africa.* Cambridge: Cambridge University Press.

———. 2003a. "Conquest, State Formation, and the Subalteran Imagination in Rural South Africa." In *The Culture of Power in Southern Africa: Essays on State Formation and the Political Imagination,* ed. Clifton C. Crais. Portsmouth, N.H.: Heinemann.

———. 2003b. "Chiefs and Bureaucrats in the Making of Empire: A Drama from the Transkei, South Africa, October 1880." *American Historical Review* (October 2003): 1034–1056.

———. 2006. "Custom and the Politics of Sovereignty in South Africa." *Journal of Social History* (Spring): 721–40.

———, ed. 2003. *The Culture of Power in Southern Africa: Essays on State Formation and the Political Imagination.* Portsmouth, N.H.: Heinemann.

Crick, B. 1959. *The American Science of Politics: Its Origins and Conditions.*

Berkeley: University of California Press.

Daily News. 1990–2008.

D'Engelbronner-Kolff, F. M., M. O. Hinz, and J. L. Sindano. 1998. *Traditional Authority and Democracy in Southern Africa.* Windhoek, Namibia: New Namibia Books.

Diamond, Larry. 1996. "Is The Third Wave Over?" *Journal of Democracy* 7: 20–37.

———. 1997. "Introduction: In Search of Consolidation." In *Consolidating the Third Wave Democracies: Regional Challenges,* ed. Larry Diamond et al. Baltimore, Md.: Johns Hopkins University Press.

———. 1999a. *Developing Democracy: Toward Consolidation.* Baltimore, Md.: Johns Hopkins University Press.

———. 1999b. "Introduction." In *Democratization in Africa,* ed. Larry Diamond and Marc Plattner. Baltimore, Md.: Johns Hopkins University Press.

Diamond, Larry, et al., eds. 1997. *Consolidating the Third Wave Democracies: Regional Challenges.* Baltimore, Md.: Johns Hopkins University Press.

Digeser, Peter. 1992. "The Fourth Face of Power." *Journal of Politics* 54, no. 4: 977–1007.

Du Toit, Pierre. 1995. *State Building and Democracy in Southern Africa: Botswana, Zimbabwe, and South Africa.* Washington, D.C.: United States Institute of Peace Press.

Duminy, Andrew, and Bill Guest. 1989. *Natal and Zululand: From Earliest Times to 1910.* Pietermaritzburg: University of Natal Press.

Dusing, Sandra. 2002. *Traditional Leadership and Democratisation in Southern Africa.* Hamburg: Lit Verlag.

Economic Commission for Africa. 2007. "Relevance of African Traditional Institutions of Governance." Addis Ababa, Ethiopia.

Ekeh, Peter. 1975. "Colonialism and the Two Publics: A Theoretical Statement." *Comparative Studies in Society and History* 17, no. 1: 91–112.

Englebert, Pierre. 2000. *State Legitimacy and Development in Africa.* Boulder, Colo.: Lynne Rienner.

Etherington, Norman. 1989. "The 'Shepstone System' in the Colony of Natal." In *Natal and Zululand: From Earliest Times to 1910, A New History,* ed. Andrew Duminy and Bill Guest. Pietermaritzburg: University of Natal Press.

Evans, Ivan. 1997. *Bureaucracy and Race: Native Administration in South Africa.* Berkeley: University of California Press.

Ex Parte Chairperson of the Constitutional Assembly: In re Certification of the Constitution of the Republic of South Africa, 1996. 1996. (4) SA 744 (CC) (*First Certification Judgment*), heard on 1–5 and 8–11 July 1996 and decided 6 September 1996.

Ex Parte Chairperson of the Constitutional Assembly: In re Certification of the Amended Text of the Constitution of the Republic of South Africa, 1996. 1997. (2) SA 97 (CC) (*Second Certification Judgment*), heard on 18, 19, and 20

November 1996 and decided 4 December 1996.

Ezimoti. 1995–2001.

Fields, Karen. 1985. *Revival and Rebellion in Colonial Africa: Revisions to the Theory of Indirect Rule.* Princeton, N.J.: Princeton University Press.

Financial Mail. 1990–2008.

Flint, Karen. 2001. "Healing the Body Politic: Umuthi (Medicine), Healers, and Nation Building in Southeastern Africa in the Early 19th Century." Ph.D. diss., Department of History, University of California, Los Angeles.

Forrest, Joshua. 2003. *Lineages of State Fragility: Rural Civil Society in Guinea-Bissau.* Athens: Ohio University Press.

Forsyth, P. 1992. "The Past in Service of the Present: The Political Use of History by Chief A.N.M.G. Buthelezi, 1951–91." *South African Historical Journal* 26: 74–92.

Fortes, M., and E. Evans-Pritchard, eds. 1940. *African Political Systems.* Oxford: Oxford University Press.

Freedom House. 2001. *Freedom in the World: The Annual Survey of Political Rights and Civil Liberties 2000–2001.* New York: Freedom House.

Friedman, Steven. 1999. "No Easy Stroll to Dominance: Party Dominance, Opposition and Civil Society in South Africa." In *Awkward Embrace: One-Party Domination and Democracy,* ed. Hermann Giliomee and Charles Simkins. Amsterdam: Harwood Academic Publishers.

———, ed. 1993. *The Long Journey: South Africa's Quest for a Negotiated Settlement.* Johannesburg: Ravan Press.

Frost, Mervyn. 1996. "Preparing for Democracy in an Authoritarian State." In *Launching Democracy in South Africa: The First Open Election, April 1994,* ed. R. W. Johnson and L. Schlemmer. New Haven, Conn.: Yale University Press.

Galvan, Dennis C. 2004. *The State Must Be Our Master of Fire: How Peasants Craft Culturally Sustainable Development in Senegal.* Berkeley: University of California Press.

Galvan, Dennis C., and Rudra Sil. 2007a. "The Dilemma of Institutional Adaptation and the Role of Syncretism." In *Reconfiguring Institutions across Time and Space: Syncretic Responses to Challenges of Political and Economic Transformation,* ed. Dennis C. Galvan and Rudra Sil. New York: Palgrave Macmillan.

———. 2007b. *Reconfiguring Institutions across Time and Space: Syncretic Responses to Challenges of Political and Economic Transformation.* New York: Palgrave Macmillan.

Galvin, Mary. 1997. "Rural Local Government in KwaZulu Natal: Development Dilemma or Disaster?" *Indicator South Africa* 13, no. 4.

Geertz, Clifford. 1973. *The Interpretation of Cultures: Selected Essays.* New York: Basic Books.

Gerhart, Gail M. 1978. *Black Power in South Africa: The Evolution of an Ideology.*

Berkeley: University of California Press.

Geschiere, Peter. 1997. *The Modernity of Witchcraft: Politics and the Occult in Post-Colonial Africa.* Charlottesville: University of Virginia Press.

Gibson, James. 2004. *Overcoming Apartheid: Can Truth Reconcile a Divided Nation?* New York: Russell Sage Foundation.

Giliomee, Hermann, and Charles Simkins, eds. *Awkward Embrace: One-Party Domination and Democracy.* Amsterdam: Harwood Academic Publishers.

Gluckman, Max. 1940a. "The Kingdom of the Zulu of South Africa." In *African Political Systems,* ed. M. Fortes and E. Evans-Pritchard. Oxford: Oxford University Press.

———. 1940b. "Analysis of a Social System in Modern Zululand." *Bantu Studies* 14 (part B): 147–74.

———. 1965. *Politics, Law and Ritual in Tribal Society.* Chicago: Aldine.

Goheen, Mitzi. 1992. "Chiefs, Sub-Chiefs and Local Control: Negotiations over Land, Struggles over Meaning." *Africa* 62, no. 3: 389–412.

Goodenough, Cheryl. 2002. *Traditional Leaders: A KwaZulu-Natal Study 1999–2001.* Durban, South Africa: Independent Projects Trust.

Grant, Evadne. 2006. "Human Rights, Cultural Diversity and Customary Law in South Africa." *Journal of African Law* 50, no. 1: 2–23.

Greenberg, Stanley. 1987. *Legitimating the Illegitimate: State, Markets, and Resistance in South Africa.* Berkeley: University of California Press.

Gumede, William Mervin. 2005. *Thabo Mbeki and the Battle for the Soul of the ANC.* Cape Town: Zebra Press.

Gump, James. 1990. *Formation of the Zulu Kingdom in South Africa.* San Francisco: Mellen Research University Press.

Guy, Jeff. 1979. *The Destruction of the Zulu Kingdom: The Civil War in Zululand, 1879–1884.* London: Longman Group.

Hamilton, Carolyn. 1995. *The Mfecane Aftermath: Reconstructive Debates in Southern African History.* Johannesburg: Witwatersrand University Press.

———. 1998. *Terrific Majesty: The Powers of Shaka Zulu and the Limits of Historical Invention.* Cape Town and Johannesburg: David Philip.

Harbeson, John. 1994. "Civil Society and the Study of African Politics: A Preliminary Assessment." In *Civil Society and the State in Africa,* ed. J. Harbeson, D. Rothchild, and N. Chazan. Boulder, Colo.: Lynne Rienner.

Harbeson, John W. 1994. "Civil Society and Political Renaissance in Africa." In *Civil Society and the State in Africa,* ed. J. Harbeson, D. Rothchild, and N. Chazan. Boulder, Colo.: Lynne Rienner.

Harbeson, John W., D. Rothchild, and N. Chazan, eds. 1994. *Civil Society and the State in Africa.* Boulder, Colo.: Lynne Rienner.

Harries, P. 1987. "Imagery, Symbolism and Tradition in a South African Bantustan: Gatsha Buthelezi, Inkatha and Zulu History." Unpublished paper, Department of History, University of Cape Town.

Hemson, David, and Michael O'Donovan. 2006. "Putting the Numbers to the Scorecard: Presidential Targets and the State of Delivery." In *State of the Nation, 2005–06,* ed. Sakhela Buhlungu, John Daniel, Roger Southall, and Jessica Lutchman. Cape Town: Human Sciences Research Council.

Hendricks, F. T. 1990. "The Pillars of Apartheid: Land Tenure, Rural Planning and the Chieftaincy." Ph.D. diss., Department of Sociology, Uppsala University.

Herbst, Jeffrey. 2000. *States and Power in Africa: Comparative Lessons in Authority and Control.* Princeton, N.J.: Princeton University Press.

———. 2005. "Mbeki's South Africa." *Foreign Affairs* 84, no. 6.

Heywood, Linda M. 1998. "Toward an Understanding of Modern Political Ideology in Africa: The Case of the Ovimbundu of Angola." *Journal of Modern African Studies* 36, no. 1: 139–67.

Hill, Christopher R. 1964. *Banutsans: The Fragmentation of South Africa.* London: Oxford University Press.

Hinz, M. O. 1998. "'The Traditional' of Traditional Government: Traditional versus Democracy Based Legitimacy." In *Traditional Authority and Democracy in Southern Africa,* ed. F. M. d'Engelbronner-Kolff et al. Windhoek, Namibia: New Namibia Books.

Hlengwa, W. 1994. "The Role of Traditional Leaders in Local Government." Seminar report. Johannesburg: Konrad Adenauer Stifung.

Hobsbawm, E. J. 1983. "Introduction: Inventing Traditions." In *The Invention of Tradition,* ed. E. Hobsbawm and T. Ranger. Cambridge: Cambridge University Press.

Hobsbawm, E. J., and T. Ranger. 1983. *The Invention of Tradition.* Cambridge: Cambridge University Press.

Holomisa, Chief Patekile. "Ubukhosi the Bedrock of African Democracy." *Mail and Guardian,* February 16, 2000.

Horowitz, Donald. 1991. *A Democratic South Africa? Constitutional Engineering in a Divided Society.* Berkeley: University of California Press.

Huntington, Samuel P. 1968. *Political Order in Changing Societies.* New Haven, Conn.: Yale University Press.

Hyden, Goran. 1980. *Beyond Ujamaa in Tanzania: Underdevelopment and an Uncaptured Peasantry.* Berkeley: University of California Press.

———. 1992. "Governance and the Study of Politics." In *Governance and Politics in Africa,* ed. Goran Hyden and Michael Bratton, 1–26. Boulder, Colo.: Lynne Rienner.

Hyden, Goran, and Michael Bratton, eds. 1992. *Governance and Politics in Africa.* Boulder, Colo.: Lynne Rienner.

IDASA. 1996. *Building a Democratic Culture in KwaZulu Natal: The Present Terrain.* Public Opinion Service no. 9. Cape Town: IDASA.

Independent Online. 1997–2008.

Isaacs, Nathaniel. 1966. *Travels and Adventures in Eastern Africa.* Cape Town: C. Struik.

Jackson, Robert H., and Carl G. Rosberg. 1982. *Personal Rule in Black Africa: Prince, Autocrat, Prophet, Tyrant.* Berkeley: University of California Press.

James, W., and D. Caliguire. 1996. "The New South Africa: Renewing Civil Society." *Journal of Democracy* 7, no. 1: 56–66.

Johnson, R. W., and Lawrence Schlemmer, eds. 1996. *Launching Democracy in South Africa: The First Open Election, April 1994.* New Haven, Conn.: Yale University Press.

Johnson, R. W., and Paulus Zulu. 1996. "Public Opinion in KwaZulu-Natal." In *Launching Democracy in South Africa: The First Open Election, April 1994,* ed. R. W. Johnson and L. Schlemmer. New Haven, Conn.: Yale University Press.

Jones, David S. 1983. "Traditional Authority and State Administration in Botswana." *Journal of Modern African Studies* 21, no. 1: 133–39.

Joseph, Richard. 1999. *State, Conflict, and Democracy in Africa.* Boulder, Colo.: Lynne Rienner.

Karlstrom, Mikael. 1996. "Imagining Democracy: Political Culture and Democratization in Buganda." *Africa* 60: 485–505.

———. 1999. "Civil Society and Its Presuppositions: Lessons from Uganda." In *Civil Society and the Political Imagination in Africa,* ed. John Comaroff and J. Comaroff. Chicago: University of Chicago Press.

Keulder, Christiaan. 1998. *Traditional Leaders and Local Government in Africa.* Pretoria: Human Sciences Research Council.

Khandlhela, R. S. 1998. "Problems Facing the Institution of Traditional Leadership in South Africa." Paper read at Good Governance at Local Level—Traditional Leaders and Rural Councillors Conference, at East London, South Africa.

Khumalo, Sipho. 2008. "Amakhosi Unhappy about Proposed Land Act." *Mercury,* April 4, 2008.

Kindra, Jaspreet. "Secret Deal Mooted for Amakhosis." *Mail and Guardian,* October 6, 2000.

Klitgaard, Robert, and Amanda Fitschen. 1997. "Exploring Income Variations across Traditional Authorities in KwaZulu-Natal, South Africa." *Development Southern Africa* 14, no. 3: 363–76.

Klopper, Sandra. 1998. "'I respect custom, but I am not a Tribalist': The ANC-CONTRALESA Alliance and 'Designer Tradition' in 1990s South Africa." *South African Historical Journal* 39: 129–42.

Klug, Heinz. 2000. *Constituting Democracy: Law, Globalism and South Africa's Political Reconstruction.* Cambridge: Cambridge University Press.

Koelble, Thomas A. 1998. *The Global Economy and Democracy in South Africa.* New Brunswick, N.J.: Rutgers University Press.

———. 2005. "Democracy, Traditional Leadership and the International Economy in South Africa." Working Paper no. 114. Centre for Social Science Research.

Koelble, Thomas A., and Ed LiPuma. 2005. "Traditional Leaders and Democracy: Cultural Politics in the Age of Globalization." In *Limits to Liberation after Apartheid: Citizenship, Governance and Culture,* ed. Steven L. Robins. Oxford: James Currey.

Krige, Eileen Jensen. 1936. *The Social System of the Zulus.* Pietermaritzburg: Shuter and Shooter.

KwaZulu Legislative Assembly. 1974. KwaZulu Chiefs' and Headmen's Act (Act 8 of 1974).

———. 1974–1994. KwaZulu Legislative Assembly Debates.

———. 1994. KwaZulu Ingonyama Trust Act (Act No. 3 of 1994).

KwaZulu-Natal Briefing. 1996. "The Clash That Had to Come: African Nationalism and the 'Problem' of Traditional Authority." No. 1: March 1996. Durban, South Africa.

KwaZulu-Natal Government. 1994–99. Legislative Assembly. KwaZulu-Natal Legislative Debates. Pietermaritzburg.

———. 1998. "An Integrated Rural Development White Paper." Pietermaritzburg.

———. 2000. Department of Traditional and Local Government Affairs. *Annual Report 2000.* Pietermaritzburg.

Kyed, Helene Maria, and Lars Buur. 2006. "New Sites of Citizenship: Recognition of Traditional Authority and Group-Based Citizenship in Mozambique." *Journal of Southern African Studies* 32, no. 3: 563–81.

Laband, J. 1995. *Rope of Sand: The Rise and Fall of the Zulu Kingdom.* Johannesburg: Jonathan Ball.

Ladley, A. 1982. "Changing the Courts in Zimbabwe: The Customary Law and Primary Courts Act." *Journal of African Law* 26, no. 2: 95–114.

Laitin, David D. 1986. *Hegemony and Culture: Politics and Religious Change among the Yoruba.* Chicago: University of Chicago Press.

Lambert, John. 1995. *Betrayed Trust: Africans and the State in Colonial Natal.* Durban: University of Natal Press.

Lemarchand, Rene. 1977. "In Search of the Political Kindgom." In *African Kingships in Perspective: Political Change and Modernization in Monarchial Settings,* ed. R. Lemarchand. London: Frank Cass.

Lemarchand, Rene, ed. 1977. *African Kingships in Perspective: Political Change and Modernization in Monarchial Settings.* London: Frank Cass.

Linz, Juan, and Alfred Stephan 1996. *Problems of Democratic Transition and Consolidation: Southern Europe, South America, and Post-Communist Europe.* Baltimore, Md.: Johns Hopkins University Press.

Lodge, Tom. 1977. *Poqo and Rural Resistance in the Transkei, 1960–65.* London: Institute of Commonwealth Studies, University of London.

———. 1999. *South African Politics Since 1994.* Cape Town and Johannesburg: David Philip.

———. 2001. *Politics in South Africa: From Mandela to Mbeki.* Bloomington:

Indiana University Press.

Logan, Carolyn. 2009. "Selected Chiefs, Elected Councillors and Hybrid Democrats: Popular Perspectives on the Co-existence of Democracy and Traditional Authority." *Journal of Modern African Studies* 47, no. 1: 101–28.

Lukes, Steven, ed. 1986. *Power.* Oxford: Basil Blackwell.

Lutz, Georg, and Wolf Linder. 2004. "Traditional Structures in Local Governance for Local Development." In *World Bank Institute's Community Empowerment and Social Inclusion Learning Program.* Berne, Switzerland: World Bank.

Mabeta, Masilo. 1998. "Traditional Leadership in a Democratic South Africa: Cooperation or Conflict." Paper read at Good Governance at Local Level— Traditional Leaders and Rural Councillors Conference, in East London, South Africa.

Mabuyakhulu, Mike. 2005. Budget Speech 2005–2006 delivered by the Honourable KwaZulu-Natal MEC for Local Government, Housing and Traditional Affairs. May 5, 2005.

MacDonald, Christine. 1998. "The Construction of State and Development in Rural KwaZulu Natal: Implications of Dominant Discourses in the KwaZulu-Natal Land Reform Pilot Programme." *Transformation* 37.

MacGaffey, Janet. 1994. "Civil Society in Zaire: Hidden Resistance and the Use of Personal Ties in Class Struggle." In *Civil Society and the State in Africa,* ed. John Harbeson, D. Rothchild, and N. Chazan. Boulder, Colo.: Lynne Rienner.

Mackay, Moses. 2003. "Mbeki defends traditional rights." *Daily News.* April 2, 2003.

MacKinnon, Aran S. 2003. "Negotiating the Practice of the State: Reclamation, Resistance, and 'Betterment' in the Zululand Reserves." In *The Culture of Power in Southern Africa: Essays on State Formation and the Political Imagination,* ed. Clifton C. Crais. Portsmouth, N.H.: Heinemann.

Magnusson, Bruce A. 1997. "The Politics of Democratic Regime Legitimation in Benin: Institutions, Social Policy, and Security." Ph.D. diss., Political Science, University of Wisconsin, Madison.

Mahoney, Michael Robert. 1998. "Between the Zulu King and the Great White Chief: Political Culture in a Natal Chiefdom, 1879–1906." Ph.D. diss., Department of History, University of California, Los Angeles.

Mail and Guardian. 1990–2008.

Makgetla, Neva Seidman. 2007. "Local Government Budgets and Development: A Tale of Two Towns." In *State of the Nation, 2005–06,* ed. Sakhela Buhlungu et al. Cape Town: Human Sciences Research Council.

Mamdani, Mahmood. 1996. *Citizen and Subject: Contemporary Africa and the Legacy of Late Colonialism.* Princeton, N.J.: Princeton University Press.

Mandela, Nelson. 1965. *No Easy Walk to Freedom: In His Own Words.* Oxford: Heinemann.

————. 1994a. *Long Walk to Freedom*. Boston: Little, Brown.

————. 1994b. State of the Nation Address. May 24, 1994.

Mann, Kristin, and Richard Roberts, eds. 1991. *Law in Colonial Africa*. Portsmouth, N.H.: Heinemann Educational Books.

Maphumulu, Siyabonga. 2007. "Chiefs Told to Work Closely with Councilors." *eZasegagasini Metro,* October 19, 2007.

Mare, Gerhard, and Georgina Hamilton. 1987. *An Appetite for Power: Buthelezi's Inkatha and South Africa*. Johannesburg: Ravan Press.

Mare, Gerhard, and Muntu Ncube. 1989. "Inkatha: Marching from Natal to Pretoria." In *South Africa: Contemporary Analysis,* ed. G. Moss and I. Obery. London: Hans Zell.

Marks, Shula. 1970. *Reluctant Rebellion: The 1906–08 Disturbances in Natal*. Oxford: Clarendon Press.

————. 1986. *The Ambiguities of Dependence in South Africa*. Johannesburg and Baltimore, Md.: Ravan and Johns Hopkins University Press.

Marx, Christoph. 2002. "Ubu and Ubuntu: On the Dialectics of Apartheid and Nation Building." *Politikon* 29, no. 1: 49–69.

Mathieson, Susan, and David Atwell. 1998. "Between Ethnicity and Nationhood: Shaka Day and the Struggle over Zuluness in Post-Apartheid South Africa." In *Multicultural States: Rethinking Difference and Identity,* ed. David Bennett. London: Routledge.

Mattes, Robert. 2002. "South Africa: Democracy without the People?" *Journal of Democracy* 13, no. 1: 22–36.

————. 2007. "Democracy without People: Political Institutions and Citizenship in the New South Africa." Afrobarometer Working Paper no. 82. Michigan State University–Afrobarometer Conference on Micro Foundations of African Politics.

Mattes, Robert, and Michael Bratton. 2007. "Learning about Democracy in Africa: Awareness, Performance, and Experience." *American Journal of Political Science* 51, no. 1: 192–217.

Mattes, Robert, and Hermann Thiel. 1997. "Consolidation of Public Opinion in South Africa." *Journal of Democracy* 9, no. 1: 95–110.

May, Julian, ed. 1999. *Poverty and Inequality in South Africa*. Cape Town: ABC Press.

May, Julian, and Chris Rogerson. 1999. "The Spatial Context." In *Poverty and Inequality in South Africa,* ed. Julian May. Cape Town: ABC Press.

Mbeki, Govan. 1984. *South Africa: The Peasant's Revolt*. London: International Defence and Aid Fund.

Mbeki, Thabo. 1997. Statement of the President of the African National Congress at the Closing of the 50th National Conference of the ANC. December 20, 1997.

————. 1999. State of the Nation Address. June 25, 1999.

————. 2000. State of the Nation Address. February 4, 2000.

————. 2006. State of the Nation Address. February 3, 2006.

————. 2007. Address at the Annual Opening of the National House of Traditional Leaders. February 23, 2007.

McClendon, Thomas. 2003. "Coercion and Conversation: African Voices in the Making of Customary Law in Natal." In *The Culture of Power in Southern Africa: Essays on State Formation and the Political Imagination*, ed. Clifton C. Crais. Portsmouth, N.H.: Heinemann.

————. 2004. "The Man Who Would Be Inkosi: Civilising Missions in Shepstone's Early Career." *Journal of Southern African Studies* 30, no. 2: 339–58.

McIntosh, Alastair. 1995. "The Rural Local Government Question in South Africa: Prospects for Locally Based Development." *Development Southern Africa* 12, no. 3: 413–22.

Mercury. 1990–2008.

Migdal, Joel. 1988. *Strong Societies and Weak States: State-Society Relations and State Capabilities in the Third World.* Princeton, N.J.: Princeton University Press.

————. 1994. "The State in Society: An Approach to Struggles for Domination." In *State Power and Social Forces: Domination and Transformation in the Third World,* ed. Joel Migdal, Atul Kohli, and Vivienne Shue. Cambridge: Cambridge University Press.

Migdal, Joel, Atul Kohli, and Vivienne Shue, eds. 1994. *State Power and Social Forces: Domination and Transformation in the Third World.* Cambridge: Cambridge University Press.

Mitchell, Timothy. 1986. *Social Facts and Fabrications: "Customary" Law on Kilimanjaro, 1880–1980.* Cambridge: Cambridge University Press.

————. 1991. "The Limits of the State: Beyond Statist Approaches and Their Critics." *APSR* 85, no. 1: 77–96.

Moore, Sally Falk. 1978. *Law as Process.* London: Routledge and Kegan Paul.

————. 1986. *Social Facts and Fabrications: "Customary" Law on Kilimanjaro, 1880–1980.* Cambridge: Cambridge University Press.

Morris, Donald R. 1965. *The Washing of the Spears.* New York: Simon and Schuster.

Moss, G., and I. Obery, eds. *South Africa: Contemporary Analysis.* London: Hans Zell.

Motloung, Boyboy, and Ronald Mears. 2002. "Combating Poverty in South Africa." *Development Southern Africa* 19, no. 4: 531–43.

Munro, William. 1996. "Re-Forming the Post Apartheid State? Citizenship and Rural Development in Contemporary South Africa." *Transformation* 24: 3–35.

Munro, William, and Justin Barnes. 1997. "Dilemmas of Rural Local Government in KwaZulu Natal." *Indicator South Africa* 14, no. 3: 75–80.

Myers, Jason C. 1999. "The Spontaneous Ideology of Tradition in Post-Apartheid South Africa." *Politikon: South African Journal of Political Studies* 26, no. 1: 33–55.

Mzala. 1988. *Gatsha Buthelezi: Chief with a Double Agenda.* London: Zed Books.

Natal. 1852–53. *Report of the Commission Appointed to Inquire into the Past and Present State of the Kafirs in the District of Natal, and to Report upon Their Future Government.* Pietermaritzburg.

———. 1891. *Natal Code of Native Law.* Pietermaritzburg.

Natal Witness. 1990–2008.

North, Douglass C. 1990. *Institutions, Institutional Change and Economic Performance.* Cambridge: Cambridge University Press.

Ntsebeza, Lungisile. 2000. "Whither South Africa's Democracy? The Case of the Rural Government in the Eastern Cape." Paper read at 43rd Annual Meeting of the African Studies Association, in Nashville, Tennessee.

———. 2004. "Democratic Decentralisation and Traditional Authority: Dilemmas of Land Administration in Rural South Africa." *European Journal of Development Research* 16, no. 1: 71–89.

———. 2005. *Democracy Compromised: Chiefs and the Politics of the Land in South Africa.* Leiden: Brill Academic Publisher.

Ntshangase, Bheka. 2003. "Brave Enough to Build Bridges through Dialogue: The Case of Chief Zibuse Mlaba." New York: Synergos Institute.

Nyong'o, Peter Anyang. 1987. *Popular Struggles for Democracy in Africa.* London: Zed Books.

Oberhauser, Ann M., and Amy Pratt. 2004. "Women's Collective Economic Strategies and Political Transformation in Rural South Africa." *Gender, Place, and Culture* 11, no. 2: 209–28.

O'Donnell. 1996. "Illusions about Consolidation." *Journal of Democracy* 7, no. 2: 34–51.

Olivier, N. J. J. 1969. "The Governmental Institutions of the Bantu Peoples of Southern Africa." In *Recueils de la Societies Jean Bodin XII.* Brussels: Foundation Universitaire de Belgique.

Olowu, Dele, and James S. Wunsch. 2004. *Local Governance in Africa: The Challenges of Democratic Decentralization.* Boulder, Colo.: Lynne Rienner.

Omer-Cooper, J. D. 1966. *The Zulu Aftermath: A Nineteenth-Century Revolution in Bantu Africa.* London: Longman.

———. 1987. *History of Southern Africa.* London: James Currey.

Oomen, Barbara. 2000. *Tradition on the Move: Chiefs, Democracy, and Change in Rural South Africa.* Leiden: Netherlands Institute for Southern Africa.

———. 2005. *Chiefs in South Africa: Law, Culture, and Power in the Post-Apartheid Era.* New York: Palgrave Macmillan Press.

Peires, J. B. 2000. "Traditional Leaders in Purgatory Local Government in Tsolo, Qumbu and Port St. Johns, 1990–2000." *African Studies* 59, no. 1: 97–114.

Peters, Pauline E. 1994. *Dividing the Commons: Politics, Policy, and Culture in Botswana.* Charlottesville: University Press of Virginia.

Picard, Louis A. 1987. *The Politics of Development in Botswana: A Model for Success?* Boulder, Colo.: Lynne Rienner.

———. 2005. *The State of the State: Institutional Transformation, Capacity and Political Change in South Africa.* Johannesburg: Wits University Press.

Posel, Deborah. 1991. *The Making of Apartheid 1948–1961.* Oxford: Clarendon Press.

Poulnic, Jacqueline, and Shrin Motala. 1997. "Reinventing Rural Local Government in South Africa: Current Status, Constraints and Options." Regional Consultative Forum on Rural Development Report. November 1997.

Przeworksi, Adam, et al. 1996. "What Makes Democracies Endure?" *Journal of Democracy* 7, no. 1: 39–55.

Rangan, Haripriya, and Mary Gilmartin. 2002. "Gender, Traditional Authority, and the Politics of Rural Reform in South Africa." *Development and Change* 33, no. 4: 633–58.

Ranger, Terence. 1983. "The Invention of Tradition in Colonial Africa." In *The Invention of Tradition,* ed. E. Hobsbawm and T. Ranger. Cambridge: Cambridge University Press.

———. 1993. "The Invention of Tradition Revisited: The Case of Colonial Africa." In *Legitimacy and the State in Twentieth-Century Africa,* ed. Terence Ranger and Olufemi Vaughan. London: Macmillan Press.

Rathbone, Richard. 2000. *Nkrumah and the Chiefs: The Politics of Chieftaincy in Ghana, 1951–60.* Oxford: James Currey.

Ray, Donald I. 1996. "Divided Sovereignty: Traditional Authority and the State in Ghana." *Journal of Legal Pluralism* 37–38: 181–202.

———. 2003. "Ghana: Traditional Leadership and Rural Local Governance." In *Grassroots Governance? Chiefs in Africa and the Afro-Caribbean,* ed. Donald I. Ray and P. S. Reddy. Calgary: University of Calgary Press.

Ray, Donald I., and P. S. Reddy, eds. 2003. In *Grassroots Governance? Chiefs in Africa and the Afro-Caribbean.* Calgary: University of Calgary Press.

Reno, William. 1995. *Corruption and State Politics in Sierra Leone.* Cambridge: Cambridge University Press.

Republic of South Africa. 1960–62. Department of Bantu Administration and Development. *Annual Report, 1960–62.*

———. 1993. Constitutional Principles.

———. 1994. Constitution of the Republic of South Africa (Act 200 of 1993).

———. 1996. Constitution of the Republic of South Africa (Act 108 of 1996).

———. 1998a. Department of Constitutional Development. *Traditional Leadership in Transition—In Search of a New Middle Ground.*

———. 1998b. Department for Provincial Affairs and Constitutional Development. *Local Government White Paper.*

———. 2001a. Statistics South Africa. 2001 Census.

———. 2001b. Independent Electoral Commission. Results. Available from http://www.elections.org.za (accessed 1999–2001).

———. 2002. Department of Provincial and Local Government. Draft White Paper on Traditional Leadership and Governance.

———. 2003. Traditional Leadership and Governance Framework Act, [No. 41 of 2003]. December 19, 2003.

Reynolds, Andrew, ed. 1994. *Election '94 South Africa: The Campaigns, Results and Future Prospects.* New York: St. Martin's Press.

———, ed. 1999. *Election '99 South Africa: From Mandela to Mbeki.* New York: St. Martin's Press.

Robins, Steven L., ed. 2005. *Limits to Liberation after Apartheid: Citizenship, Governance and Culture.* Oxford: James Currey.

Rose, Laurel. 1992. *The Politics of Harmony.* Cambridge: Cambridge University Press.

Rothchild, Donald, and Naomi Chazan, eds. 1988. *The Precarious Balance: State and Society in Africa.* Boulder, Colo.: Westview Press.

Rouveroy van Nieuwaal, E. Adriaan B. van. 1987. "Chiefs and African States: Some Introductory Notes and an Extensive Bibliography on African Chieftaincy." *Journal of Legal Pluralism* 25: 1–46.

———. 1996. "States and Chiefs: Are Chiefs Mere Puppets?" *Journal of Legal Pluralism* 37–38: 39–78.

———. 1999. "Chieftaincy in Africa: Three Facets of a Hybrid Rule." In *African Chieftaincy in a New Socio-Political Landscape,* ed. E. Adriaan van Nieuwaal van Rouveroy and R. van Dijk. Leiden, Netherlands: African Studies Centre.

Rouveroy van Nieuwaal, E. Adriaan B. van, and R. van Dijk. 1999a. *African Chieftaincy in a New Socio-Political Landscape.* Leiden, Netherlands: African Studies Centre.

———. 1999b. "Introduction: The Domestication of Chieftaincy: The Imposed and the Imagined." In *African Chieftaincy in a New Socio-Political Landscape,* ed. E. Adriaan van Nieuwaal van Rouveroy and R. van Dijk. Leiden, Netherlands: African Studies Centre.

Schaffer, Frederic C. 1998. *Democracy in Translation: Understanding Politics in an Unfamiliar Culture.* Ithaca, N.Y.: Cornell University Press.

Schapera, I. 1956. *Government and Politics in Tribal Societies.* New York: Schocken Books.

Schatzberg, Michael G. 1988. *The Dialectics of Oppression in Zaire.* Bloomington: Indiana University Press.

———. 1993. "Power, Legitimacy and 'Democratization' in Africa." *Africa* 63, no. 4: 445–61.

———. 2001. *Political Legitimacy in Middle Africa: Father, Family, Food.* Bloomington: Indiana University Press.

Schedler, Andreas. 1998. "What Is Democratic Consolidation?" *Journal of Democracy* 9, no. 2: 91–107.

Scheepers, Theo. 1998. "Constitutional Provisions: The Role of Traditional

Leaders and Elected Local Councillors at Rural Level." Paper read at Multi-party Democracy "Effective Governance at Rural Local Level," May 13–14, 1998, in Mmbatho.

Scott, James C. 1998. *Seeing Like a State: How Certain Schemes to Improve the Human Condition Have Failed.* New Haven, Conn.: Yale University Press.

Shively, W. Phillips. 2005. *Power and Choice: An Introduction to Political Science.* New York: McGraw-Hill.

Sithole, M. 2000. "Traditional Leaders Turn Down State's Offer." *Sunday Independent,* September 2, 2000.

Sklar, Richard L. 1999. "African Polities: The Next Generation." In *State, Conflict, and Democracy in Africa,* ed. R. Joseph. Boulder, Colo.: Lynne Rienner.

Skweyiya, Z. S. T. 1993. "Chieftaincy, the Ethnic Question and the Democratisation Process in South Africa." Community Law Centre Occasional Paper Series. University of the Western Cape.

South African Institute of Race Relations. 1965. "Race Relations Survey." Johannesburg.

———. 2006. "South Africa Survey." Johannesburg.

South African Press Association. 1990–2008.

Southall, Roger. 1998. "The Centralization and Fragmentation of South Africa's Dominant Party System." *African Affairs* 97, no. 389: 443–69.

———. 2007. "The ANC State, More Dysfunctional than Developmental?" In *State of the Nation, 2005–06,* ed. Sakhela Buhlungu et al. Cape Town: Human Sciences Research Council.

Sowetan. 1990–2008.

Sparks, Allister. 2003. *Beyond the Miracle: Inside the New South Africa.* Jeppestown: Jonathan Ball.

Starr, June, and Jane F. Collier, eds. 1989. *History and Power in the Study of Law: New Directions in Legal Anthropology.* Ithaca, N.Y.: Cornell University Press.

Sunday Independent. 1990–2008.

Tapscott, Chris. 2005. "Democracy and Trust in Local Government." In *Trust in Public Institutions in South Africa,* ed. Steinar Askvik and Nelleke Bak. Burlington, Vt.: Ashgate.

Temkin, B. 1976. *Gatsha Buthelezi, Zulu Statesman: A Biography.* Cape Town: Purnell.

Thompson, Leonard. 1995. *The History of South Africa.* New Haven, Conn.: Yale University Press.

Thornton, Robert. 2005. "Four Principles of South African Political Culture at the Local Level." *Anthropology Southern Africa* 28: 22–30.

Tripp, Aili. 1994. "Rethinking Civil Society: Gender Implications in Contemporary Tanzania." In *Civil Society and the State in Africa,* ed. John Harbeson, D. Rothchild, and N. Chazan. Boulder, Colo.: Lynne Rienner.

———. 1997. *Changing the Rules: The Politics of Liberalization and the Urban Informal Economy in Tanzania.* Berkeley: University of California Press.

Union of South Africa. 1951. Bantu Authorities Act (Act 68 of 1951).

———. 1957. Proclamation No. 110.

United Nations Development Programme. 2003. *South Africa Human Development Report 2003*. Oxford: Oxford University Press.

Uthungulu Regional Council. 1999–2000. Financial Year Projects Report.

Vansina, Jan. 1990. *Paths in the Rainforests: Toward a History of Political Tradition in Equatorial Africa*. Madison: University of Wisconsin Press.

Vaughan, Olufemi. 2000. *Nigerian Chiefs: Traditional Power in Modern Politics, 1890s–1990s*. Rochester, N.Y.: University of Rochester Press.

———. 2003. *Chiefs, Power, and Social Change: Chiefship and Modern Politics in Botswana, 1880s–1990s*. Trenton, N.J.: Africa World Press.

Vilakazi, Herbert. 2003. "Traditional Leader and Contemporary South Africa." Unpublished document.

Villalon, Leonardo A. 1995. *Islamic Society and State Power in Senegal: Disciples and Citizens in Fatick*. Cambridge: Cambridge University Press.

Villalon, Leonardo A., and Peter VonDoepp. 2005. *The Fate of Africa's Democratic Experiments: Elites and Institutions*. Bloomington: Indiana University Press.

Von Trotha, Trutz. 1996. "From Administrative to Civil Chieftancy: Some Problems and Prospects of African Chieftaincy." *Journal of Legal Pluralism* 37–38: 79–107.

Walker, Cheryl. 1994. "Women, Tradition, and Reconstruction." *Review of African Political Economy* 61: 347–58.

———. 2005. "Women, Gender Policy and Land Reform in South Africa." *Politikon* 32, no. 2: 297–315.

Webb, C. de B., and J. B. Wright, eds. and trans. 1976. *The James Stuart Archive of Recorded Oral Evidence Relating to the History of the Zulu and Neighboring Peoples*. Vol. 1. Pietermaritzburg: University of Natal Press.

———. 1979. *The James Stuart Archive of Recorded Oral Evidence Relating to the History of the Zulu and Neighboring Peoples*. Vol. 2. Pietermaritzburg: University of Natal Press.

———. 1982. *The James Stuart Archive of Recorded Oral Evidence Relating to the History of the Zulu and Neighboring Peoples*. Vol. 3. Pietermaritzburg: University of Natal Press.

———. 1986. *The James Stuart Archive of Recorded Oral Evidence Relating to the History of the Zulu and Neighboring Peoples*. Vol. 4. Pietermaritzburg: University of Natal Press.

Weber, Max. 1978. *Economy and Society: An Outline of Interpretive Sociology*. Berkeley: University of California Press.

Weir, Jennifer. 2005. "Whose Unkulunkulu?" *Africa* 75, no. 2: 203–19.

Welsh, David. 1971. *Roots of Segregation: Native Policy in Colonial Natal, 1845–1910*. Cape Town: Oxford University Press.

Whitaker, C. S. 1970. *The Politics of Tradition: Continuity and Change in Northern*

Nigeria, 1946–1966. Princeton, N.J.: Princeton University Press.

Williams, J. Michael. 2004. "Leading from Behind: Democratic Consolidation and the Chieftaincy in South Africa." *Journal of Modern African Studies* 42, no. 1: 113–36.

Wunsch, James S. 2000. "Refounding the African State and Local Self-Governance: The Neglected Foundation." *Journal of Modern African Studies* 38, no. 3: 487–509.

Wunsch, James S., and Dele Olowu, eds. 1989. *The Failure of the Centralized State: Institutions and Self-Governance in Africa.* Boulder, Colo.: Westview Press.

Yawitch, Joanne. 1981. *Betterment: The Myth of Homeland Agriculture.* Johannesburg: South African Institute of Race Relations.

Young, Crawford. 1993a. "The Dialectics of Cultural Pluralism: Concept and Reality." In *The Rising Tide of Cultural Pluralism,* ed. C. Young. Madison: University of Wisconsin Press.

———. 1994. *The African Colonial State in Comparative Perspective.* New Haven, Conn.: Yale University Press.

———, ed. 1993b. *The Rising Tide of Cultural Pluralism.* Madison: University of Wisconsin Press.

Young, Crawford, and Thomas Turner. 1985. *The Rise and Decline of the Zairian State.* Madison: University of Wisconsin.

Zartman, William I., ed. 1995. *Collapsed States: The Disintegration and Restoration of Legitimate Authority.* Boulder, Colo.: Lynne Rienner.

Zulu, P. M. 1984. "An Identification of Base-Line Socio-Political Structures in Rural Areas, Their Operation and Their Potential Role in Community Development in KwaZulu." Durban: University of Zululand.

INDEX

access to services: conflicts over,
185–92, 197–216; equality of,
122–24, 201–202, 226; levels of,
170–71, 197; local delivery of,
140–43, 174–85; and performance
legitimacy, 28–30, 141–42, 197–98;
research on, 36–38
accommodation, triangle of, 15, 143
African National Congress (ANC):
and chieftaincy, 9, 148; delivery
of development by, 122, 140–42,
169–75, 248n1; and democracy, 1–2;
vs. Inkatha, 82, 84–85, 109–14, 126,
129, 142, 152, 239–40n18, 249n13;
and mixed polity, 30, 81, 83–89, 103–
104, 219; policies of, 14, 83–89; as
"transformative movement," 81–82
amabutho military units, 47, 49,
65–66, 76
ancestors, chief as link to, 8, 41, 48
Anglo-Zulu War of 1879, 48, 65–66
anti-apartheid movement, 84–85, 121
apartheid: Bantustans under, 6, 61;
bifurcated state under, 13–14; consultation under, 72–73; end of, 78;
establishment of, 61; legacies of,
1–2; and mixed polity, 219; traditional principles under, 67–79
attitudes surveyed: on chieftaincy,
198–203, 208, 214–16, 222, 247n51;
on democracy, 114–17, 135, 227–29,
242nn31,32; on development,

145–47, 149–51; on local government, 138–39, 141–42, 163–67
authority: autonomous, 2; balance
of, 204–205; contextual view of,
55–56, 78; expansion of, 222–24; of
king, 46–47; in local government,
137–67; limits of, 147, 195–96; in
mixed polity, 132–36; over people
vs. land, 44; overlapping, 137; of
state, 13–15, 64–67; supernatural,
47–48; as syncretic, 4, 19, 21, 23

Bambatha uprising, 69, 76
Bantu Authorities Act of 1951, 6, 61,
64–66, 72–73, 77, 102–103
Bantustan system, 6, 41, 77, 82, 225
Bayete salute, 65
Biyela, Bhekabelungu, chief: background of, 36; and Chamane,
133–34, 249n19; death of, 231; and
development, 176, 180–81, 183–84,
189–90, 192; on elected council,
147; in election of 1999, 125–29,
221–22; and politics, 111, 112; public
perceptions of, 199–205, 213
Biyela, Hashi, 69–72
Biyela, May, 231
Biyela, Zalaba, and Zimva Biyela,
70–72
Biyela, Zimva. *See* Zalaba Biyela
boundaries: blurred, 19, 137–38,
153–54, 162, 224–25; political,

137–67; pre-colonial, 44; set by law, 5–7, 247n56; territorial, 76–77
Bratton, Michael, 15
British rule, establishment of, 59–62
Buthelezi, Gatsha, 9, 41, 48, 75, 82, 84, 121–22

Cape Colony, 60
case studies, 30–38
cattle, as wealth, 54–55
Cetshwayo, king, 60–61, 64–66, 236n8
Chamane, Vusi: and Biyela, 133–34, 231, 249n19; and development, 176, 180–81, 183–85, 189–92; in election of 1999, 125–29, 221–22; on *induna* role, 250n27; and Inkatha, 152; and regional council, 155–56, 161
chiefs: allegiance to, chosen, 44, 54; daily responsibilities of, 7–8; and development, 167–216; dispute resolution role of, 7, 44, 51, 53–54, 74, 120–21, 185–92, 207–208; education of, 36–38; and elected councilors, 146–53; election of, 196, 198, 209–10; as government representatives, 67; judicial role of, 73–74, 120–21, 147; and king, 46–49; land allocation role of, 8, 12, 14, 66, 86, 94, 104; and local government, 87–107, 137–67; other elective offices held by, 111–12, 154; policeman role of, 66, 205–206; protocol around,153–54; ritual role of, 7, 44, 47–48, 94; wealth of, 54–55
chieftaincy: abolition of, 2, 104, 152; across Africa, 11; attitudes on, 198–203, 208, 214–16, 222, 247n51; in colonial rule, 60–62, 76; co-opted by/co-opting of state institutions, 76, 90, 143–67; and democracy, 116–18, 132–36, 218–30; and development, 28–30, 105, 168–69, 174–75, 181–82, 197–216; historical development of, 39–79; as institution,

39–43; and kingship, 46–49; legitimacy of, 2–4, 192–230; and ongoing change, 221–33; number of members, 5–6, 233n1; as syncretizing, 227; as term, 5; territorial definition of, 76–77; theories on resiliency of, 12–17; as tier of government, 105, 157; urban awareness of, 4
Citizen and Subject (Mamdani), 13–15
Comaroff, John, 223; and Jean, 27
Communal Land Act of 2004, 80, 104, 168
community welfare principle: in colonial and apartheid periods, 67–79; in development projects, 204–206; in pre-colonial period, 50–52, 54–55; as principle of unity, 42
Congress of Traditional Leaders of South Africa (CONTRALESA), 82, 84–89, 99–102, 239–40n18
Constitution of South Africa: final, 1–2, 97, 105–106, 121–22, 157, 238n3; interim, 80, 83–89, 239n7
Constitutional Court (CC), 88–89
consultation principle: in colonial and apartheid periods, 67–79; and democracy, 117, 120–21; and local government, 93; in pre-colonial period, 50–54; as principle of unity, 42
council: local, 90–92, 96–97; regional, 138–39, 155–62; traditional, 6, 101–102, 130–33, 231–32
Crais, Clifton, 27, 104
culture: and legitimacy, 164–65, 223–24; reflected in constitution, 84–89; and rights, 12, 15
customary law, 13, 87, 88, 98–100, 120–21, 237–38n20
Cyprian, king, 72–73

democracy: African, 227–30; ANC and, 1–2; attitudes on, 114–17, 135, 227–29, 242nn31,32; chiefs' need

pre-colonial period, 50–52; as principle of unity, 42

incrementalism policy, 83–89, 107, 143–44

Independent Electoral Commission (IEC), 126–29

indirect rule: and apartheid, 13; establishment of, 59–62; and order, 62–67; Shaka and, 49–50; traditional roles under, 67–79; and unity, 26–27, 62–67

Induna/izinduna (headman): consultation role, 52–53; dismissal of, 72, 131; dispute resolution role, 8; election of, 129–33, 225–26; state sanction of role, 66; as term, 5; and ward system, 130–33, 177–78, 183, 190–92, 201–202, 209–10, 225, 246n36; in Zulu Kingdom, 44–45

Inkanyezi Regional Authority, 34, 77

Inkatha (grass coil of the nation) symbol, 48–49

Inkatha Freedom Party (IFP): as advocate for chieftaincy, 82, 84–86, 148; vs. ANC, 82, 84–85, 109–14, 126, 129, 142, 239–40n18, 249n13; dominance in KwaZulu-Natal, 33, 36, 82, 148, 150–52; in Mvuzane, 126–29, 244n70

Inkatha KaZulu, 41

Inkatha National Cultural Liberation Movement, 84–85

institution: chieftaincy as, 39–43, 78–79; co-opting of, 143; in hierarchy, 33; legitimacy of, 215–16; traditional vs. modern, 17–18, 31–32; trust in, 115

Integrated Sustainable Rural Development Programme (ISRDP), 170–71

isigungu (advisory group), 118–20, 130, 133, 154

izikhulu (advisors), 52–53

judicial role of chiefs: under apartheid, 73–74; in democracy, 120–21, 147

Keulder, Chistiaan, 15

Kholweni Tribal Authority: attitudes on local government in, 145, 163–67, 174–75; as case study, 30–38, 250n2; delivery of development in, 139–43, 178–79, 197–203; democracy in, 115–21; legitimation process in, 214–16; meaning of chieftaincy in, 26; resignation of chief in, 196–214

king role: development of, 5–6, 9–10, 45–50, 62–67, 236n7; politics in, 109–14

kinship ties, 57, 76–77

Koelble, Thomas, and Ed LiPuma, 16, 226–27

Krige, Eileen, 45

Kutshwayo, chief, 50

KwaZulu Bantustan Government (KZG), 33–34, 61–62, 162

KwaZulu Chiefs's and Headmen's Act of 1974, 67

KwaZulu Ingonyama Trust Act, 86

KwaZulu Legislative Assembly (KZLA), 74–75, 159, 231

KwaZulu Territorial Authority (KZTA), 74

KwaZulu-Natal (KZN): chieftaincy in, 5–9, 67; civil war in, 109–14; under constitution, 86; regional councils in, 158; research in, 30–38; unity concept in, 40–43

Lambert, John, 68

Land Act of 1913, 61

land allocation role of chiefs, 8, 12, 14, 66, 86, 94, 104

legitimacy: and culture, 164; and democracy, 19; and development, 192–94, 202; evaluations of, 20–21;

weak-state theory, 14–15, 162–66
witchcraft, 26, 51, 196, 230
women: in age-sets, 47; as chiefs, 119, 175, 213–14, 226; as council members, 99–102, 119, 127, 202, 203; and development, 170, 180–81, 200; married to chiefs, 207, 226; as political actors, 91, 118–20, 240n19; as queens, 5–6
world-views, competing, 108, 220–23

Ximba Tribal Authority: access to services in, 38, 171–72; attitudes on chieftaincy in, 198, 202, 208, 214–16, 222; attitudes on local government in, 145, 162–67, 174–75; blurring of authority in, 162; as case study, 30–38; delivery of development in, 139–43, 178–79; democracy in, 115–21; meaning of chieftaincy in, 26; politics in, 109–14
Xulu, Theodore, 181

Zulu Kingdom, 5–6, 41–79
Zululand Joint Services Board, 36, 200
Zuma, Jacob, 232
Zwelethini, King Goodwill, 5–6, 75, 84, 85, 164, 228
Zwide, king, 45–46

J. MICHAEL WILLIAMS is Associate Professor of Political Science at the University of San Diego.

Printed and bound by CPI Group (UK) Ltd, Croydon, CR0 4YY

13/04/2025

14656548-0004

.